THE STORY OF
DION FORTUNE

THE STORY OF DION FORTUNE

As Told To
Charles Fielding
And
Carr Collins

THOTH PUBLICATIONS
Loughborough, Leicestershire

First published 1985
New Edition with Explanatory Introduction 1998

A CIP catalogue record for this book is available from the
British Library.

ERRATA

Cover design by Rebecca Mazonowicz

ISBN 1 870450 33 7

Printed and bound in Great Britain

Published by Thoth Publications
64 Leopold Street, Loughborough, LE11 5DN

CONTENTS

Dion Fortune
(Violet Mary Firth Evans)

INTRODUCTION
TO THE SECOND EDITION

J.F.K. New York is not the ideal place for a tired soul in the wet evening of a September day. I cannot remember why I had chosen to get to Dallas in this way, but I had, and the "commuter block" as they called it was in full swing and my flight was already two hours late. And the ceiling of the optimistically named "departure" lounge had a big crack in it and there was plaster on the burger-stained carpet. So I had plenty of time for a thoughtful assessment and nothing distractingly pleasant to look upon.

It had all started nearly a year before, when I first met Carr P. Collins Jr. in a rather seedy little hotel in London. But to make any sense of what followed, a little more history is called for.

Dion Fortune died in 1946. I joined her Group, the Society of the Inner Light, in 1954 while still serving in the R.A.F. About 10 years later I left to set-up my own organisation, which later came to be known as the London Group: it is still thriving.

Some time later. Carr contacted me through a mutual friend (we will call her Petra) with a view to my giving an exploratory series of talks to a small collection of his friends in Dallas. It came about like this. Carr had been corresponding with several British occultists for some time; a couple of them were writers on the subject. He arranged to meet them on his next trip to England. They met him for tea in the Grosvenor Hotel. Petra was with them. Carr desperately wanted occult contacts and someone to bring them over to the U.S.A. Now on the staff of his London bank was no other than the mysterious Petra and through this circumstance they met on many occasions. All the time, the subject was the same. Petra knew me well and recommended me. Carr's aim was to get me to set-up an American offshoot of the London Group. Subsequently I found that he had several other projects in mind: one of them was this book. Carr Collins was rich; he had time to spare and all the necessary resources. My expenses were paid. This was the first day of September and the initial lecture was to take place on the morrow.

Ultimately, all bad things come to an end. My flight was called and, three hours later, I alighted in the warm and alkaline-scented environs of Dallas-Fort Worth airport. To meet me was a tired Carr Collins and his wife Lucia, who had been waiting over the long delay.

Carr was casually dressed, a tallish thin figure topped with a crop of white hair. Lucia, his wife, was petite, attractive and immaculately modelled. Both belonged to the North Dallas area of Highland Park, the upper crust.

The hour was late but Carr had a *schedule*. "Schedules" were sacred to Carr and midday or midnight, he would not deviate from them - as I was to learn to my cost.

The Cadillac moved smoothly out of the airport precincts towards Dallas itself. I felt the lure of bed and oblivion if not in the "arms of Morpheus" then rather in the environs of some nice quiet goddess. But it was not to be. The schedule ruled. First I was exposed to the delights of "the ice-cream parlour with the biggest selection of flavours in the known world" - and was required to eat four of these delights; then conveyed to "the biggest dough-nut bar in the world" (with free unlimited coffee). Two such experiences later I was, at last, delivered to Carr's Highland Park residence, confused in mind and digestion.

Ultimately, I retired to bed in a self-contained penthouse flat - kitchen, shower, wet bar (drinks) and glorious, glorious bed.

I was asked to awaken my host over the intercom when ready the next morning. I slept.

The next morning, prepared to deliver my first exploratory talk to the embryonic occultists of Dallas. I found it was not yet to be. The assembly had been arranged for the afternoon. It was 6.45 a.m. local time. After an "English muffin" and two cups of surprisingly bad coffee, I was taken on what later turned out to be the standard tour of Dallas. Apparently, all would-be gurus to the proposed Dallas Group had been exposed to this ordeal, and I found out later that several had preceded me but none had been chosen. The itinerary included the original log hut (the first building in Dallas) carefully preserved, the Kennedy assassination site, two museums, the old long-horn cattle pens at Fort Worth ("the beginning of the West"), a "real American drug store" with the obligatory ice-cream sodas, a new shopping mall, various stores, a mechanical oscillating bull which I was required to mount and stay mounted for the duration of the "ride"; two restaurants and the family ranch. Carr called this 'the death march" and judged his would-be gurus' esoteric suitability by their stamina and reactions. It seems that I was weighed in the balance and apparently not found wanting.

And in the afternoon the introductory session went ahead.

My talk seemed to go very well. The group of about 15 souls was biased toward the female sex. They came from all walks of life and, with a few exceptions, were either rich or very rich. One robust and generously proportioned woman was in the processes of selling her second factory for a cool million. There was a delightful southern belle, a computer software expert-cum-alchemist and other interesting people. But, outstanding among them was a one-time professor of psychology, a practising Jungian analyst, one of the foremost exponents of the Jungian school in the U.S.A. In the event, he turned out to be a sort of sane anchor-point to the group, a source of stability and common-sense. He soon became a friend and ally and remains so today.

After the talk and its subsequent socialising, Carr called me to his den (study). It was the only room in this opulent house that had a door; the rest, bedrooms and all were open-plan. Here, Carr prepared to discuss the true matter of his heart, a book, jointly authored, about Dion Fortune, the *true* "Story of Dion Fortune" no less.

A vast vessel of Jack Daniels whiskey which must have contained half a gallon was brought forth from his personal "wet bar", duly dispensed, and the talk commenced and continued, lubricated at intervals by the sour-mash whiskey.

Carr Collins' interest in Dion Fortune amounted to a minor obsession. His concern in things esoteric went back for many years. An omnivorous reader, he had ploughed through everything he could lay his hands on - and he had the resources to support his quest. The voluminous works of Regardie and Crowley were absorbed, if not understood but, when he met the writings of Dion Fortune, the process stopped. He had met his guru and his High Priestess.

His only fear was that she would not be properly recognised as he saw her. He wanted someone who had worked within her system and experienced the results. He finally alighted upon me.

The idea of a Dallas offspring of the London Group was still very active and he was using his resources to bring this about. An American Study Course based on the Dion Fortune philosophy was in his mind. But the core of all his hopes was a biography of Dion Fortune.

His project was theoretically simple. I, having been in Dion Fortune's group for many years and (presumably) understanding her esoteric philosophy, would provide the substance. Any other relevant writings could be included. He, Carr, would add what he thought necessary and act as general editor.

Money was no object. The project must go ahead. And it did.

At the end of this strenuous two-day session, I returned to England and my normal academic duties.

Evidence of Carr's dynamism soon arrived dramatically in the form of a red felt bag from the bank, containing £5000 in five pound notes for the purchase of an Apple computer system with all peripherals. The same was to be provided at the Dallas end at three sites. The first was to be with Carr in his "den"; the second with his secretary in Euless, Texas (for the real work) and the third with Dr. James Hall, the psychiatrist mentioned earlier who was to monitor the project and give the benefit of his own experience.

Computer discs were to be airmailed, audiotapes transported and telephone communication maintained at all times - day or night - regardless of the six-hour gap or the expense.

Carr was a frequent visitor to Britain, and rendezvous were arranged for intensive tape sessions at various hotels in London.

The pace accelerated madly and I couldn't understand why. It was only a 'phone message from Dr. Hall in Dallas that enlightened me. Carr's need for speed was indeed genuine and urgent. The Mayo clinic could do no more for him: he was dying.

Cystic Fibrosis is an insidious disease. It progressively destroys the working surfaces of the lungs, rendering breathing more and more difficult and resulting in an increasing disablement. Ultimately, the simplest movements such as standing or walking a few paces become a gasping agony.

Oxygen helped somewhat and Carr had a cylinder in his study: that, a large bottle of Jack Daniels and very little else, sustained him during the last few weeks of his life.

Meanwhile, I was shuttling back and forth from Norfolk to Dallas every few weeks at first and, towards the end, every weekend.

It soon became obvious that Carr's excellent secretary in Euless was producing material from my tapes and discs that I could sometimes barely recognise. I found later that he was "improving" the material to suit his own ideas of what was acceptable and saleable in the American market.

The situation became farcical. Every weekend in Dallas was spent restoring what Carr had "improved". And, of course, he was always ahead of me! An example may help. In the appendix which deals with Dion Fortune's "Guild of the Master Jesus", Carr altered the liturgy in any section that he thought might offend American Episcopalian norms. Also, his secretary was not a highly literate woman and tended to transcribe audio-tapes without paying too much attention to the actual context.

By the time I saw Carr for the last time, he was more or less immobile, but still seated in his study breathing oxygen and nourished by sour-mash whiskey. But he was triumphant. The final copy was being prepared. From his viewpoint, the book was complete.

I had to return to Britain. A few days later I heard that Carr was dead. His last words were, "Damn! Damn! Damn!" probably a frustration from not being able to see the final published book.

That was it. The text had gone straight to the printers and, I found out later, distribution arranged by Weiser[1].

No editing had been possible; all one could do was wait and hope.

On the 17th December 1985, Lucia, Carr's widow, assigned the copyright of "The Story of Dion Fortune" to me. Carr had completed his book.

---

[1] Samuel Weiser Inc., Box 612, York Beach, Maine, 03910-0612

When the usual author's copies arrived, my worst fears were realised. In addition to all my other worries, the last few pages were devoted to exuberant (and often inaccurate) promotions of the Study Course that I was still in the process of writing.

But the back cover surpassed itself. In lurid transatlantic hyperbole, it promised the purchaser that the book explained how to:

* become a trance medium
* contact the Inner Planes
* work with the Christ Force
* alert the Occult Police
* accomplish "Rising on the Planes"
* work with the Elemental Ray
* contend with Magical Bodies

- and there was more.

Again, nothing could be done. The truth is that the text is descriptive rather than explanatory. It relates how Dion Fortune and some of the more advanced members of her group worked, together with a little of their modus operandi. The actual abilities mentioned are partly a result of the individual's esoteric evolution and largely the consequence of long and arduous training. One cannot make silk purses out of sows' ears - on this side of the Atlantic at any rate. This edition comes forth without those excrescences, at least!

The present publisher will have removed many of the typographical errors in the first edition, but the reader's tolerance will be needed in certain passages, particularly those resulting from (fairly obvious) unedited tapes.

There are also occasional intrusions of apparently irrelevant material. For example, in the chapter "The Magical Body" on page 126 of the first edition, two paragraphs emerged which described inconsistencies in Zener card experiments. The origin of these paragraphs is unknown to me.

The last paragraph of the "Editor's Note" prefacing "The Guild of the Master Jesus" material reads, "It is noted that minor changes have been made to the original text material and certain Bible verses substituted in the Mass itself." Not guilty! What Carr P. Collins Jr. did not like, he changed.

Naturally enough, most of the spelling was American.

But, toward the end of his life, Carr and I became warm friends. He trusted me. He gave me the pick of his considerable library and drove me (incredibly, in view of his condition) to the Dallas Post Office to send my selection to the U.K. via six boxes in two U.S. Mail sacks. Ultimately, it all arrived safely in Britain.

If this consideration of my co-author Carr P. Collins Jr. seems unduly biased, then the fault is mine. I can only report what happened. Without him, this book could not have been produced. Without his resources and energy the American Study Course would never have emerged. Without his dynamism and money, the newly fledged American occult group would never have existed.

Carr was an idealist with a vague "idea"; he was probably a natural mystic. He hoped to crystallise his aspirations and, by his drive and determination, he largely succeeded for others - but not for himself.

His wealth was his greatest enemy. Too many had taken advantage of his generous support and hospitality. But in the end, he trusted something that he saw as "real" - but he somehow denied himself access to it. He once said to me, "this is all REAL inside me, but I somehow can't get to it, and now I never will in this life".

Subsequently, he spent his resources and time and rapidly depleting energy in helping others to approach that Light he felt he could not yet attain. His generosity and commitment are beyond praise. If I were called upon to give a dedication to Carr P. Collins Jr., it would be in this form:

Greater love hath no man than he who, while in darkness, seeks to help others toward the Light

---

Publishers Note: - These were the last words from the pen of Charles Fielding. Just before this second edition was to go into print he was rushed into hospital. Three days later he entered the Light.

INTRODUCTION
TO THE FIRST EDITION

The horror and carnage of trench warfare was still in everyone's mind. The old order of the Edwardians had gone forever. The Liberal Prime Minister Lloyd George headed the government of the day and King George V was on the throne of England.

Theosophy and the Hermetic Order of the Golden Dawn had been the centres of a great occult revival which had survived the war. Spiritualism, with its promise of communication with the many war dead, was thriving and charlatanism was rife.

This book is about an outstanding woman who lived in those times. The outside world knew her as Mrs. Penry Evans, a doctor's wife, who died nearly 50 years ago. She achieved her fame in the shadowy world of the occult as a strong, fearless champion of commonsense and sound scholarship and an implacable enemy of the rogue, the charlatan and the ineffectual.

Certainly one of the foremost figures in her field, her books are considered as essential reading by all aspiring occultists and have been translated into several languages. She was a strong woman, but she had her weaknesses and follies. Yet despite difficulties and the constraints of the age that she lived in, she managed to lift occultism out of the 19th Century miasma into a clearer air. To understand the story of her life and achievements it is necessary to consider the age she lived in and understand some of her beliefs and motivations.

She first became interested in the occult in her young womanhood, but it was not until the First World War was about to end that she became seriously involved.

In more respectable quarters, psychology was also experiencing a great surge forward. *War neurosis, shell shock* and *Mother fixation* had become household words in middle class homes. Dion Fortune herself (or Violet Evans as she was then) trained and practised as a lay Freudian analyst. Society was in a state of flux; things were never to be the same again.

It was Dion Fortune's interest in the enigma of human consciousness that led to her involvement in psychology. But she soon realised that there was more within the nature of man than any textbook could tell her. So she started research on her own account and was soon in the thick of a search for the unseen inner worlds of Man and Nature. She had already been introduced to the occult through Theosophy, but her new investigations soon took her deeper into the subject, revealing a system of thought which answered many of her questions and which set her off on a great psycho-spiritual quest. Subsequently, she founded her own occult group and devoted the rest of her life to experimentation, writing, lecturing and developing her own interpretation of the Western Esoteric Tradition.

Dion Fortune was no mere occult dabbler but a profoundly religious person. She conceived of man as a god-in-the-making, and the Universe as the unfolding of a great plan in the mind of God. These were the foundation stones of her belief and no understanding of the significance of her work is possible without some examination of her terms of reference.

In her comparatively short life she wrote many books and articles and gave many lectures but in all of them certain fundamental ideas appear repeatedly. She defined the Western Esoteric Tradition as the sum-total of the spiritual experience of the Western Culture. Different cultures had different work to do and the task of the Western races was quite different to that of the East.

Because of this basically different orientation she discouraged Western occult students from attempting to follow Eastern practices, such as Yoga, without a thorough knowledge of what they were doing. She maintained that there was an authentic Yoga of the West, based upon the Tree of Life of the Hebrew Qabalah, and entirely suited to the temperament and life-style of Western Man.

Naturally, when she established her own esoteric group she incorporated her beliefs and the results of her own experimentation. The essence of her teaching was as follows. First, there was an *invisible reality* behind the outer appearance of things. Material forms and forces were merely the end results of hidden causes. And the inner principle and motivator of the invisible reality was God.

Next she taught, as many had before her, that *man is an evolving spiritual being* — immortal, indestructible and essentially of the same nature as God, although vastly junior in development.

She taught that *man has freewill* within the limits of the universe in which he is evolving. Life is not a random matter but the working-out of a *Master Plan* held in the mind of God. Ideally, man should contribute his own unique creativity to the plan.

Thus each individual has his or her own part to play within the evolutionary scheme, and this unique contribution she called his *destiny.*

Dion Fortune saw man as a vital intelligent life-form evolving with the Universe who took physical form as a means of working within the material world. As one short life could not provide enough experience within the school of matter, the essence of man periodically *reincarnated* to continue his work.

In his evolution, man sometimes made errors of motive and judgement and acted contrary to his destiny. Action generates reaction; thus man set in motion forces which opposed him in varying degrees. This reactive effect, Dion Fortune called *karma,* a term introduced into the West by the Theosophical Society.

From this it followed *that man is entirely responsible for his present state and environment.* It was no use blaming others.

When man, an essentially spiritual being, acquired the skills of handling dense matter, there was no longer a need for further reincarnation, evolution could continue on non-physical levels. Continued evolution produced a highly developed human being, unfettered by the restrictions of a physical body. Some of these super-humans, Dion Fortune believed, were concerned with helping their fellows who were still in the flesh; she called them *inner-plane adepts.*

She taught that *initiates,* that is, those who understand something of their own true nature and purpose and who are trying to cooperate with the unfolding of God's plan, had a duty to help their fellow humans toward light, freedom and eventual godhead.

Dion Fortune devoted her life to preparing a psycho-spiritual system that would assist man on his spiritual journey. In this respect. she followed many others: but her unique combination of dedication. drive and commonsense placed her in a special position.

She was a great woman.

EARLY YEARS

Dion Fortune came into this world as Violet Mary Firth, the daughter of Arthur Firth and his wife, the former Sarah Jane Smith. She was born on the 6th of December 1890 in the area of Bryn y Bia, Llandudno, on the north coast of Wales.

The name Dion Fortune was a pen name that Violet adopted for her occult writings. It was very appropriate for these writings and it is interesting that Dion Fortune is a contraction of "Deo, non fortuna" a family motto which means "God, not luck."

Her father, Arthur Firth was a solicitor. When Violet was about five years old the family moved to Highbridge, Somerset, near Burnham-on-Sea. Here the family operated a superior rooming house which catered to the more elite gentlemen and ladies of the middle class. The Firth family appeared to be of the upper grade middle class that normally would not have to earn a living and had probably been of a higher social strata but for reasons unknown seem to have lost their money and social prestige.

The situation produced a curious childhood for Violet Firth and even though she went to comparatively normal schools, her parents always isolated her as being better than her classmates. Consequently, Violet had few friends and playmates as she grew up. This lack of friends made an introvert of her and she enjoyed writing poetry. Her first book of poems was published when she was thirteen and was called *Violet*. Being alone also encouraged her to use her imagination and enjoy her fantasy world which turned out to be a boon to her when she was writing romantic "pot-boilers" in her twenties.

Violet Firth was given more freedom than most girls of that period, and spent much time with her parents and other adults, who respected her thoughts and encouraged her to think and take part in

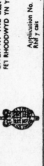

Birth Certificate: Violet Mary Firth, 6 December 1890

WBC 21910

A poem from

"VIOLETS"

Within the forest's dim arcade,
Where sunlight filters through the shade,
Making patterns soft and green,
The winged songsters of the air
Are singing softly everywhere
All hidden and unseen.

The trilling of the thrush responds
To the willow-warblers by the ponds,
In softly blending harmonies;
A blackbird singing far away,
Seems to praise the dying day
In sweet celestial melodies.

The sunset is gilding the forest and hill,
Turning all blood-red each rippling rill
With his soft and ruddy light.
The Moon is rising in the sky,
To bid the setting sun good-bye,
And rule as the Queen of the Night.

And now the Moon rules all alone -
A silver queen on a silver throne,
With her page the Evening Star.
The birds are sleeping in the trees,
But, borne upon the evening breeze,
A sound comes from afar.

The nightingale, on soft brown wings,
Like an ancient troubadour he sings,
Praising the Queen of the Sky.
She looketh down from her throne above
On the amorous singer of joy and love,
And the night winds softly sigh.

by Violet M. Firth
age 13

their limited activities. This freedom helped to build her confidence and ability to make decisions. Her only outside interest was in horses and she regularly attended any function in the neighbourhood that involved ponies. These local horse shows were called gymkhanas and she thoroughly enjoyed them, not only for the ponies, but also as an opportunity to be away from home for the afternoon.

She was said to be a rather difficult child and this could have easily have been a result of too much freedom before she was capable of accepting it properly.

The picture we have of Violet in her early teens shows her to be a slim and attractive young girl. Later in life Dion Fortune told friends that she really was not very attractive when she was young but in her early twenties and as she began to recover the knowledge of her past lives, she changed inwardly and this reflected in a more attractive outward appearance. When she was in her early forties, Dion Fortune's appearance changed again to the stout figure we associate with her. This change was thought to be due to changes in metabolism resulting from the trance and magical work she was doing.

Dion Fortune was a woman's liberation type of female who had decided not to go through the usual channels of marriage, a home, and children, but to strike out on her own behalf. Since she was going on twenty, some sort of profession was indicated and she decided to enter the residential commercial school in nearby Weston-Super-Mare.

As far as commercial training schools were concerned, this school was probably as good as any and close to home. The woman in charge had lived for many years in India and seemed to have acquired some knowledge of the occult, particularly of the subtle bodies of man and the techniques of hypnosis. This woman was an extremely domineering person and seemed to control her staff by a knowledge of mind-power.

By now, Dion Fortune had grown into a very strong-minded young woman, full of confidence in her own abilities. She got into arguments with the directoress of the school and a certain amount of ill feeling built up between them.

At this point, Dion Fortune attempted to do a good turn for a

Miss Violet M. Firth
Drawing by Betty Matil

fellow student whom she suspected was being swindled out of a sum of money by the directoress, so Violet just packed the other student off home and resolved to do the same thing herself.

In those days this was quite a step to take because the failure by the young woman to complete the training course was some indication that she was not much good and it is doubtful if she would have received references for employment. Violet actually had completed her training program but she was still there as the school arranged for such upper class students to work in the school office for practical experience (and as free help to the school).

Before she had finished her packing to leave, she was called for by the directoress. Violet went to the office about nine or ten o'clock in the morning and was questioned and harassed there for many hours. When the directoress finally let her leave. she was a nervous wreck. The technique the directoress had used was the reiteration of certain destructive phrases such as, *"You have no self-confidence. You are incompetent. You have no self-confidence — admit it and I will let you go! You are incompetent"*. and on and on.

Whatever could be said about Dion Fortune. self-confidence was not her weak point. In fact she rushed in where angels feared to tread. There might have been deficiencies in her ability but that is also doubtful. Nevertheless, the reiteration of these simple phrases went on to the point where she was reduced to a condition of near hysteria. Something inside warned her to pretend to collapse and she did this while attempting to maintain an inner barrier against the suggestions. She pretended to give way and collapse, and when she did, the directoress purred over her like a happy, contented cat and let her go. She went back to her room and then really did collapse on her bed. The window had been left open, the weather was cold, and it had commenced to snow and freeze. With snow blowing in on her as she lay on top of the bed with no covering, she slept in this semi-conscious state for thirty hours.

Another student of the institution got in contact with Violet's parents who came to fetch her from the school. Although they were exceedingly suspicious, nothing could be proved. As far as Violet Firth was concerned the entire episode in the office had ceased to exist; she had completely repressed it. Her parents took her home a nervous wreck.

The family doctor unfortunately gave her something like bromide as a sedative, and this made matters worse. He did, however, give as his opinion, that she had been hypnotised. Only when she realised that this was a possibility and began to face up to the consequences, did she get some degree of relief. She could not do any form of work: her mind raced and she was afraid that if she gave it its head there would be some sort of complete mental disintegration. She used to spend hours doing simple sums in an exercise book to try and give her mind something to bite on. This condition gradually abated but she was left in a depleted condition subject to extreme nervous prostration when put under any stress whatsoever. However, she did at least nominally recover to the point where she could take up some sort of employment.

Violet Firth (or Dion Fortune) was not very well educated. She had done no foreign travel and had little experience though she had worked during World War I in the capacity of a lay Freudian analyst. Having seen some of the results of the war, she never wanted to travel. Consequently, she was somewhat narrow in her outlook. She always suspected scholarship when it appeared heavy, as she thought there must be something very illuminating in its depths that she could not understand. Because of this feeling, she very carefully *avoided subjects that she did not feel qualified to talk about.*

She was also terribly snobbish which was a trait her parents had developed in her by not letting her play with other girls of lower class, and who probably in those days would have been very painfully aware of their own position.

Dion Fortune was not close to anyone. She seemed only to mix with people in the Mysteries and had few friends outside of the occult world to which she gave all her energies.

She had no significant connection with the Orthodox Church but she had been raised nominally in the Church of England.

This was a time of great interest in *new thought* and the tendency was to replace established religion with "new thought" affirmations and things of that sort. Violet's mother had joined the Christian Science Church so it was very easy for Violet - a pragmatic young woman, full of new thought, new psychology, and new liberation for women - to ignore religious matters until she was brought face to face with the extremely painful revelation of her lack of development on the devotional nature. This came about through a rather profound experience in a dream from which she realised that the significance of much of the Christian message applied to her.

At this same time she began to develop a deeper interest in the Theosophical Society. The attraction here was probably triggered by her own unfortunate experience at the commercial school. Until that time she had not realised that there were things going on which could not be explained by normal, physical means. She had also come into contact with other people who associated with a group called the Hermetic Order of the Golden Dawn and this piqued her interest in the mystical-occult even further.

MYSTICAL EXPERIENCE

One night Dion Fortune had a dream where she saw herself reading in the library of the Theosophical Society Headquarters in London. As she raised her eyes from her book, a section of the wall solid with books and shelves faded away revealing a stairway out into space. Some inner force made her rise and start climbing this stairway. The building apparently disappeared after a while and she was walking up the stairway through space with only emptiness on either side of it. She continued, and finally came out on a plateau where three great figures were standing. These entities were a blend of columns of pulsating and moving force represented as coloured lights and shaped into a semblance of humanoid form.

Their confidence and bearing radiated a feeling of extraordinary power and love. They could communicate at the human level but were obviously super-human beings. Dion Fortune was compelled to move toward them and of her own volition knelt before them. She understood by the colours of the light that made up their robes that one represented the elemental contacts and the forces of Nature, another was devotional and represented the inner powers behind the Christian Church (the Master Jesus in the occult sense), while the third figure also bathed in colour was essentially Hermetic, representing what we know as the Western Mysteries.

Dion Fortune was made to understand that her natural path was probably Hermetic but she also would require the forces of Nature and devotion to do the work she was to do in this lifetime. These three great entities pointed out that she was severely and dangerously deficient in the spiritual qualities exemplified by the Master Jesus. If she elected, she should follow the devotional path of inner development for a time. This undertaking would be painful and difficult and result in little outward progress, but it would balance out her inner nature and in some way make her a more acceptable leader for the future. She accepted this challenge and was filled with an enormous amount of emotion which was quite foreign to her ordinary nature.

When she awakened, she was in a state of great emotional shock; a condition so filled with peace, joy and extreme exaltation that it resulted in a sort of dementia, and incredible exhilaration.

The feeling of this vision never left Dion Fortune. Even in her worst moments it remained with her to guide her. She mentions something similar in her book *"The Sea Priestess"*, where she makes Wilfred have a minor experience of this sort while he is sleeping off a heavy Sunday lunch in the fort that he built for his Sea Priestess. But, it is obviously only a reflection of what she went through earlier.

There is no doubt that largely as a result of this dream experience Dion Fortune's future was decided. She would devote the rest of her life to the service of the Mysteries through writing, lecturing, serving as a Priestess, and also establish a group of her own.

It was undoubtedly this experience that caused the Society of the Inner Light to take a completely different form from the structure of the Hermetic Order of the Golden Dawn into which she herself was later to be initiated into, at least into the lower grades.

Editor's Note:

Dion Fortune officially had but this one significant dream which she writes about in the foreword to The Cosmic Doctrine. This is what she wanted the public to know, but in actual fact, she had two dreams separated by about a month in time. The second dream seems to have provided the spur for her future activities. The first dream had not produced enough reaction to get her moving and the second was needed to kick her and tell her to do something.

In the second dream it was notable that there were only two adept figures, the Green Ray figure had been withdrawn and only the adepts of the Hermetic and the Devotional Rays remained for the intense discussion.

Dion Fortune's writing reveals that she had a deep inner sympathy with Green Ray elementals and it is quite possible that had she been left to her own devices, she might well have gone strongly onto the Green Ray contacts and to some extent on the Hermetic, but largely would have ignored the Devotional. Removing the Green Ray contact from this dream experience puts stress on the fact that while it was recognised that she would have to develop her Hermetic side in order to run an occult group she was also strongly urged to make the Devotional Ray a real part of her life because this was something that was considered to be dangerously deficient in her.

After the Society of the Inner Light was organised, Dion Fortune had the three distinct divisions operating: Green Ray, Hermetic and Devotional Rays. Although she personally had many Green Ray experiences, and organised some of the Green Ray work, she did not direct its activities — she did most of her work on the devotional and hermetic side. Other people like Colonel Seymour did a tremendous amount of work on the Green Ray but Dion Fortune did not. This would seem to back-up the idea that she had far too great a natural sympathy for it and could have become unbalanced.

It is also well to note that in one of the Dr. Taverner stories, "A Daughter of Pan," the hero is falling in love with this strange, elfin girl and is having a very difficult job in pulling himself back to normality. She spends a good deal of descriptive time talking about how the smell of the drugs in the dispensary and the sight of medical instruments refocused his mind on the intellectual side of things, and helped him to draw back from involvement on the Green Ray where he would have stopped being a full human being and would have ended up being taken over by the forces of Nature. She makes quite a point of this, rather more than is necessary for the literary purposes of the story.

One consideration for this Green Ray attachment is the fact that Dion Fortune was very strongly Nordic through her bloodstock. The theory of Root-Races has much to do with the development of different phases of evolution on the surface of the earth and it is said that the origins of races came about at the time when certain conditions were being laid down on the earth. One of these conditions was connected with the establishment of the etheric matrix, or net, which holds together the physical matter of which the earth is made. It is said that the races have their origins at different times and they develop in cycles and that some Root-Races are therefore much more strongly connected to the earth's development than others. The Nordic race was said to have its roots in times of this particular epoch when the etheric stresses were being laid down and before the earth became firmly physical. This period, or the forces governing this period, were called the Red Ray and were the immediate forerunner of the Green Ray, or Elemental Ray. Very likely one of the fears on the part of the adepts was that Nordic Dion Fortune, if allowed to regress to the Elemental Ray would automatically pass through this and back onto the Red Ray. The Red Ray is a very primitive ray which obviously in terms of time must relate to a period in the ice evolution and to the tooth and claw standard of ethics and morals which applied then.

This tendency was made very plain in the "Psychic Self-Defence" story about the famous wolf which was materialised while brooding on an injustice that had been done her. This wolf was made out of her own etheric substance in the way that a medium can sometimes materialise the figure of someone departed. It is notable that the opportunity for revenge on the person who had done her wrong came about after the wolf had materialised. That is a typical Red Ray phenomenon, the wolf being in fact etheric and made up of nothing more substantial than a set of stresses. Nevertheless the wolf would have a very real negative action upon anyone to whom it was directed. This story appears to bear out the fact that Dion Fortune had a tendency to regress, as it is going back to an earlier human condition.

DR. MORIARTY

There is an old saying in the occult that "when the pupil is ready, the Master will appear."

About 1917, toward the end of World War 1, Dion Fortune came into contact with a man who had a tremendous influence on her future, a man by the name of Moriarty. He was a most remarkable personality and the prototype from which her fictional character of Dr. Taverner later developed.

Moriarty had some connection with the Order of the Golden Dawn but he was by nature a solitary occultist. His special interest was in astro-etheric conditions and psychology and healing. He thought that disease or mental affliction could only be properly explained by an understanding of the inner nature of man and possibly by an investigation into past incarnations where the originating cause might be found. He was a doctor of medicine and at one time had served in the medical service in India.

Dr. Moriarty's techniques and treatments were unusual and to get away from his orthodox colleagues he set up a training school in the Hampshire Barrens, the country between London and Southampton. It is a great area of heather, sandy ground, and pine trees, and somewhere in the middle of this was his centre. It consisted of a series of cottages in a small hamlet and those who wanted to be trained could come and stay in one of the cottages and become a member of his community for a period of time.

Moriarty had some strange characteristics that would not endear him to modern occult students. His establishment seemed to be run on the lines of the Gurdjieff Institute for the Harmonious Development of Man, which was located near Paris. Gurdjieff believed that one of the conditions for occult enlightenment was dedication and a concentration of all the inner abilities upon a single

Dr. Taverner

Dr. Taverner was not a healer of bodily ailments,
he was a physician of souls.

"The Royal Magazine", Vol.48, No.287. September 1922.

It is said that the similarity between this drawing
and the real Dr. Moriarty is uncanny.

goal. In training his students Gurdjieff would frequently employ hard physical labour such as chopping trees, constructing buildings, and other things requiring strenuous exercise. The idea was that the student who concentrated upon the physical things he was doing was in effect tying up the lower levels of his psyche, and this in turn allowed enlightenment to flood in at the higher levels which were no longer preoccupied with mundane concerns. Certainly some of the characteristics of Moriarty's establishment did resemble Gurdjieff's.

At Moriarty's the student interns were made to work at unaccustomed tasks. For instance anyone who by nature was an outdoor person, who did well in sports, liked healthy exercise, and so on, would be confined to do secretarial and household tasks. While another, who was essentially an intellectual type and whose world was bounded by books, was made to work in the garden and chop down trees.

There was a Mrs. Amy Campbell who was at the Moriarty training centre at the same time as was Dion Fortune. Mrs. Campbell's interest lay in the Theosophical Society and later in her life she was head of the East London Lodge of the Theosophical Society in South Africa. After both had attained prominence, Mrs. Campbell enjoyed telling of Dion Fortune's enthusiasm in the garden assignment and the fact that Dion Fortune not only wanted to clear the area thoroughly but also tried to chop down as many nearby trees as possible.

One of Moriarty's techniques was not very pleasant for those who were on the receiving end. The technique assigned the trainee a great deal of work calculated to achieve perfection in the house or garden duty. When the work was completed Moriarty would then in some way destroy it. For example, work in the garden to restore order was rewarded by setting the dogs upon it to dig it up. The idea was that when one ceased to react to his work being destroyed, then a certain stage of development, of detachment, had been reached in the soul. Unfortunately, human nature being what it was, people very rapidly ceased to react outwardly, while fuming inwardly. Whether or not this particular type exercise really achieved its ends is not known.

Despite some of his ideas, Moriarty was undoubtedly a genuine adept in the occult sense. Many of the accomplishments recorded of Dr. Taverner have been watered down considerably. Some of the cases he worked on while training Dion Fortune, were of a nature that could not be easily written about because they involved *unnatural vice of a sexual nature* and one could not write about such things at that time.

Moriarty was quite interested in the condition of *vampirism*. This is a strange pathology which flared up after World War I involving a situation in which one human being feeds upon the energies of another. These energies can be of various levels but in some of the cases recorded of Dr. Moriarty, they actually involved the drawing of blood in the traditional Transylvanian manner. Quite often these cases of vampirism were allied in some way to other forms of unnatural vice.

Dion Fortune mentions that Taverner considered this curious type of psychic contamination to have originated in certain troops from the area known as Transylvania, the traditional home of the vampire. The carnage in World War I needs no commentary. It was not uncommon for a mentally deranged person to be tempted to drink the blood of severely wounded soldiers. Taverner's idea was that this pathological urge originated from a newly dead person who for reasons of his own sought at all costs to avoid leaving this physical world and going onto the plane of the dead. The semi-dead soldier achieved his ends by associating himself psychically with a fairly unstable or shell-shocked soldier and then causing that soldier to make the actual physical contact with the source of energy, the blood of the wounded or dying soldier. Dr. Moriarty, through his knowledge and ability in psychiatric medicine, was in many cases able to break this contact and restore the person to normal life.

Dion Fortune was associated with Moriarty for various periods of time until the end of the war and beyond and maintained this close contact up into 1919 when she joined the Order of the Golden Dawn and their paths separated.

Probably the most valuable thing that Moriarty did for Dion Fortune was to help her to bring the great mass of memories and knowledge of her past lives into the present and to see a regular plan behind it. This unconscious material had been brought close to the surface as a result of her psychic shock at the hands of the school directoress.

Moriarty had trained Dion Fortune up to the point where she had a very clear understanding and a good outline in her mind of the Western Mysteries. Because of her studies, experience as a lay Freudian analyst, her two years under the guidance of Moriarty, her recall of previous incarnations, and her recovery of training and competence in these prior lives, Dion Fortune was now ready to go out on her own.

Dion Fortune was a very powerful personality while she was still the young woman of thirty. She was essentially a practical, doing person. She would never just listen. If something was good, she wanted to put it to practical use. Essentially she was not of a mystical nature but her experience in the Theosophical Society library dream had placed her under the care of the Master of Love and Compassion.

Moriarty died in 1921 and Mrs. Amy Campbell reports that Dion Fortune appeared in a purple robe before a number of Moriarty's students attending one of the memorial gatherings and said: "Our master is dead, follow me." Most of them did not chose to do so as Dion Fortune was so very young, just thirty at the time. Some half-a-dozen did follow her and this little group were some of the earliest members of the Society of the Inner Light. These members were quite a boon to Dion Fortune's early efforts as these followers were all sincere and well-trained students of the mysteries.

OCCULT POLICE

Dion Fortune particularly disliked one Indian guru who had come to England in the early twenties to cause unrest and confusion in the British group-mind. His plan was to trick unsuspecting women out of their money, abandon them and then use the money in activities to cause unrest. All of this was done at the unconscious levels of the mind and there were no laws broken for the local police to act upon.

She was so angry that she kept picking at the problem until she remembered that there was a group within the occult world that oversaw all magical activities and took action when black magic practitioners got too far out of line. She decided to appeal to this surveillance group and proceeded to put out a clairvoyant call to them for help. Dion Fortune projected her thought through willpower that was filled with emotion and mentally sent it out with all the force that she could muster.

Very shortly she received a message through a clear, inner voice that said to her: "Go to Colonel Y." She did not reveal Colonel Y's name but he was an eminent official in the government, so prominent in fact that she was afraid to approach him. Really even more than his importance was the British custom that would not allow her to speak to him without a proper introduction. So she talked back to the inner-planes and told them: "That is impossible as I have not been introduced. Give me a sign." With that the inner-planes said that the sign would be that "Colonel Y will be at your next lecture." Again Dion Fortune argued that it was impossible because Colonel Y's regiment had been ordered abroad and he would not be in England. The inner voice reiterated firmly: "Colonel Y will be at your next lecture."

Dion Fortune was due to lecture in a certain town and when the day of the lecture came around, she went to the town. As she was going up the steps to the lecture hall she saw Colonel Y was just ahead of her. This more or less cleared up all of her doubts. Immediately after the lecture was finished, she went from the hall and approached him. "I have a message for you," she said. To which he turned quite naturally and replied: "Yes, I know. I have been told to expect it." She then told him everything she knew and all her fears and misgivings. He replied: "There is rather more to it than that, but do not worry, leave it in my hands, and thank you."

When later she spoke to her inner-plane sources and asked if any more action was called for? They replied, surprisingly: "No action now, later, not yet."

Shortly thereafter she heard that this rather undesirable Indian occultist had left the country within a few days of her contact with Colonel Y.

There were basically three types of occult abuse according to Dion Fortune. In the first category came the fools, and on these 'she did not waste her powder and shot'. Then there were the charlatans, and finally those she called the gray and black occultists.

The charlatans were basically occult con men and tricksters. They were mysterious adepts who had just returned from the continent or from the East (both rather vague addresses) and charged large sums of money to the gullible for so-called initiation into the higher degrees of an occult order of which they claimed to be the head. This was a typical malpractice of the day. In her own words she thought that if people were stupid enough to pay perhaps three hundred pounds for a certain bogus initiation, then they deserved all they got. Apart from writing about them in her articles, she considered them beneath contempt.

The group she really disliked were those who, by using debased occult methods, gained advantage over other human beings, often reducing them to a nervous breakdown or insanity and usually taking their life savings in the process. A typical group of this sort would be drawn to and surround a magnetic, charismatic figure. The group would consist very largely of women. Nowadays, it is very doubtful if such an organisation could exist because of greater education and the emancipation of women generally, but in those days, not only was it a distinct possibility, it was all too common.

The practice that was generally adopted by these undesirables was to involve the members of the group in some sort of hypnotic rapport with the leader, under the excuse that this furthered the development of an occult group-mind and knit together the fabric of the group so it could act more cohesively. This in itself was very unethical. It was followed by many other practices which developed very strong and unhealthy attachment to the group leader by these unsuspecting women. The system operated in such a manner as to keep those people bound to the group through the *projected transference* onto the group leader.

Unfortunately the women were encouraged to give large sums of money for the support of the organisation, would get caught up in the emotion of it all, and would end up quite destitute, as well as psychologically deranged. Certainly, most of them were in bad shape when they left the group because when they ceased to provide psychic energy and money they were frequently expelled and were left with no financial resources and in a psychotic state.

Sometimes this sort of operation was less on a group basis and more specific. In *"Psychic Self-Defence"*, Dion Fortune gives details of a man who ran a strange sort of group where he and several colleagues were attempting to use hypnotic techniques and other occult practices to attract women to his group, and then excite them into a peculiar emotional state. When the women were sufficiently aroused on this level the leader would make use of this emotional rapport and use it for his own purposes, generally in building up his own magnetic magical personality. This resulted in the members of the group becoming enraptured by the leader and their energy was magnetically drained and depleted for the leader's own use. In ordinary psychological language it maintained the members in a state of perpetual *projection*.

Sometimes this went further and the more nubile of the ladies concerned were frequently encouraged to engage in an operation which is called *congressus subtilis*, or subtle sex. The young woman was developed in such a way as to loosen the bonds between the astro-etheric body and the rest of the psyche. This training resulted in a sort of debased ability to project the astral body. The lady concerned would be told to meditate strongly upon the leader of the group, before going to sleep. By various practices, the bonds between the astro-etheric soul and the rest of the psyche were progressively loosened. If the method succeeded, astral projection would frequently take place and congressus subtilis, or astral sex with the group leader would occur.

It may be argued in our present emancipated state, that astral sex is in no way more central than physical sex. But it has to be remembered that this was done in an unethical manner and that the young woman concerned frequently had no idea that her occult practices would lead to astral sex. It was also done in a manner that resulted in a sort of debased love affair between the woman concerned and the leader of the group. She was projecting onto him her emotional energy which was being progressively drained away. This process was a type of etheric vampirism.

Practices of this nature were reportedly very common during the 1920s, and we should ask ourselves if they could happen now. The answer is probably no because most young women, and certainly young men, are much better informed, not only about the physical details of the sex life but also have more experience from quite a young age of relationship and the emotional side of sex. To most young people nowadays there would be little advantage in going through a series of complex, mental procedures to achieve what could be done physically in full consciousness.

Another category of abuse concerned simple homosexuality. Some groups were considered gray or black, because of their magical use of sodomy or unnatural sex in one form or another. The technical details of this sort of operation are fairly complex, but basically it must be remembered that in normal sex a flow of force passes between the male and female participants and is grounded by polarity in a natural way. In unnatural sex or magical abuse, the flow of force is short-circuited by the deviated act and instead of passing cleanly through the system and being grounded, as in natural coitus, it is made available for debased use by the occult practitioner. It does not go to ground; it does not pass into circuit with the forces of the universe; it is held up, short-circuited, and thus made available for gray/black purposes.

Dion Fortune often stressed how infrequently really high-powered black magic was encountered. She was fond of quoting: "The Christs of Evil are as rare as the Christs of Good, and that most so-called black magic was just dirty gray." The truth is that she had a rather low opinion of many of her occult contemporaries, believing them to be too ineffectual for either good or evil.

It was in her initial research into occult abuses that she became aware of the existence of an inner-plane and an outer organisation of initiates which was called the Occult Police. Most of its operations were on the inner-planes with adepti whose job it was to try to seek out occult abuse and spiritual wickedness and then to put an end to it wherever possible. Certain occult groups in the physical world had their own inner section to work with the Occult Police and these were called *hunting lodges*. They were the physical plane terminals for the inner-plane Occult Police organisation.

Another inner-plane group to help control abuse was called *The Watchers*. They seemed to act as part of the Occult Police and their specific role seemed to be to seek out occult abuse, misuse of the powers of the mind, and general misconduct in the field. The Watchers would then hand over the information either to the Occult Police or to suitable individuals on the physical plane who would then take the necessary action to put the matter right. The Watchers appeared to spend their time searching out abuse and did not actually act to correct it, they passed it on.

The Watchers and the Occult Police did not die with Dion Fortune; in fact, they are still very much in evidence. One example of this was that there had been some rather bad misuse of certain occult powers by a man who ran a small lodge from his house near Cambridge. This man said that he was a black occultist and that he could exercise considerable power over people, as well as bring them wealth and everything they desired. Not a terribly prepossessing figure in his own right, he nevertheless enjoyed considerable popularity for a time. Unfortunately he used animals and one of the things he did was to torture them ritually.

The Watchers had been aware of his activities but had not been able to learn his name or the location of his lodge until he was arrested for some trivial local offence. When the inspectors looked over his house they found the temple and the story of his activities appeared in one of the popular newspapers. A copy of the paper was left upon the seat of a railway train leaving Cambridge and was found by a good occultist whom the Watchers had alerted. Now with the name and the address of the man known, it was a simple matter to call it to the attention of the Occult Police. Within three days the man was arrested for indecent assault, prosecuted and sentenced. He was completely removed from the scene and the temple was dismantled.

This is a clear indication of the sort of cleaning up action that continually goes on. The Watchers make the initial discovery as it were and bring the matter to the attention either of the Occult Police or to someone on the physical plane who is capable of action. Then corrective action is taken. The circumstances are sometimes very strange, but the poison is removed.

Dion Fortune was instructed in the procedure to use should she ever need to get in touch with the Occult Police to report abuse or to ask for protection. She was told that she should visualise a black Calvary Cross with a circle imposed upon it (similar to the Celtic Cross) against a scarlet-red background, while mentally or clairvoyantly calling for help. *This is the legitimate symbol for that purpose and should never be used except in time of need or emergency.*

While using the resources of this inner organisation, Dion Fortune was able to obtain a great deal of information about occult malpractice as the Occult Police headquarters seemed to be the clearinghouse for all messages. Her connection with the Occult Police continued throughout her lifetime and it was always her wish that when the Society of the Inner Light was well established, that they would be able to set up their own hunting lodge to be affiliated with the inner Occult Police organisation.

THE GOLDEN DAWN

During World War I, Dion Fortune was again being depleted of energy and suffering from recurring spells of mental exhaustion which undoubtedly was a throw back from her encounter with the directoress of the commercial school. The work she was doing as a lay Freudian analyst was occupying more and more of her time. World War I ended and Dion Fortune had renewed her links with the Theosophical Society while moving away from the close association with Dr. Moriarty.

It was at this time that Dion Fortune met one of the members of a Brodie Innes' offshoot of the Golden Dawn, the Alpha et Omega. Innes was a writer and his works were very popular at the time. He would write mostly about mystical subjects, generally along the lines of the Celtic tradition and the elementals.

Brodie Innes did not run a breakaway movement from the Golden Dawn. He was quite well regarded within that organisation and was allowed to run his own particular version of the Golden Dawn system and was given considerable latitude to do so. He certainly was not a bad ogre and in no way was it schismatic. His group was the Alpha et Omega and was a duly accredited branch of the main order. The lodge in the Weston-Super-Mare area was an Innes type lodge and followed his modified system.

With the encouragement of her new acquaintance Dion Fortune decided that the correct thing for her was to enter an organised magical group of the Western Tradition and proceeded to join the Innes lodge of the Hermetic Order of the Golden Dawn.

She was accepted and initiated into Alpha et Omega about the end of World War I, and immediately following the ceremony, her problems of energy depletion and mental prostration vanished, and never returned. Apparently what had happened was that in the course of the peculiar type of etheric hypnotism practised by the headmistress of the commercial school, Dion Fortune's aura had been damaged and leaked in the way that a faulty vessel will leak. Hence, energy was being perpetually lost and she was also prone, in a reverse way, to the invasion of negative forces through the same faulty part of her aura.

As far as we know, Dion Fortune was a model neophyte within the Golden Dawn until she decided that the people who ran that particular lodge knew very little about the inner workings of what they were doing. One description was that they were a set of bearded old men more interested in the antiquities than in the living force of the Tradition. She asked more and more questions and got fewer and fewer satisfactory answers.

In 1920, Dion Fortune moved to London and transferred to the branch of the Alpha et Omega under Mayia Curtis-Webb who later became Mrs. Tranchell-Hayes. Mayia Curtis-Webb was an excellent teacher and had a great influence over Dion Fortune's future and Dion Fortune regarded her and Moriarty as her great teachers.

Dion Fortune next moved to a lodge of the Stella Matutina, (Star of the Morning), which was run by Moina Mathers, the widow of MacGregor Mathers, one of the founders of the Golden Dawn. Moina Mathers was another remarkable woman, very powerful, very self-opinionated, and it was inevitable that there would be a clash of personality between Moina Mathers and Dion Fortune.

Moina Mathers was a very cultured woman, the sister of Bergson, the Norwegian philosopher. She was very attractive, vivacious, and yet something was a little odd. She married MacGregor Mathers and they agreed to have a platonic relationship, she believing that the sexual act was intrinsically unlovely. She believed that the highest part of the self could only be developed if the lower practices, as she called them, were put away.

This was not an uncommon viewpoint of the age, but she had this very strange relationship with Mathers who apparently declared to her that had she showed any signs of sexual interest, he would not only have got rid of her as a wife but thrown her out of the Golden Dawn as well. She agreed totally and appeared to have had no sexual experience whatsoever.

Some of her rather violent reactions to Dion Fortune could well have come from this enormous pool of dammed up emotion, which was released when she came face to face with someone as dynamic as Dion Fortune.

At this time Dion Fortune was writing some articles which would later be combined into a book, *"The Esoteric Philosophy of Love and Marriage"*. This caused an immediate reaction from Moina Mathers who tried to expel her for betraying the inner secrets of the Order. However, when it was pointed out that Dion Fortune had no access to the fraternal information, Moina Mathers recanted and allowed her to remain. Soon after this Dion Fortune was writing for publication a series of articles on occult abuse and after the essays appeared individually, they were published as *"Sane Occultism"*.

Dion Fortune always maintained that she wrote better than she knew — and she was right. Some of the information did not come through the conscious mind but through her psychic faculties from inner-plane sources. Unknown to her, the material she wrote involved some of her new lodge friends. On hearing of the articles Moina Mathers became very angry indeed and instructed Dion Fortune to withdraw them before publication. Dion Fortune considered this for some time but refused to do so on the grounds that the abuses were real and brought the occult movement into disrepute. Probably the inner source of the information she had recorded came from the Watchers, as she called them, an inner-plane group who looked after the integrity of the human race.

Moina Mathers wanted her to withdraw the essays she had written on the subject of abuse in the occult world and in *"Psychic Self-Defence"*. Dion Fortune details what happened and claimed that upon her refusal to recall the articles from publication she was viciously and astrally attacked by Moina Mathers.

Dion Fortune did not advance very far up the ladder of the esoteric grades, and like Israel Regardie, author of *"The Complete System of the Golden Dawn"* (Falcon Press, Phoenix 1984), she had a low opinion of the ability of those who were supposed to be her elders and betters within the fraternity.

She was fascinated by the Qabalah and realised that in it lay the key to the Western Mystery Tradition. Dion Fortune found that the

mundane information to which she had access was fragmentary
and rather poor in quality. To satisfy herself, she was forced to
spend a great amount of time researching the subject and finally
wrote a Qabalah series, which was published in the *"Inner Light
Magazine"*. Later this material became her well-known book,
possibly the most famous of them all, *"The Mystical Qabalah"*.

Dion Fortune was only thirty-two at this time, a mature woman
with considerable experience in practical occultism. A person who
had recovered many past incarnations in detail and had acquired,
or reacquired, the occult capabilities of those lives. Now she found
herself in a decaying offshoot of the Golden Dawn surrounded by
ineffectuals, widows, and greybeards. A woman of her temperament
could hardly accept that.

Curiously, despite her arguments with Moina Mathers, and
despite the antagonism which Moina Mathers undoubtedly had for
her, Dion Fortune suggested starting a lodge of the Theosophical
Society which would act as a recruiting base for Moina Mathers'
Alpha et Omega, which was at that time woefully short of members.
It seems to have been a very curious arrangement but one that gave
Dion Fortune access to the Golden Dawn library and the Alpha et
Omega lodge obtained a screening source for new members. In 1922
Dion Fortune opened the Christian Mystic Lodge of the Theosophical
Society in London and managed to refer to Moina Mathers a number
of potential recruits.

With increasing disillusionment in the Golden Dawn system,
Dion Fortune became independent. Her small group of esoteric
followers consisted of those she had gathered from Dr. Moriarty
graduates, and some she had attracted into the Christian Mystic
Lodge of the Theosophical Society. From this small and brave
beginning grew her own society, the Society of the Inner Light.

THE BEGINNING

The training Dion Fortune had received in past lives prepared her for leadership now. She was largely untrained and had little apprenticeship in other organisations. She would not have considered her current experience and awareness in any way adequate and she once said, that had she sat down and thought, she never would have started because she did not consider herself to have the required qualifications.

Dion Fortune was essentially a Way-Shower and a builder. She was a person who could break the ground, get things going, get the group together, and then at that point, she would logically withdraw. She was the builder.

Her initial group consisted mostly of retired schoolmistresses, ladies of uncertain age whose fathers had left them certain amounts of money, and women who had been tied to an ageing and ailing mother until the mother died. Most of the group was of the middle and upper middle classes, with the class system working very strongly in England at that time. To balance it out the group was able to recruit a couple of able-bodied men into the project and off they started to challenge the world.

This little group did most of the spadework in getting organised. It is very easy to underestimate people like this but they were the backbone and the work that they did enabled the group to start off on a solid foundation.

Their first major project was acquiring land in Glastonbury at the foot of the Tor and then buying an old Officers' mess hut from the army to erect on the property. This property was named and is still known as Chalice Orchard. Later they rented a big old house at No. 3 Queensborough Terrace, London. The QueensboroughTerrace

Chalice Orchard, Glastonbury, at the foot of the Tor.
Photo by Martin Staines. Glastonbury.

address became the group's headquarters and Glastonbury was used for special trance elemental work.

By now, Dion Fortune had with her a number of associates, many of whom were women of middle age, with private means who did not need to work. They followed her about in a sort of hero worshipping condition which Dion Fortune disliked intensely. Nevertheless, she put up with it because they were good workhorses and did much of the initial work in establishing what later became known as the Society of the Inner Light. The house at No. 3 Queensborough Terrace was used as a community house for people interested in the occult, a place where they could live and work. It was referred to within the group as *The Community*.

Dion Fortune gradually became a sort of cult figure with her very powerful personality and all those other capabilities that she had and the other ladies had not. Many of them were unmarried ladies and this raised difficulties because of their asserting some independence in following an inner need, but the group progressed. Each of the women had a particular set of tasks assigned as her responsibility.

In the early days of hard work the members of the group became very friendly and in turn they acquired some most curious nicknames. There was one woman, the daughter of a well-known general and the sister of another, who was a very competent organiser and she was put in charge of household. It was she who had to organise everything to do with cooking, cleaning, services, and laundry. She was a super housekeeper and was known as "Dragon" first because of an imagined likeness to the picture of a dragon on a tea tray that they used, and secondly, because of her tendency to breathe fire upon anyone who would not take their dirty shoes off, or in other ways fail to observe house rules.

Dragon had known and worked with Dion Fortune from earlier days but because Dion Fortune considered her of low esoteric grade, Miss Lathbury never operated at the centre of things. She was a small woman about five feet tall, fairly slight, with extremely piercing, dark brown eyes. She had a ready turn of humour and organising abilities so enormous that it appeared that whenever she set her mind to a task, the job somehow completed itself.

Another lady of an even more uncertain age, who because of her habits of dilly-dallying and failing to make decisions promptly, was known as "Doo-dah". But it should be noted that this lady, despite her shilly shallying and peculiarities, was in fact vigorous enough to indulge in sea-bathing at all times of the year, including mid-winter and even breaking the ice on occasions. She continued with her weekly swim even in later life. She was really an extremely hardy lady. Among her other accomplishments was the ability to translate technical Russian at very high speed. Toward the end of her life, while still within the Society of the Inner Light, she made a comfortable living translating technical documents from Russian into English.

Dion Fortune, at the time, flourished under the nickname of "Fluff" as she would go around the rooms detecting small pieces of dust fluff which had not been removed at cleaning.

The healthy male influence came from a man who worked for the Tramways Corporation, which was a forerunner of London Transport. He was a highly dedicated fellow with a strong grasp of accounting and financial principles, and an excellent organiser as well. He probably kept Dion Fortune from the worst demands of the women and it was he who provided a note of male stability. He was Mr. Thomas Loveday and was known as "Nibs". It was he who arranged the leasehold of No.3 Queensborough Terrace in the early days of the group and had very much to do with Glastonbury, in fact, he ultimately died there and was buried there next to Dion Fortune. Nibs was largely responsible for getting the affairs of the organisation into order. Subsequently a number of other men came in but for a while it was he on whom they all depended.

Nibs was also the one who bought an old army officers' mess hut in 1924, had it transported to Glastonbury and then erected it on land he acquired at the foot of the Tor. There were plenty of temporary army buildings available at that time and many people bought them to use as holiday places by the sea or in the mountains.

Meanwhile Dion Fortune was using Glastonbury with the little army hut, the chalet as it was called, as a focus for an increasing amount of inner-plane work. In that place and with this strange group, much of the early esoteric material came through Dion

Fortune's developing mediumship. She considered Glastonbury or *Avalon* as she called it, to be the holiest earth in England and considered it as a centre for both an enlightened mystical Christianity and also very powerful in elemental contacts. The Tor was the centre of this power.

Another lesser figure was a woman known as "Lummy" due to her habit of using the cockney term, when she was disturbed, of "Oh, lummee!" Her true name was Miss Lonsdale and she occupied one of the rooms in the basement at No. 3 Queensborough Terrace and for quite a long time she took charge of Chalice Orchard at Glastonbury. She was a comparatively insignificant figure in the esoteric life of the group but one who was totally trustworthy and had enormous dedication. Much of the routine work fell on her and Nibs Loveday.

During the time that she was housekeeper, members did most of the work within the house, no outsiders were allowed in because this was the phase of *the closed group*. Hence, she had to organise members to do anything from cleaning out drains, scrubbing kitchen floors, carpentry, painting, and so on. This she did admirably with tremendous discretion and a good sense of humour, and no matter what time a member might finish their tasks, they would always find a tray of coffee and biscuits awaiting them.

SOCIETY OF THE INNER LIGHT

Dion Fortune's original group consisted of possibly a half dozen people who worked with her in setting up the Glastonbury magical operation. When this was done it was thought a London headquarters was needed, so they leased No.3 Queensborough Terrace, London, and subsequently bought it. No.3 Queensborough Terrace is a typical London townhouse, Victorian or early Edwardian, a high narrow house on a tree lined street with one end of the road abutting onto Kensington Gardens where Dion Fortune spent quite a lot of time walking. The house was on four floors with a sub-basement. An access to the basement which would have been the kitchen quarters in the old days was gained by a short flight of steps leading down from the street. Any caller at the house would normally approach the front door by going up a short flight of steps and then through quite a large door to enter a narrow hall. On the left was a door leading to a well-proportioned room of fair size that was used as a library and for Dion Fortune's lectures as well. On this same floor were several other rooms and at the end of the narrow passage there was a flight of stairs leading upwards and another staircase leading down to the sub-basement where there were four rooms.

The first two floors above the main level were divided into two rooms each, one quite large looking over the street and a smaller one to the back. On the top floor you had a labyrinth of small rooms that would once have been the servants bedrooms. All in all, the house provided the newly formed group with plenty of space, probably a great deal more space than they needed at that time.

The significant thing about the acquisition of No.3 Queensborough Terrace was that now the group had a home where they could perform steady occult work and build up a system. The only proper way of doing ritual was to have a building dedicated to that single purpose. Now they had it.

The condition of the house when they moved in was appalling. There was little money but there were eager hands, and it was remarkable what they did with soap and water followed by a lot of paint.

No.3 Queensborough Terrace remained the group's principal headquarters from the time it was bought, sometime in 1924 or 1925, right up until 1960 when it was sold and the present quarters at 38 Steeles' Road was purchased.

The Society was publishing a magazine now, *"The Inner Light Magazine"*, and in its pages toward the end was a small section for advertisements. One frequently appeared there advertising a bed-sitting room at No.3 Queensborough Terrace for anyone who was sympathetic to the esoteric work of the group. They would be told that here was a place where they could live in a community atmosphere and sample something of what was going on esoterically without feeling the need to become more closely committed. This idea was very rapidly dropped for the common sense reasons that it was impossible to control people who were unsuitable and secondly because it was difficult to get the outsiders to move when asked to leave. By eliminating all outsiders, things got under control again.

After the group grew in size, was not as pinched for money and No.3 Queensborough Terrace became better organised, they hired a full time domestic staff. These were not members of the group but domestic servants and a cook, and the Society was able to afford them well into World War II. It was only after the War that the last of the domestic staff were finally dismissed and given a formal presentation to mark their years of service.

Meanwhile the group had grown to a size of about thirty. As the group grew there were quite naturally a number of different special interest sub-groups developing. Dion Fortune's aim was to have the three main strands of the Western Tradition — the Hermetic with ritual magic, the Elemental or nature contact, and the Devotional representing the spiritual side — all working together within the Society. The inner-plane adepti told her that in order to get a balanced group these three aspects must work together. The Hermetic Ray

Group picture at Chalice Orchid, Glastonbury, Mid - 1930s. Gentleman in centre back row is Col. C.R.F. Seymour, second from left on seated row is Dr. Penry Evans, then Dion Fortune, and next to her Thomas Loveday. Seated on ground is Miss Lathbury, *'Dragon'*.

would synthesise the apparently complementary Devotional Ray on the one side and the Nature Ray on the other. So she started to organise sub-groups within the Society with each specialising in a single Path of either the elemental, devotional or hermetic. Dion Fortune was really building up three separate organisations, but it must be very carefully noted that they were not chapters or sub-lodges or anything like that, they were merely specialised occult groups within the one organisation. Fundamentally there exists the Devotional Pillar and the Elemental Pillar with the Hermetic Pillar to reconcile them.

But to make something like this work you have to have a good development in all the people taking part. Dion Fortune was always aware of the shortage of time. She had this enormous pressing urge to move, almost as if she knew that her life would be a comparatively short one. Consequently she was building up the Society as fast as she could, feeling that she had to get a structure of some sort going, and that she could correct the deficiencies and problems afterwards. She was not able to do this, and these ideal conditions for the three Rays to manifest were not realised at that time.

Like many people of her stature and intelligence, Dion Fortune was a bit naive as far as human nature was concerned. She failed to appreciate that these sub-group people would want to build up an organisation of their own to practice the Nature Ray within these specialised conditions and would tend to develop a sort of internal hierarchy of their own. What happened within the Society of the Inner Light was the development of three rather uncomfortable bedfellows, and it finally got to the point where people working with the Nature Ray would not talk to those working with the Devotional Ray, who in turn, would not talk to the Hermetic Ray people, and vice versa. This certainly points to an underdevelopment of the group's structure and the problems it caused had not been satisfactorily reconciled by the time she died in 1946.

The problems were temporarily reconciled by World War II, 1939-45, because many activities had to stop as a number of the members were away in the Services. The War shook them all up and harmony was temporarily restored, but Dion Fortune was never actually able to reconcile the concept of developing all three rays.

The thing to note here is that there never were any schisms or offshoots of the Society and there never were any mandates given to open other lodges of the Society of the Inner Light. It was always one central operation and the only operating lodge was centred in London. Glastonbury was simply a specialist operation where people went to do certain work mostly connected with the Nature Ray and sometimes with the Devotional Ray. The nearest Dion Fortune got to specialised sub-organisations were these three rather uncomfortable sub-groups within the Society itself.

Dion Fortune was completely against the idea of having chapters and mandates to open other lodges because she had seen the abuse that had occurred within the Golden Dawn organisation. In some instances, persons only scantily qualified were empowered to open Golden Dawn lodges in some distant part of the United Kingdom and it was extremely difficult to keep one's finger on what these semi-official lodges were doing. Under the right circumstances, the concept would work well and could develop into a healthy group, but often the emphasis was more on maintaining numbers than developing quality. Consequently, many chapters of the Golden Dawn system deteriorated to where, in one instance, two of the officers, a husband and wife, engaged in a full scale family squabble in the middle of one of Dion Fortune's initiations in the Golden Dawn system! Frequently, a number of candidates were initiated together and stumbled over each other due to untrained officers who were unfamiliar with the ritual.

Dion Fortune's organisation was always well disciplined and had a standard of ritual that was effective, efficient, and produced results. She had raised the whole magical procedure several levels.

The purpose of the Society of the Inner Light was originally two-fold. The first was to train people from the standpoint of regeneration so that they could become better examples of what they ought to be and hence have an effect directly on the world. The second objective was to direct a propaganda organisation to produce literature and books, to offer lectures about the work, and to spread the word in a manner that could be clearly understood by the public at large.

However, once the Society got going and the inner-plane contacts were established, the adepti quite plainly stated that: "We are not going to spend a lot of time and trouble playing around with you — we want results. We are going to use you and in the process you will get developed." It was not to be a mutual admiration society with people sitting around going in for a bit of self-development. Thus the purpose of the organisation tended to change, the regeneration part was obviously necessary but the propaganda part was largely withdrawn apart from the books Dion Fortune wrote. The inner-plane adepti placed an enormous stress upon regeneration of the group consciousness and upon talismanic and magical action. The bias and stress of the group had now passed over from propaganda to the magical regeneration of the group mind.

The Society of the Inner Light came in for an enormous amount of criticism because the Society was never represented at occult conferences. No one from the Society of the Inner Light would lecture or appear as a representative, they were completely isolated. Hence, the Society was considered to be stuffy and possibly incompetent. The objective had changed following inner-plane instruction so that now the prime function of the organisation was to operate on the group mind consciousness and ultimately on the world condition.

Dion Fortune had publishing as a legitimate and mundane channel into the ordinary life of the culture because people were interested in buying books. Books have an interesting effect because they act as filters. If you read a book and like it, then presumably you are in tune with most of the ideas, so the book gathers together those of a like mind and eliminates the disinterested. Whoever read Dion Fortune's books and approved was quite likely to go along with the practices and precepts of her group. She found that this was a legitimate way into the group mind quite consciously and quite normally. This was a propaganda channel and it also acted as the sole recruiting tool for the Society. The books acted as a useful filter and they were at least one step in that person's selection.

In the early days of the organisation, Dion Fortune did give a lot of public lectures and a study course was set up which consisted of a mixture of lectures by her and other senior members of the group. Certain homework had to be done which consisted mostly of visualisation and the study of the Qabalah. The Society maintained this program for some time, but as the organisation grew and became more withdrawn, the public lecture part of the study course stopped as well. It is interesting to note that the Society was getting more and more inquiries from interested people who had read Dion Fortune's books but lived in fairly inaccessible parts of the United Kingdom and some of them from abroad. These letters showed a need for another form of training course available to all which could be completed at home prior to invitation and initiation into the group.

A correspondence course was developed and it went through various forms, but normally consisted of some printed material which the student had to work through, plus a recommended book which provided most of the essential reading material. The student would read and answer questions on the lesson from both the duplicated material and the book, and he would also perform a daily meditation and record it. The study course was divided into three or four parts and an essay on each part had to be submitted and accepted before the next part could be undertaken. The final part was a screening or a threshold-conditioning course, which was supposed to give additional information that would enable the student to decide whether he or she wanted to go into the group. When all of this had been satisfactorily completed and the neophyte was accepted by the Society, a ritual initiation followed.

It is important to note that at the end of the study course but before the threshold or linking course, there was always an interview with one or more senior people in the organisation. This normally took place in the library of No.3 Queensborough Terrace. The technique would be that the potential candidate was invited along at eleven o'clock in the morning or some time like that. Possibly coffee and rolls were provided and one of the interrogating members would be present. This member was generally male. Another member who was a psychic sensitive would be in the room as well, but would take no part in the discussion. The interview went on for anywhere from twenty minutes to more than an hour and gave an opportunity for the candidate to ask questions as well. It was a very searching but deceptive meeting. At the end of the discussion, the members would withdraw from the room and decide if the candidate should be invited to continue. If the answer was satisfactory, the members would immediately produce "the threshold course material" and give it to the student before he went his way.

This method worked quite well with these perceptive people in the Society. The threshold course took eight weeks to complete and the Society always had that period of time in which they could change their minds, so the threshold was a buffer as well as advanced neophyte training.

It must be stressed that in the heyday of the Society the neophyte student had absolutely no contact with the organisation at all, save through the material of the study course and the one short interview, prior to initiation. Therefore the candidate had no opportunity to assess the members or anything else about the organisation. Almost everything was taken on trust. It is possible that a slightly arrogant attitude did pervade. The assumption was that the privilege of entering the group was so great there was never any question in anyone's mind as to the ethics of the situation. So it was accepted automatically that the privilege would more than compensate for any inconvenience.

In the next step the candidate would receive a letter inviting him to come for initiation on a particular date. It was as simple as that. The candidate was asked to respond immediately saying that the date was suitable as it was not expected that there would be any problem. In other words, the Society of the Inner Light would give a date and, generally speaking, it would be understood that it would be accepted. However, in the case of people travelling from abroad or on duty in the armed services, the Society was quite flexible.

People came from all over the country and the continent as well. It speaks well of the reputation of the Society of the Inner Light that they were able to maintain this attitude for some ten or fifteen years.

It is possible to find a great number of faults with this training plan on looking at the material with the benefit of hindsight. The program looked woefully inadequate but it worked. The fact was that the Society did seem to produce quite reasonable people who suffered from a shortage of basic information but made up for it with their dedication and enthusiasm. Success was remarkably consistent, possibly due to the fact that most of the neophytes came into the group through reading some of Dion Fortune's books and were already sympathetic to the general ideas.

In later years the study course was re-written several times. Some of the versions were a curious mixture of the occult and of a sort of neo-Catholicism. By and large, during the Society's heyday the study course was quite short and intellectually simple. The course contained the basic precepts in an easy to understand manner.

Additional books were recommended and varied according to the time. During one period Mallory's *"Morte d'Arthur"*, a twin-volume work on the Arthurian tradition was recommended. Most students found this very difficult to understand because of the archaic language and some of the rather quaint expressions. At another time, Jacobi's book on *"The Psychology of C. G. Jung"* was highly promoted. Dion Fortune's *"Mystical Qabalah"* was always included and was one of the standard books. In earlier times the *"Cosmic Doctrine"* had been used but was discontinued because most people found it confusing and hard to comprehend.

THE INNER-PLANE ADEPTS

Dion Fortune founded the Society of the Inner Light and guided its development on the basis of direct communication with the inner-plane adepti. She declared openly that the bulk of her rituals and knowledge papers were of inner-plane origin in contrast to the material used by the Golden Dawn initiate, which was written by the human superiors in the lodge.

Dion Fortune was an iconoclast and, like Martin Luther, believed that every man and woman should be his own priest. Despite the framework of discipline necessary to any organised group she encouraged individual approach to the inner-plane adepti implementing their dictum: "What you now are, we once were; what we are, you may become; whence we come, you may go." By this approach she hoped to overcome the fossilisation of truth and the superstitious approach to esoteric practice that had become commonplace.

Dion Fortune saw the Society of the Inner Light as the physical plane terminal of an organisation that had its origins, not in this world, but on the inner-planes. That is an important concept and here the fundamental difference between the Hermetic Order of the Golden Dawn and the Society of the Inner Light is highlighted and the cause of much misunderstanding explained.

The truth is that the Golden Dawn and the Society of the Inner Light had completely different aims and their terms of reference were quite different. The Golden Dawn was a society founded to investigate magic, the so-called hermetic science, the hidden forces in relationship to man and nature. The Society of the Inner Light on the other hand, took magic as incidental to its true purpose which was the implementation of the next phase of human existence, the bringing to earth of the Great Plan in the Mind of God. Magic, it was taught in Dion Fortune's group, was simply a set of tools to help man get to grips with the inner realities. It was taught with the aim of making the initiate more efficient so that he could properly use these techniques more effectively just as a man with a bulldozer could clear a forest better than a man could with an axe.

Dedicated work with occult forces should improve the stature of a man, enhance his abilities, increase his capabilities and rid him of at least the main psychological blockages and personality problems. But all of this is simply incidental. The operation of the occult forces upon him will produce these effects, but the object of the exercise is not simply self-improvement, but to make him a better tool to be used for the regeneration of mankind.

The term regeneration means "rebirth" and it is considered that if a man co-operates with these great natural forces which are used within occult fraternities, he will experience changes within himself that could be called rebirth. Carl Jung used the term *individuation* to mean a person's becoming more himself and Jung saw the goal of the psychological therapeutic process as enabling man to become more perfectly what he should be. This viewpoint would be shared by occult organisations. But it should be stressed that this is incidental to the work of the organisation. The object of the training is to prepare him for service to others.

The Golden Dawn lodges were like a group of abstract researchers, fascinated by the details of their methods and apparatus, while the Society of the Inner Light sought to use esoteric science to help the human condition. Dion Fortune's work represented in its day an evolutionary breakthrough in esoteric group development. It was a product of its age, as was the Golden Dawn before it, and the importance of each should be understood as such.

The inner-plane adepti were absolutely essential to Dion Fortune's work. Her original impetus came from such a contact and the development of her Society was based entirely on inner-plane direction.

An inner-plane adepti by Dion Fortune's definition is a human being who has evolved beyond the need for further experience in the physical world and who is continuing to evolve on non-physical levels of existence. The men and women who have evolved to this point have a choice of leaving behind all contact with physical human beings and journey on through the realms of glory for their own growth, or, if they decide to follow the path of an inner-plane adept, they voluntarily forego the personal freedom in order to help their brothers and sisters still in the flesh.

The inner-plane adepti are grouped together into like-minded association as we are on this plane. Thus, those who work in the areas that we call occult, continue to do so after they cease to need physical bodies. The inner-plane adepti have evolved to different degrees of perfection just as in the physical world we recognise that some men are nobler and wiser than others. Thus there is a continuous graded hierarchy between man in his various stages on this plane and God.

These great intelligences have developed beyond the need to incarnate and all the experience of their lives on earth have been absorbed into the essence of their present makeup. They no longer live on earth, they are no longer incarnate, and the tales of their living on the earth in remote places are quite groundless.

There are of course, high adepts, highly developed and illuminated men of this world, but these are not yet inner-plane adepti. It may be that in the future as evolution proceeds, illuminati of the grade of inner-plane adept may remain on earth instead of passing on to the inner-planes and remain in full contact with both inner and outer planes in order to accomplish certain work. In which case they will remain in incarnation as long as the physical vehicle remains effective. But these would be very special conditions at sometime in the future and certainly do not apply at the present time.

The inner-plane adepti have given certain guidelines to assist those who want to make contact with them. If a student sets out to look for the Path, he shows a desire, which will be noted by those who watch on the inner-planes, and he will be assigned to a group-class according to his temperament. After he has gone a certain way under that tuition, he will be put in the care of what is called a *guide* who is not to be confused with a spiritualist guide.

A *guide*, in this terminology, is the first work assignment given to souls when they leave the physical plane for inner-plane work. The *guide* will try to impress the teaching he wishes to convey on the soul of his pupil by what we would call telepathy and the pupil must try to catch what is said. Later the pupil will be put in touch with one of the lesser inner-plane adepts and be one of the number of pupils for whom that inner-plane adept is responsible. A *guide* has only one pupil at a time but an inner-plane adeptus has many and is much more concerned with groups than individuals.

As the pupil advances further he will be passed to inner-plane adepti of higher grades and different specialities. His problem will always be to listen and hear what his inner-plane adept says. The higher the grade of the inner-plane adeptus, the more remote he is from earth beings.

What are the inner-plane adepti? Beings like yourselves, but without bodies. They have gained wisdom through experience and desire. They are not gods, they are not angels, they are not elementals, but are those individuals who have achieved and completed the same task as you have set for yourself. *What you are now, they were once. What they are now, you can be.*

Have you so little belief in the survival of bodily death that you cannot conceive of the existence of the inner-plane adepti? Have you so little belief in the doctrine of evolution that you cannot conceive of beings as greatly superior to your soul as you are to the animals? Have you so little knowledge of the power of the mind that you do not believe in the possibility of communication between you and them? If there is nothing higher than yourselves, what are you striving for? And if you accept the possibility of entities being higher than yourselves, why should you not also accept the possibility of communication with them? If you accept the possibility, why should you not try it? And if you try for it, why should you not expect that your first achievements would be rudimentary and imperfect and inaccurate? If you never make a beginning you will never arrive at completion. You must be content to speak in broken tones before you can speak fluently. If you do not try, you will never learn to speak thus. You shall learn the language.

You must understand that the inner-plane adepti as you picture them, are all imagination. Notice well, that the inner-plane adepti were not said to be imagination, but the inner-plane adepti *as you picture them* are imagination. What the inner-plane adepti really are you cannot realise and it is a waste of time to try to do so, but you can imagine the inner-plane adepti on the inner levels and contact can be made through your imagination. Although the mental picture you may have is not solid or actual, the results of it are very real. As long as you are a concrete consciousness you will have to use the imagination to reach the abstract. It is the Laws of the Constructive Imagination that are taught in occult science.

Constructive imagination is the use of the image building faculty of the human mind in a definite, planned way. The inner-plane adepti stress that it is impossible for a human being in incarnation to understand what the real state of inner-plane existence is. Nevertheless, if the image building faculty of the human mind is used to make a workable image of the inner-plane adepti, then the inner-plane adepti can contact the individual by using the image as a channel. Though the actual image is not real, the effect of the process is true because the inner-plane adept has used the image to establish a working relationship with the person on the human plane. What is happening is that the laws of the astral plane, on which the image exists, are being used in developing a channel for communication between the planes.

It should be recognised that the greatest privilege a human soul can receive is to be accepted by the inner-plane adepti as a pupil. The attitude towards such training on the part of the pupil should be that of gratitude for the privilege. The pupil is trained simply in order that he may help others, not for himself alone. The soul that is ready for the training will not need any persuasion or special treatment. If it should be required, the soul is obviously unready. A teacher on the physical plane may pass a pupil out of pity but be assured the inner-plane adepti will not. The pupil must come up to the standard or be put back into the lower class to try again. The pupil can try as often as he likes but to advance a soul to a stage to which it has not attained is a most cruel thing to do, as the forces it will meet will shatter it.

In one sense there is no hurry, you have all time. In another sense and on another plane the work presses and you are urged forward. So, have patience on the outer but on the inner, press onwards for God awaits you.

Dion Fortune would have said that a true occult group is a fraternity of people dedicated to helping humanity and such a fraternity is founded by one of the inner-plane adepti. It is a very difficult process for the inner-plane adept is on the inner-planes and has to make contact and work through someone on the physical plane in order to found a physical esoteric group. Some of the necessary requirements are:

1) The person on the physical plane will need a fair degree of developed psychism in order to establish contact with the inner-plane adept.
2) The earth person must have a strong personality which is able to overcome the practical difficulties of starting an occult group.
3) The individual must be a comparatively advanced person esoterically.

There are few people who have all three of these qualifications. There are many dominant personalities about, quite a large number of psychics and a fair sprinkling of spiritually advanced people — but the combination of all these in any one person is rare because psychism goes almost invariably in hand with the sensitive temperament which cannot cope readily with all the administration and finance problems involved in starting a group from scratch. H. B. Blavatsky was one example of a person who succeeded and Dion Fortune was another.

As those in touch with the inner-plane adepti proceed in their evolution they are given certain work to do for themselves and by those assignments, they themselves continue to learn. Such work given to a pupil by an inner-plane adepti might not always sound very interesting but the pupil has to begin with small matters.

Very often, such people who are given lesser tasks are the *guides*. The occult guide on the inner-planes is usually entrusted with a certain pupil to help him, report on him, and watch carefully over what he does. But also, those people in physical bodies on the physical plane who are developing contact with inner-plane hierarchy are also given these tasks and for them it is harder than someone who is permanently on the inner-planes because they have to attempt to get a clear telepathic impression of the duty to be carried out.

It should be remembered that contact with an inner-plane adept does not usually manifest in hearing particular words in the inner ear or seeing wonderful visions with the inner eye, but in a telepathic type of contact on an abstract mind-level. As all contact with the inner-planes is subjective, there is of course much room for error and delusion, and a very high degree of training is necessary before someone can bring through a message undistorted and untinged by his own pre-conceptions, prejudices, or unconscious complexes. This must account for a lot of the discrepancies in inspired writings. (The word subjective, in the way it is used here, means within the consciousness of the person concerned, while objective means outside the individual consciousness and in the world.)

It is not until a group is sufficiently established to have a team of competent communicators whose work can be cross-checked by others who have enough telepathic contact to be able to judge intuitively what is true or false.

There is a great difference between Eastern and Western teaching on this subject. The situation has not been clarified by the efforts of the Theosophical Society despite the great good they have done, because they have taught Western people ideas that applied predominantly to the life-style of the East.

In the esoteric it is necessary to work according to the conditions where the work is being done. In the hurry of modern life in the West, with its increasing mechanisation and the general noise and bustle, force cannot be concentrated as easily as in the more passive East. Nor are the bodies of Western men fit for constant going in-and-out of the physical body in doing the esoteric practices of the East. There is too much strain from the noisy world of the West, and for that reason *ritual* has been widely used as a powerful technique for concentrating power in certain channels and bringing it down to the physical plane in that way.

It has often been said that certain adepti have been such and such a well-known historical figure in some incarnation. Very possibly they have, but there is always another possibility; namely, that the spirit of the inner-plane adept may well have worked in a very dedicated pupil and have been so incorporated in that pupil's mind and spirit that it may give all the appearance of an incarnation, though in fact, it was not one. A particular pupil who makes an effective contact with an inner-plane adept may undertake certain work for that adept and devote perhaps the rest of his life to it. If he remains true to his dedication, then he will become so attuned to the particular attitudes, experience, and dedication of the adept, that he will develop so many characteristics that when looked at historically, it may make him capable of being confused with the adept whose force he is mediating.

Dion Fortune considered that the inner-plane adepti who are in contact with dedicated groups on the physical plane help to bring in the next phase of human evolution and it is interesting to take the development of the spiritualist movement and the Theosophical Society as examples of how this comes about.

In the Victorian Era, the occultists felt that the cycle of evolution had reached its most materialistic point and now it was necessary to change direction and give new impetus in order to swing around the nadir and to move onward and up the evolutionary scale. First of all it was necessary to wake up the ordinary Victorian who was rather dull and respectable and somewhat unimaginative and obsessed with a mechanical idea of science and the universe. They had no particular faith in the Protestant worship they practised and many did not believe in continuity of life. Therefore, that side of things had to be awakened in them.

For that purpose a movement known as spiritualism was set afoot by which, through mediums, those people could get into touch with their departed friends. This established a contact with the inner-planes which the Victorians were able to believe with a conscious mind and it really did not matter that this activity was often associated with the uneducated, the curious and the sentimental. The point is that in order to investigate this movement, persons in authority went out to look into these matters and found the inner-plane adepti of higher grade and of different teaching. So the spiritualist movement actually prepared the ground in two ways: first, it started to move the stolid and unimaginative population of that time into considering that there might be other levels of consciousness in addition to that of the physical plane; and second, it prepared the people for a higher level of teaching which the inner-planes began to send through. Therefore was the Theosophical Society begun through spiritualism and provided this meeting of the cultures of the East and West. Although the terminology was often confusing and living conditions were not right for the Eastern teaching, nevertheless a great movement was started to regenerate the group-mind of the Western cultures at that time. The great inner-plane forces began to penetrate the mundane minds of ordinary people all over the world and particularly in the West.

Madam Blavatsky popularised the inner-plane adepti, mahatmas or masters, and there was much talk of their activities. It was believed that some of them lived in the mountain vastness of Tibet and that one or two of them walked about the streets and even attended Oxford University. There was quite a lot of nonsense taught and it was the legacy of this misunderstanding of the inner-plane adepti and their purpose that Dion Fortune set out to correct.

As a rule the inner-plane adepti do not like details of their past lives to be given out as this tends to limit people's conception of what they are now. An example often given is that of the Master Rakoczi. This great being is often connected in popular occult books with the Comte de St. Germaine, but anyone who knows much about the life of St. Germaine and of what the Master Rakoczi really is, will realise the irrelevance of associating the two together. The truth is that Rakoczi was not St. Germaine in a previous life, as popular theosophy would have one believe. St. Germaine was simply used by the Master Rakoczi for certain work in a manner mentioned elsewhere. One must remember that the inner-plane adepti have to use what tools they can get. The Comte de St. Germaine, himself, was by no means a Master.

The inner-plane adepti are of course, numerous. Koothoomi and Morya were the Eastern Masters behind the early Theosophical Society. The Venetian Master was one who specialised in healing and was known as the Master of Medicine. He was a member of the Great Inner Asklepian Order and had little patience with dabblers and meddlers. The Master Devid, who was one of the lesser English inner-plane adepti, whose last incarnation ended on the battlefield during World War I, takes a great interest in youth. There is one particularly powerful being who is much concerned with esoteric groups in the Western World and who twice served as Lord Chancellor of England. The Master Hilarian, another interesting inner-plane adept, is said to be particularly concerned with religions and movements effecting the mass of humanity. Some are Masters of Strength, others of Compassion, and yet others, Masters of Wisdom. Greater even than these are the Masters of the Masters, of whom the Lord Jesus is said to be one.

It was to these great beings that Dion Fortune dedicated her life. Whether one considers them fact or fiction does not matter. Throughout the teaching she received from these beings, the one thing stressed was the great spiritual journey. The powers of magic and occultism were simply to be regarded as a technology to serve that end.

TRANCE CONTACT WITH THE INNER-PLANE ADEPTS

Early in her occult studies, Dion Fortune attempted to use magic powers to free a girlfriend from the domination of her mother's actions. To do this she gathered together a group of acquaintances who were either curious or mildly interested in the subject but completely untrained. They were instructed to make up some sort of a circle along spiritualistic lines with Dion Fortune seated in the leader's place and then when things settled down, she gaily commenced to go into a trance. She left her body easily, did what she thought she had to do to accomplish the task at hand, and as she returned to her body...

Dion Fortune found that she had been flung to the floor and was up against the wall, a man had been thrown on top of her and he was shivering with fright and terror, and the room was totally wrecked. She had loosened some type of uncontrolled force, which was still tearing about the room and creating an eerie feeling. Not only had the experiment done the immediate damage to the room but also the presence of this force had awakened all of the babies in the town and all of the dogs had started to bark. Chaos was rampant.

As soon as Dion Fortune had left her body, the control group started hearing voices, bell-like clinking noises and other spiritualist type phenomena. They lost their heads and ran from the premises. In breaking the circle the force was released to do its active damage. It appeared that this was the type force that Dion Fortune was trying to combat and destroy and now it became quite obvious that this sort of thing was difficult to control and definitely not to be played with.

Luckily no personal harm came from the experiment but Dion Fortune learned many lessons: inner-plane forces are powerful;

knowledge and ability are required to work with them; reliable and knowledgeable assistants are required; and occult work is not a toy or plaything and is to be respected and used only for worthwhile purposes.

She continued to train herself as a trance medium, and when questionable mystical or occult information was given to her, Dion Fortune would check it out in trance and through her new friends on the inner-planes. This contact was important as it gave her first hand knowledge, which most others in the occult knew only from books.

Later when she was active in the Theosophical Society she was able to question whether the ways of the East were proper for the West, and when a new member in the Order of the Golden Dawn she searched for the answer as to whether the wisdom and knowledge of the Golden Dawn was in fact the true information or whether it had been misinterpreted and changed as it passed down through the years.

Through this inner-plane work she determined that the ways of the East were not for the West and also found that some of the teachings of the Golden Dawn were suspect. Dion Fortune thought these findings were true and decided it would be best to go back to inner-plane sources and start anew in building a base for future occult work.

Dion Fortune is a fundamental and important figure in the Western Esoteric Tradition because she was able to go back to the source and was the first person in the West who was able to produce a new magical system that was workable and usable.

The principles incorporated in her organisation, the Society of the Inner Light, were based on information and instructions that were *revealed* to her from inner-plane sources and were not revisions of material gathered from previous sources. The fundamental precepts of the Order of the Golden Dawn and other societies which preceded it came from ancient texts and therefore were *based upon authority not revelation.*

Dion Fortune felt that much of the Golden Dawn material came from manuscripts which had been copied, amended, abridged, and conjured-on so much that in its present condition it bore little resemblance to actual inner-plane reality. Secondly, she thought that much of it was out-dated and did not fill needs of the 20th Century Man. The essence of the Golden Dawn was a 19th Century phenomenon and much of it went back earlier than that.

She felt that she was now forced back on her own resources and because Dion Fortune had trained herself as a medium, she was able to develop her own system from material that was given or revealed to her from the inner-planes. The ritual material, instructions, and knowledge papers which came through her own mediumship were some of the finest examples of trance work that have come through. The quality of the best was exceptional.

Quality of inner-plane material can be judged two ways. First, if the information given stands the test of pragmatic trial, the information is verified and is capable of being used because it works. Secondly, and in Dion Fortune's own words, such valid instruction "would cause the heart to burn within one, and there would be a deep intuitive reaction to the material, and one would feel that this was essentially something that was vital and something which was not simply a commentary on old information." Nearly all of the better material that Dion Fortune obtained in this manner would excite the person reading it.

One of the prime reactions to the material was a feeling that there was a very powerful entity behind it; in fact, one would feel the presence of the living being who was transmitting this information. The information being received was unique, had immediate relevance, and was inspiring.

The inner-plane adepti are beings who have evolved beyond the need for incarnation and have achieved relative perfection. They are fully evolved human beings but instead of entering into the divine union, which is the final goal of evolution, they have elected to remain within reach of the earth sphere in order that they may serve humanity upon its evolutionary journey. By thinking of them a student makes an initial contact and this contact is capable of development as the student advances. Therefore a student was told that when he made his salutation, he was to think of the inner-plane adepti as his elder brothers who were organised into a graded hierarchy for the service of God and man and the earth on which we live.

The inner-plane communications came through with a style that was completely different from Dion Fortune's normal writing, making it evident that some other personality, whether from within herself or external, was concerned with their transmission. Through her mediumship and with an untrained group of people supporting her, Dion Fortune brought over new material on many subjects of which the ritual part and the formal instruction papers were only a fraction. It is said that she brought through over 10,000,000 words as a medium, enough to fill 100 books. Whatever else might be said, she was very prolific, and something was moving her.

The type of trance she used meant that she was totally unconscious and therefore required assistance. She normally had a small group surrounding her, from at least three to a maximum number of probably twenty at any given session.

In going into a trance she would take precautions that she was not to be physically disturbed at anytime, that the area was properly sealed, and only then would she go into a self-induced trance and leave her body entirely. The procedure she used was one she taught herself, claiming that she had no natural mystic powers. She would get into a totally horizontal position, lying on a couch positioned in the centre of the room in which she was operating. Traditionally, this was within the temple and her couch formed an extension of the central altar towards the East and in a line, east-west. In trance work it was usual for Dion Fortune's head to be toward the East and her body on the couch would effectively form the extended altar. The technical name for this is *"pastos"*, the name coming from the pythonesses of old in Greece.

When the temple was secure, Dion Fortune would lie down, take a few deep breaths and get generally relaxed. She would then withdraw her consciousness from the physical plane by concentrating in turn upon a succession of symbols. Each symbol was more abstract than the previous one. This process, although essentially simple, is by no means easy to do, but she had developed a very high degree of concentration and was able to succeed.

The symbols she used were a mixture of the symbolism from the Golden Dawn (which she used in the early days) and certain inner-plane symbols that had been revealed to her through her early mediumship. As she progressed beyond a certain point, consciousness of her physical surroundings quite suddenly left her and she would be aware of fear and the feeling of a constriction in her throat. The throat centre was obviously affected here as she felt as if it were necessary to swallow some sort of obstruction and anyone observing her would notice that she kept swallowing spasmodically. After this quite suddenly her respiration would slow down, her pulse beat would drop to about half speed, and she would start to produce a rather acid perspiration.

From Dion Fortune's point of view she would feel that she had detached herself from the body and she would then journey to an inner-plane temple of some sort which was apparently provided for her by the communicator. Remember, the people with whom she was in contact on the inner-planes were not spiritualist guardians or anything like that, but far higher beings. The general surroundings and the general conditions of her trance were under a much more controlled situation and of a much higher type than the spiritualist trance mediums of that time. Hence she did not just lapse into unconditioned unconsciousness but was taken to a suitable temple where she remained throughout the trance session.

Next the inner-plane communicator would attempt to make contact with her physical body. Sometime during the early period when she was in this inner-plane temple she still had some residual consciousness of the physical body. She was aware of this physical body as if it were something belonging to her but was very far away. She would feel in herself that attempts were being made, by the inner-plane communicating entity to activate the contact and she supported this by attempting to move her vocal cords. Generally those who were watching and listening on the physical plane heard the entranced body say in a very low and sometimes rather croaky voice some words of greeting or possibly just a simple word.

As soon as the physical plane group around her responded and that seemed to be an essential part, it was as if the channel of communication had opened up between the entity and the group. Then immediately Dion Fortune resting in her inner-plane temple would lose any remaining consciousness of her physical body and the inner-plane communication would proceed from that point to the scribe and observers on the physical plane. The essential thing appears to be that the inner-plane entity had to get a response from the group and then it was as if an interchange was set up and the communication began to pour through.

If the communication is considered as the substance and the contact as being a sort of modulation of a force, then the circular force was established when the attention of those surrounding the medium was directed not toward the medium, but toward the communicator. It is an inner-plane force and the action is like completing the circuit.

The inner-plane link was through the medium to the group, but initially to the medium only. If the inner-plane communicator was to talk to the group a conduit also needed to be opened between the medium on the physical plane and the group surrounding the medium. That came about as the group responds vocally with "greetings" or some similar salutation and immediately a channel is built, consciousness is tuned in and communication is set up. It seems essential that the flow had to pass through the physical plane and become grounded. It is significant that the quality of the communication, the strength, certainty, freedom from interference, and so on, depends very much on the quality and response of the group surrounding the medium. It is as if the common pool of the mental energy, shared by the group, determined the overall quality and the depth of understanding.

Undoubtedly the quality of the group understanding, the inner development of the group, will determine very largely the communication coming through this type of trance medium. The group pulls through the communicator material, which is appropriate to its development. There is no doubt that the right conditions in the group can establish great depths of communication. Sometimes communication is extremely positive, very fast moving, and there is an enormous flow of energy that passes through the channel. Such great energy forces can produce unusual physical phenomena.

The phenomena that occurred during trance were generally of two types: sound phenomena and changes in physical objects. One of the most common curiosities affected candles or altar lights where during the mediumistic sessions the flame would frequently well up to enormous heights. These were physical phenomenon, they were not astral. On one particular occasion the altar lights flame rose to about five or six feet in height where normally the light only came up about an inch. This occasion was during reception of certain parts of the *"Cosmic Doctrine"*. The scribe working the session almost fainted as there was also a great rush of wind within the room as the flame increased. Wind and air movement was not uncommon because the communication is basically an energy transference. In this one instance, the altar flame did not flicker but held absolutely steady as it increased up to the great height. They were working in one of the sanctuary bungalows at Chalice Orchard in Glastonbury and the inner-plane communicator said that in order to bring the *"Cosmic Doctrine"* material through it was necessary to use certain elemental forces as a back-up to provide a more solid channel and that these elementals were very active on the Tor.

Other easily observable phenomena included very loud knocking sounds, bell-like sounds, and on several occasions pieces of paper used by the scribe were lifted and wafted around the room.

At other times using different group members and other types of group mind surrounding the medium operation, these phenomena could be entirely absent and yet the quality or depth of the communication might be enormously enhanced. It definitely has something to do with the components of the group-mind surrounding the operation of mediumship.

From Dion Fortune's point of view she relaxed and enjoyed the inner-plane temple provided for her until the time came to return. Then she just experienced the classic situation of returning to the body sometimes with a jerk and at other times smoothly when she would enter her physical body totally unaware of what had occurred. In general, the most she would experience on re-entry was the approach to the physical body in which she would appear to hover over her body for a moment and then would drop into it. Conditions would determine how smooth this re-entry was. Under certain conditions it could be rather violent and she would snap into the body and wake suddenly with a splitting headache. On other occasions there would be a slight sinking feeling in the solar plexus. Re-entry could be extremely turbulent and sometimes very unpleasant. Dion Fortune never had any major problems after she established her working group. *It is quite unsatisfactory to attempt this type of mediumship on one's own or with a few untrained people.*

It appeared that as Dion Fortune's work progressed, communication of high level material was impossible using this comparatively simple technique. Inner-plane communicators suggested to her that a relay system should be employed, similar to that used in FM radio and television. There would be present an inner-plane entity of modest grade who could make easy contact with Dion Fortune after she left her body. This entity acted simply as a relay station. Some higher being would pass the previously unrevealed information down and the second lower grade entity, nearer the earth, would relay the message through the medium. When the material of the *"Cosmic Doctrine"* was received, two such relays were used because the source was so remote that it was almost inaccessible.

The technique has its in-built dangers for it involves a chain of people who, like dispatch riders of the armies of old, had to relay information frequently by voice to ear. Consequently, it is probable that a certain amount of distortion crept in, but that was the system used.

She described the simple induction of trance in *"Through the Gates of Death"*, which was an instruction paper which was never intended to be followed. In this book she was trying to contact and enrol spiritualist group members and therefore was writing material they could understand while at the same time pointing out to them the very different nature of occult trance communication.

As time went on, the inner group developed and the method of trance changed. By the time of her death Dion Fortune was experimenting with what would later become mind-to-mind communication. In the mind-to-mind communication, the trance method was abandoned and she would withdraw consciousness from the physical universe around her. She would appear to operate a form of telepathy and there was no withdrawal from the physical body.

She considered that in mind-to-mind communications, the

channels offered to the communicating entity were in danger of being distorted by psychological problems of various sorts in the medium. It is an old occult saying "power works through the operator", consequently, the communication presumably coming through her would be conditioned by the content of her unconscious. Dion Fortune thought that in a pure transmission, where the communicator operated the vocal cords directly, there was no danger of this as the inner-plane entity was simply using the physical body as a voice. In other words, the inner-plane was using the human being as a robot.

The trance method is only suitable for very low level communicators and as soon as she started to deal with higher level entities whose natural habitat was on rarer and rarer planes, this method became less possible to use in the pure sense. Consequently, more material had to pass through part of her own consciousness before it reached the vocal cords and came out as speech.

By the time of her death, Dion Fortune had never managed to get the mind-to-mind technique fully established, at least for public consumption within ritual conditions. She simply had experimented with it and had been forced to return to the trance method for most communications.

In an occult group of the type that she had, there were two occasions where trance communications would take place. On one occasion, the communication would simply be for information, perhaps knowledge papers to explain some point, or perhaps to gain ritual material that was to be used for the group. In this case, an extremely small and select group of possibly three people could be used. In the second instance, the trance would be in a full ritual condition, *ex cathedra*, with twenty or thirty people present. The medium functioned as a loudspeaker system to allow an inner-plane communicator direct contact with the group for inspirational purposes.

Hence there are two different conditions: in the first instance, through Dion Fortune was relayed special information which was taken down by a shorthand writer—the communicator would speak through the medium, and the stenographer would write it down; in the second case, communication was performed under ritual conditions and was intended as an open address to the group. From Dion Fortune's point of view, the real leaders of the group, which she organised and supervised, were the inner-plane adepti. Consequently, the inner-plane "boss" would come through via a general communication to the entire group on certain occasions. These occasions were normally at the equinoxes or quarters of the year. They were inspirational talks and quite different from that which was being done in private to gain information for the entire occult movement.

During the war years, Dion Fortune had been experimenting with an alternative form of mediumship. Inner-plane communicators were transmitting more and more material of an abstract philosophical nature. Also, the classical trance method required the communicator to take over the speech control mechanism of the medium. High level communications can very rarely take place in this way because when the communicator is an inner-plane adept, there is no body dense enough to make a link. The inner-plane adept's most dense body is on the abstract mental level. Remember, when the *"Cosmic Doctrine"* was transmitted from a very high source, at least one relay had to be employed.

The new method involved the medium's raising consciousness to a much higher level equivalent to Tiphareth on the Tree of Life. This was more like meeting the communicator face to face and involved first progressively shutting off the outer layers of consciousness. Thus far, it was the same as for the classical trance, but instead of stopping at the level of the lunar consciousness, Yesod on the Tree, the second stage of the operations continued with a further inner journey ending with the junction point of individuality and personality, the condition which Qabalists call Tiphareth.

Here, the link with the communicating entity was made. Here, a mind-to-mind contact was established and the medium never relinquished control.

Margaret Lumley-Browne began to use this technique under Dion Fortune but developed it to the full under Chichester. Lumley-Browne had trained herself in a form of automatic writing, and sometimes when she returned to normal consciousness, her pile of paper had been covered with her elegant script. On other occasions she remembered the details and language of the contact and committed it to paper when she returned to normal. Occasionally a thread of normal consciousness remained during the contact and she wrote semi-consciously. She never used a tape recorder for these personal one-to-one sessions.

Once the initial contact had been made, the type of communication would itself further tune the medium's consciousness. Thus, if some very abstract material was coming through, the medium could be drawn more deeply into her own unconscious to a level corresponding with the source level of the contact.

Eventually, under Margaret Lumley-Browne, this method entirely replaced the old trance technique. However, it always demands a medium of high occult grade who is also very highly trained in this work.

PERSONAL LIFE

One of the interesting things said about Dion Fortune by modern commentators is that she had a tremendous interest in the etheric or magnetic interflow between man and woman and essentially in the sex relationship. As expressed in her many novels, she saw the psychological sanitation of modern civilisations to be akin to the physical sanitation of the medieval World City. She felt as one of her tasks, the duty to put right the sexual interflow between man and woman, not merely on the physical plane, but on the inner-planes as well. The time frame for this was the 1920s and 1930s.

Earlier in the century, Marie Stopes had instituted the first family planning clinic in the United Kingdom and had created somewhat of a revolution with her liberal ideas on the sexual emancipation of the female. Up until that time the wife, particularly in the cases of the lower middle classes and working classes, was constrained to sex and producing children to the point of exhaustion.

Dion Fortune was brought up in this climate and thought that she should do the same for the emotional life of women as Marie Stopes had on the physical side; hence the emphasis placed in her many novels — starting even with *"The Demon Lover"*, but particularly in the case of *"The Goatfoot God"* and leading up to *"The Sea Priestess"* and *"Moon Magic"* — to represent a happy, healthful relationship that could occur between man and woman. She saw the woman as the Egyptian goddess Isis and having the more dynamic role in the inner magnetic interplay of the sex exchange.

It was impossible to put these things into plain words in the 1930s and some of her early books appear extremely funny and have drawn a lot of criticism. It must be remembered that the time in which she wrote a publisher would have rejected them instantly had they been more explicit.

Dion Fortune wrote a book on *"The Esoteric Philosophy of Love and Marriage"* and another called *"The Problem of Purity"* which viewed in the light of present day morality gives a young man and woman an impression that causes much laughter. In fact she was trying desperately, through the veiled channels available to her, to portray an ideal relationship between a man and a woman. She insisted an essential magnetic component was frequently missing from what were considered to be stable and normal middle class relationships. Remember that the girl in a middle class relationship was frequently introduced to the man because of some linkage between the two families and almost all of the marriages at that time were arranged. The actual functional side of the marriage went well enough — that is to say the couple produced children — but there was no magnetic link between the two and the lower emotions which provide instinctual freedom and joy were missing. She saw it as her job to get this sort of flow going into society and believed that as a Sea Priestess or Moon Priestess it was her natural task.

Theory is one thing and practice is another.

At one of her lectures she was introduced to a doctor of her age, mid-30s, who had a Diploma in Psychiatric Medicine in addition to his other medical qualifications. This was Thomas Penry Evans, and best of all, he had a sincere interest in the psychology of the esoteric work they were doing. Dion Fortune was very impressed with him as he was with her. She was convinced that Penry Evans was of a high priestly rank and she regarded him as a priest-companion that she had known in previous incarnations.

Dr. Evans was equally taken with this sort of young group, and within a short time had moved into No.3 Queensborough Terrace and was spending most of his time in esoteric work and withdrawing almost completely from his medical practice. She realised the importance of having a medically qualified person within an esoteric group because someone could help many of the problems in the psychophysical makeup with expert medical knowledge.

Dion Fortune was still a slender young lady and even though she exuded power and her natural woman's liberation tendencies, she was still a very attractive person. Later she became stout and this was thought to be the result of endocrine imbalance caused by the psychic changes within her body. During her mature years, she was a fairly large lady, Nordic appearance, blond hair pulled back with a bun, piercing blue eyes, a clear complexion, and a ready sense of humour.

Thomas Penry Evans was a well-set figure, the very embodiment of manly virility and who undoubtedly formed the basis for Dr. Malcolm in the book "Moon Magic".

He was fairly heavily built with a dark, rather Welsh complexion. In medical school Penry Evans had been a very enthusiastic rugby player, and up to the time of his death used to make a point of watching as many rugby matches as he could. He appeared to be somewhat slow moving, but was a powerful figure and those who knew him always said he was kind and considerate.

It seemed to be natural that Thomas Penry Evans and Dion Fortune should have been drawn together personally and they were married in London on 7th. April 1927 with Dion Fortune's father, Arthur Firth, as one of the witnesses. This was the first marriage for each of them.

Mr. and Mrs. Thomas Penry Evans set up their home at No.3 Queensborough Terrace and then later moved to No.21b Queensborough Terrace, which was rented by the Society and used by the higher grades.

Little is known of their married life but several people close to both of them say their life was congenial and compatible although somewhat of a disappointment to Dion Fortune as far as the magnetic side of sex was concerned. All in all it seemed to be entirely harmonious. It must have been apparent to her that she had not married the ideal, magical sexual partner because many of the things she spoke about — such as the importance of the magnetic side of the sex function — did not appear to work out too well with the good Dr. Evans. It will be noted that when she wrote "Moon Magic", she was still looking through the pages of her book for an ideal magical partner.

Dion Fortune was convinced that he was a priest of considerable magical potential and proceeded to initiate him through the grades

Dr. Thomas Penry Evans

THE MEDICAL DIRECTORY 1959

115TH ANNUAL ISSUE

PART I
GENERAL ALPHABETICAL LIST A - L

LONDON

J. & A. CHURCHILL LTD

104 GLOUCESTER PLACE W.1

EVANS, Thomas Penry, "Pan," Weedon Lane, Amersham, Bucks. (*Tel.* Amersham 902)—M.R C S. Eng., L.R.C.P. Lond. 1924; D.P.H. Eng. 1940; (*Char. Cross*); C.P.H. 1924, Char. Cross Hosp.; M.O.H. Amersham R.D.C., Beaconsfield U.D.C. & Chesham U.D.C.; Sch. Med. Off. Amersham & Chesham Div. Educat. Exco.; Asst. Co. Med. Off. Bucks. C.C.; Fell. Soc. M.O.H. *Late* Med. Regist. Char. Cross Hosp.; Asst. Tuberc. Off. Metrop. Boro. Southwark; Tuberc. Off. S.E. Bucks. (Slough) Area. Author, "Smallpox with minimal lesions," *B.M.Jl.* 1947; "Rep. upon milk from a pub. health point of view, esp. bovine tuberc." *Ib.*; "Undulant fev." *Ib.*

Credentials of Dr. Thomas Penry Evans

Dr. and Mrs. Thomas Penry Evans

CERTIFIED COPY OF AN ENTRY OF MARRIAGE

Given at the GENERAL REGISTER OFFICE, LONDON

Application Number .. R19425

Registration District Paddington

1927 . Marriage solemnized at Register office
in the District of Paddington in the County of London

No.	When married	Name and Surname	Age	Condition	Rank or profession	Residence at the time of marriage	Father's name and surname	Rank or profession of father
141	Seventh April 1927	Thomas Penry Evans	34 years	Bachelor	M.R.C.S L.R.C.P	3 Queensborough Terrace	Kerry Evans	Tin Plate Manufacturer
		Violet Mary Firth	35 years	Spinster		3 Queensborough Terrace	Arthur Firth	Solicitor

Married in the Register office according to the _____ of the _____ by licence before me

This marriage was solemnized between us,
{ T P Evans
{ V M Firth
in the presence of us,
{ Arthur Firth
{ H D Evans

Percival E Kirk Registrar
Frederick P Jordan Superintendent Registrar

CERTIFIED to be a true copy of an entry in the certified copy of a Register of Marriages in the District above mentioned.

Given at the GENERAL REGISTER OFFICE, LONDON, under the Seal of the said Office, the _____ 29th _____ day of January _____ 19 86.

MB 320318

Marriage Certificate of Thos. Penry Evans and Violet M. Firth

Certificate of making Decree Nisi Absolute (Divorce) Folio N° 111

No.   of 19

IN THE HIGH COURT OF JUSTICE

FAMILY DIVISION

PRINCIPAL REGISTRY

Between   THOMAS   PENRY EVANS   Petitioner

and   VIOLET   MARY   EVANS   Respondent

and   Co-Respondent

Referring to the decree made in this cause

on the 18th day of January 19 45

whereby it was decreed that the marriage solemnised.

on the 7th day of April 19 27

at Paddington Register Office in the County of London

between THOMAS PENRY EVANS the petitioner

and VIOLET MARY EVANS then Firth Samuel the respondent

be dissolved unless sufficient cause be shown to the court within six ~~weeks~~ months from the making

thereof why the said decree should not be made absolute. and no such cause having been

shown, it is hereby certified that the said decree was

on the 30th day of July 19 45

made final and absolute and that the said marriage was thereby dissolved.

Dated this 31st day of January 19 55

Divorce Registry, Somerset House, Strand, London, WC2R 1LP.   D.242

Divorce Certificate: Decree Nisi Absolute
Thos. Penry Evans and Violet Mary Evans
Final decree 30 July 1945

CERTIFIED COPY OF AN ENTRY OF DEATH

Given at the GENERAL REGISTER OFFICE, LONDON.

Application Number. R.194.25

REGISTRATION DISTRICT   Amersham

1959. DEATH in the Sub-district of   Amersham   in the County of Buckingham

No.	Columns:— 1. When and where died	2. Name and surname	3. Sex	4. Age	5. Occupation	6. Cause of death	7. Signature, description, and residence of informant	8. When registered	9. Signature of registrar
337	Twentieth August, 1959 General Hospital, Amersham	Thomas Penry Evans	Male	66 years	of Pen Wisdom Lane Amersham Retired Medical Officer of Health M.R.C.S. L.R.C.P. D.P.H.	1(a) Cerebral Embolus (b) Auricular Fibrillation (c) Mitral Stenosis Certified by R.G. Wraughan, M.R.C.S.	V. N. Williams cousin Delfryn, Oakfield Road Pontardawe, Swansea	Thirty first August 1959	H.G. Piggin Registrar

CERTIFIED to be a true copy of an entry in the certified copy of a Register of Deaths in the District above mentioned.
Given at the GENERAL REGISTER OFFICE, LONDON, under the Seal of the said Office, the 20th day of January 19 85.

This certificate is issued in pursuance of the Births and Deaths Registration Act 1953. Section 34 provides that any certified copy of an entry purporting to be sealed or stamped with the seal of the General Register Office shall be received as evidence of the birth or death to which it relates without any further or other proof of the entry, and no certified copy purporting to have been given in the said Office shall be of any force or effect unless it is sealed or stamped as aforesaid.
CAUTION:—Any person who (1) falsifies any of the particulars on this certificate, or (2) uses a falsified certificate as true, knowing it to be false, is liable to prosecution.

DA 779374

Form A509 Dd. 236425 20M May(2160)

Death Certificate: Thomas Penry Evans, 13 August 1959.

6 BUCKS EXAMINER, Friday, September 4th, 1940

'DOC' EVANS DIES AGED 66

DR. THOMAS PENRY EVANS, of Pan, Weedon-lane, Amersham, died at Amersham General Hospital on Sunday, aged 66 years. The funeral was held at 11.30 a.m. yesterday (Thursday) at Ruislip crematorium. . . . Those are bare words. Dr. Evans was a leading character in the Amersham, Beaconsfield and Chesham Local Government districts for 17 years; he was, in fact, a character to be reckoned with, all his life.

But his association with this area began in 1941, when he took up his office as Medical Officer of Health for Beaconsfield. He assumed the responsibility of the other areas after the war.

His health began to fail in the latter years. He had been a wonderful person to work with, a health department official said this week. "I can think of nothing but good to say about him . . . he was really well liked by the whole staff."

Dr. Evans' retirement came in September last year. A few months earlier, when this had been announced, we gave the brief outlines of his life, and added at the end: "Ironically, his future activities will depend on his health."

He had been in hospital twice during the weeks before his death on Sunday, although when revisiting his old colleagues he had never made any fuss about his health.

Dr. Evans qualified in 1924, and took on a "house job" at Charing Cross Hospital. His next duty was that of Assistant Medical Officer in the County Borough of East Ham; then Medical Superintendent at East Ham Sanatorium. Here he became Tuberculosis Officer.

He was looking for something new, and, at his own factory, began research on foodstuffs—especially products of the soya bean. This work continued until 1938. In that year the Spanish Republican Government invited Dr. Evans to go out to try to deal with the nutrition problems of children in Spain.

He accepted the invitation, and set up his equipment; but he had been in Barcelona only eight weeks when Gen. Franco returned.

"I had to fly for my life," . . . leaving equipment valued at the time at £2,500. It was never recovered. Dr. Evans was proud of the eight weeks he spent in Barcelona—"Though it was a failure, I am more pleased with that failure than I am with anything else I've ever done."

Anyway, he had to start off again, and he became Assistant Tuberculosis Officer at Southwark Borough Council until the outbreak of war. Then he was appointed Deputy A.R.P. Warden in Southwark and the Elephant and Castle district. And so to 1941, when he came to this district. And on to his retirement.

of the Society as fast as she could. She took every shortcut in his advancement through the Lesser Mysteries. This speed was something that she found to be a mistake, and would not consider such action in her later work.

Dr. Evans undoubtedly had real magical ability and this was rapidly brought back into consciousness but not at the speed he was being advanced. Dion Fortune seemed to be forcing him through the various grades of the system at such a fast rate that he was confused and bewildered. Then he was initiated into the Greater Mysteries of which he had no concept whatsoever. The problem came from the fact that the preliminary training, the foundation work, had been skimped and this lack would not support the advanced magical work.

Undoubtedly Dion Fortune's enormous drive, enthusiasm, and magical ability must have helped to involve him more deeply than he probably would have become if left to himself. After some years of marriage with Dion Fortune and close involvement in the affairs of the Society of the Inner Light, he sometimes appeared to be bewildered by the weight of the esoteric knowledge and responsibility placed upon his shoulders.

Dion Fortune worked with Thomas Penry Evans on the Isis Formula, an Egyptian ritual work to enhance the Goddess's powers, emphasising the feminine potency of God. Many of the exerts from the Rite of Isis, which appear in *"The Sea Priestess"* and *"Moon Magic"*, came from her work with Penry Evans.

Dion Fortune and Dr. Penry Evans married in 1927 and separated some 10 years later. They were divorced in 1945, just six months before her death. As far as is known, the separation between the two of them was amicable.

Dr. Evans was well qualified medically and after their separation in the mid-1930s, he returned to his medical work. During the Spanish Civil War he was asked to go to Spain to advise on nutrition, but had only been there a few months when the tides of war changed and he was expelled from the country and sent back home. Later he had a small factory where he experimented and produced health foods; particularly those based upon the Soya bean. Dion Fortune had written a book on the subject of Soya beans and whether Dion

Fortune interested him in the Soya bean or whether he was the one who told her about it, is not known.

However, there was of course, the question of the group. Because he was a member of the group, how was the resignation from the group to be effected? There was some trauma associated with this, and certain of Dr. Evans' possessions were inadvertently left behind in Queensborough Terrace when he moved out. These were ceremonially and ritually burned and exorcised after his departure, in case he should use them as a channel back into the group or to bring in adverse forces.

Little mention is made by Dion Fortune of him, except obliquely, up to the time of her death. Some people have suggested that had she had a more adult relationship with him it is possible that her death in 1946 could have been avoided. Some say that she failed to work through the very psychological and magnetic stages she advocated for the heroes and heroines in her various books.

For a while after he actually moved out of Queensborough Terrace around 1937, nothing was heard from him. He separated himself completely from the occult and devoted himself once again to medicine. If there is any blame to be attached to this relationship, it must be placed on Dion Fortune herself; poor Dr. Evans appears to have been completely blameless.

Several modern authorities looking at the life of Dion Fortune and the work of the Society of the Inner Light have never been in an esoteric group. These commentators do not know the conditions therein, and have suggested that the whole thing was some sort of rather dirty joke. It was not. Without a doubt, she held within her hand a very precious key to the freedom of the human individual and his future progress. It is almost axiomatic in the modern occult society that no one whose personal psycho-sexual life is not relatively free can make progress within the mysteries. These things we now take for granted but it must be remembered that in the 1930s such things would have been almost unspeakable and therefore she did a very great service in this area. Nowadays the attitude of modern mysteries would be to regard the whole matter with a good sense of humour. There is a sense of proportion in all this and it is unlikely that the modern mystic would be in any way as confined within his own psycho-sexual structure as were people in the 1930s in the United Kingdom.

Dion Fortune has been castigated for preaching a sort of infantile sexual freedom but this criticism is not justified as it was due almost entirely to a misunderstanding of the principles on which she was forced to operate at that time.

GENERAL SOCIETY OPERATIONS

Circa 1935

By the year 1935, the Society was on a sound footing. It was financially stable, had good membership, and the headquarters at No.3 Queensborough Terrace was functioning satisfactorily both as a base for its general activities and also as an *enclosed community* with very limited access to outsiders.

If one was to look at the group at this time and analyse the membership, there would be two broad categories of members. By far the largest category would be those members who were attached to the society because they had been initiated into some grade within the group and were in fact working through the grades of the Lesser Mysteries. Almost all of these initiates would have ordinary jobs to go to and ordinary homes where they lived. Some lived in the London area but quite a few lived some distance away. As far as the London and distant members were concerned, their participation in the Society of the Inner Light and the headquarters at No.3 Queensborough Terrace was quite different from the second group who lived more intensely within the *enclosed house, the "house of the order"*, as it was called.

A typical member who was working his way through the grade system would probably attend one ritual a month and that would be the ritual of his particular grade. Dion Fortune's group used three grades in the Lesser Mysteries, and if the initiate were in the second grade then he would have the right to attend rituals of his own grade and the grade below him. So, by arrangement with the officer in charge, he would be able to attend first-degree rituals as well as his own. Again, if he were judged fit to take some office in the First-Degree Lodge then he would be required to attend the first-degree meetings in order to perform his function as an officer. From

No.3 Queensborough Terrace, London.
Photo by Donald Brooks. Enfield.

his point of view, the group headquarters would be a place where he came to attend the lodge of his grade and perhaps to act as Officer in a grade lower than his. He would meet the fellow members there, join in a certain amount of social interaction but this was not encouraged because a ritual was considered to finish only an hour or so after the actual meeting. Therefore, apart from a quick cup of coffee and some light refreshments, there was no encouragement of random talking, or casual chat. Nevertheless he would have social opportunities and many members who came up to London from a distance enjoyed renewing their acquaintanceship with other members and perhaps went out to dinner later in the evening to talk about subjects of mutual interest.

If they only attended a meeting once a month or perhaps twice a month, what did they do for their esoteric development the rest of the time? When a person came out of the world into the first degree of Dion Fortune's fraternity, he or she would already have attended lectures, possibly taken one form of the supplementary study course and would be familiar with the discipline of daily meditation. On entering the Society, the initiation ritual would have made an impression on the initiate. Each new initiate was given a quite thick envelope of knowledge papers and a set of procedures they were asked to follow. They were instructed to continue to perform daily meditation along given subjects. They were asked to visualise the temple layout appropriate for their degree, and to work with considerable dedication and one pointedness upon the subject matter of the particular degree, which probably referred to an aspect of consciousness. The stress laid upon the teaching material for that degree, plus the psychological and inner-plane pressure upon the initiates, would force them into an increasing contact with the uncomfortable realities of the mundane world. In short, the new initiates would be put in a position where they had to become aware of the world around them. Circumstances would no longer permit them to drift above the surface, they would have to come down into the world and get on with it.

The actual formal work, daily meditation, attendance at rituals and so on, was only a small part of their involvement in the mysteries. The very pressures of their mystery life would be changing their inner being at the same time. When they actually arrived at *the house of the order* for their ritual they would normally be allowed to spend a small amount of time in the library when they could return or change a book for example. Remember, they probably came up from the country, perhaps a hundred or so miles, and therefore this time would be the only time they had to make such arrangements.

Then they would enter a Robing Room and would come under the direction of the Robing Room Mistress whose job it was to make sure that everyone was properly robed and that robing was completed in time for entry into the lodge. On arrival, their name would have been recorded in a register kept for the purpose so their attendance would be noted because attendance at a certain number of meetings was an essential part of the requirements of any grade of the Fraternity. At the same time the register would enable those concerned with the layout of the temple to make sure that there was adequate seating and not too many or too few places.

The robing procedure was done in complete silence. There would normally be a period of about ten minutes after robing before the brethren of the Fraternity were called into the lodge. Robing was considered an essential part of the ritual procedure, as was the disrobing at the end of the session. On entering the lodge the member would sit in silence, meditating upon the symbolism appropriate to his or her degree and await the ceremonial sealing of the lodge, using some variation of *the lesser pentagram ritual.*

The ritual proper would then proceed and be followed by the closing sealing, the exit from the temple, and the disrobing, again in silence.

There would have been refreshments laid out in the dining room in the basement where the members would have been allowed to congregate for a brief period of time to restore themselves to normality before many of them had to rush back to trains and travel back to the homes where they lived.

Meanwhile, the burden of the work of preparing the temple for the Lesser Mysteries which involved assembling the entire lodge must now be disassembled and this task fell again upon the members who lived in the house and whose duty it was to make the conditions possible for the Fraternity to operate.

There was a distinct sense of removal; there was a distance between the outside members and the central core of the group who lived on the premises. A member who came in occasionally in this manner would probably regard with a certain amount of awe those dedicated and privileged people who lived in the centre of things in the house itself. And, in fact, to some extent they were right. Outside members had very little idea as to what actually went on and practically no concept of the pressures and the pace of life that went on within the restrictions of a closed esoteric fraternity.

It is tempting to compare a closed community such as Dion Fortune was running in 1935 with that of a monastic community. Undoubtedly there are certain similarities. There is the sociological similarity where a number of people are confined in a limited space and have to get along as best they can when each of them may have a very distinct and quite strong personality. Then there are the psychological constraints as in a monastic community where presumably the members are dedicated, have a common goal, and so on, and have a sort of group psychology working as well.

The difference lies in the fact that a monastic community in the established church is normally organised around what is called *the rule*. The rule is generally a set of procedures, which are supposed to lead the members of the community in the quickest possible way toward the light, in the case of a Christian community, which is to the Christ-like state. The rule has to be obeyed in a monastic community and all breaches, whether minor breaches of etiquette or major breaches of obedience, are breaches against the rule. Consequently obedience is paramount, also of course, poverty, chastity, and so on are an added part.

In this respect the esoteric community differs markedly. First, the members are encouraged to show the greatest possible amount of free will and self-enterprise. With the working out of a man's individual part of the great Plan it is natural that a person showing his or her own personal enterprise may clash with someone else's personal enterprise and the two matters may have to be reconciled. The vow of poverty also is obviously not applicable. If any member of the enclosed community was wealthy, then so be it. If one was poor, then so be it. The vow of poverty would be really interpreted in a different sort of way where the emphasis would be on not being dependent upon the resources of the world, which is quite a different thing to a vow of perpetual poverty.

Chastity is another subject which must come up and this naturally is rigidly enforced in an enclosed religious order, and just as naturally not enforced in an enclosed order of an occult type. However, there are interesting side issues on the matter of chastity within an occult enclosed group. Although there will be no question of chastity as a virtue, in fact it might almost be described as a vice in many conditions, the members of the group by the very life they led would not find it easy to make contact with members of the opposite sex who were not in the Society, not in the enclosed group, and not even of the required grade. So, in fact, there was a sort of invisible filter put upon the operations and the emotional lives of the members of the community. For practical reasons, due to the fact that they spent much of their time in *the enclosed house,* they could hardly meet members of the opposite sex who were not interested in the same subject. They could never invite non-group members back to the house because it was a closed place to people from the outside. Because of the strange life that they lived, and their unusual beliefs, it is doubtful whether easy communication and relationship would have built up with anyone who was not interested in the same line of country.

Anyone living in this privileged, closed community, would have been again, in one or two categories. The first category were those who lived and worked in the house and whose entire life was dedicated, twenty-four hours a day, to the practical application of the precepts of the mysteries. Such people had no external employment and were engaged in esoteric-specialist jobs within the community most of their time. Such people were given a small allowance, unless they had their own money, and were normally paid a nominal amount to take an annual holiday. In that sense I suppose they would come under the condition of enforced poverty but it was not a natural enforcement. The people in this category tended to spend almost all of their time apart from a required period of exercise or leisure in active esoteric work.

The other category of enclosed order members were those who

had work in the outside world, who pursued a normal profession, but who lived and spent the rest of their time entirely within the walls of *the house of the order*. The relationship in 1935 was roughly 4 to 1. There would probably have been about eight or nine people in the enclosed part of the order and of those seven or eight would spend all of their time within the house. One or occasionally two of the enclosed members would fall in the second category and go out during the day to pursue a normal profession. In a way the strain on those who had to go out and do an ordinary job and then return to the very special, very rare and heightened conditions, would be considerably greater. But they did have additional freedom and the ability to meet people in the world and broaden their lives.

In this connection, the second type who pursued their vocations in the world had a problem like that of deconditioning a diver who goes down into the depths of the sea. If you bring him up too fast he gets the bends due to an excess of nitrogen in the bloodstream. It is really the change of conditions, the change of pressure that causes the problem. The same sort of thing happened to those who spent part of their life in the world and part within the order. The change of pressure of their environment was so marked that in many cases special sealing of rituals were employed to seal the aura of the person concerned so that he did not take out into the world forces which would have caused disruption, and in a reverse sense, it was necessary to divest himself of the influence of the world quickly by using this sealing procedure when he re-entered the house at the end of the day. The sealing procedure was a variation of the well-known Lesser Ritual of the Pentagram and it was employed in an outward direction in the person's aura on leaving the house - that is a barrier was made stopping things from going out from the aura, and on returning, a banishing was made to push out from the extremities of the aura any remaining influences from the outside world.

At all times in the enclosed group's history there seems to have been at least one person who worked in the world. Certainly one of the foremost members of the Society, Mr. Thomas Loveday, worked for many years for the Tramways Corporation and had to go out and do a hard days work, come back in the evening and take up his very considerable esoteric duties. As time went on and the group expanded, more members came into this category.

Looking at the lives of the members in the enclosed group and taking first those who were permanent residents and who devoted all their time to the work, it is necessary to have some idea of the layout of the house in order to get an idea of what was going on. The house at No. 3 Queensborough Terrace was a typical thin London house, tall and rather narrow, but it had a large number of rooms in it and these were pressed into service in two different ways. There were first of all, the public rooms. One of these would have been the library and the room above the library where Dion Fortune would give public lectures. These rooms were pressed into service for other purposes when she was not actually in contact with the public. To these areas of the house the public had limited access.

There were the rooms set aside for the ritual operations of the Society of the Inner Light, that is to say the Lesser Mysteries, which, of course, comprised three degrees. The large room set aside for this was occasionally used for other purposes and had to be set up as a ritual temple before each meeting took place. Sometimes when there was public involvement soon afterwards the temple had to be taken down again. This unsatisfactory state of affairs, amazingly enough, persisted through much of Dion Fortune's time. As far as the members who came in from outside were concerned, it was always seen as the temple properly set up and to them it would have appeared permanent. But, to the people who lived in the house it was quite a hassle in setting it up and taking it down to fit in with the other obligations that the household had.

Quite apart from this room there were a number of other rooms. These were of two types; those rooms devoted to esoteric purposes, and other rooms, which had a dual purpose. The dual-purpose rooms were for the residents to live in and for them a number of smallish rooms were set aside. These rooms were dual purpose because they were used as a bed sitting room some of the time, and they doubled up as specialist temples at other times. To make this clearer, suppose a person was living in the group permanently, he would have certain occult work to do for the group in general, and other esoteric work to do for himsel,f such as meditation, visualisation, and so on. In both of these cases the room could be pressed into quick service by the use of certain hangings, curtains and symbols. The result would be quite an effective small temple. In fact, the members were encouraged to dedicate their rooms as temples to different types of force. The force being that considered most appropriate for their own self-development.

For a good percentage of the day some of these living-in members would be performing routine clerical tasks, but at intervals from half an hour to one hour in length, there would be intense esoteric activity perhaps going on in three or four separate members' rooms at the same time. The sort of thing that went on could have been anything from meditation work upon different subjects, some for personal development and some of it to lay stress upon a particular subject to help the group-mind of the group itself. Other type of work would consist of definite directive work such as Rising on the Planes - changing the levels of consciousness, doing experimental work, investigating different planes of existence, and so on.

A large dining room was used for communal meals and in 1935 there was also a lay staff who prepared meals and served them. Therefore, all members of the enclosed community who were there at the time, ate together. Discussion of esoteric matters at meals was frowned upon. Meals were a time for complete relaxation.

Members living-in were involved in two types of work— the general routine, running of the house type and everyone had a duty to play in this, and there was the esoteric work which was a mixture of personal and group effort. Also there were major group rituals which could involve all of the people living in the house and which were performed in the Great Mystery Temple, a dedicated room that was never disturbed. A major ritual could involve considerable preparation — meditation beforehand, special robing arrangements, and the ritual itself.

At the end of a normal day there could have been anything from two to six periods of intense occult work carried out by a member living inside the group in addition to his household chores.

For those who worked outside, the problems were greater. They missed some of the esoteric work during the day but had to come home, have a quick meal, and then they were flung into the occult work of the enclosed group. They did not normally have the nominal household tasks to perform but, on the other hand, were fully involved in any ritual work, meditation and research going on in the same way as the full-time members.

One person who spent a considerable time living in the house and who was working out in the world, actually made a calculation and worked out that he spent more time dressed in robes than out of them. This gives some idea of the amount of esoteric involvement there was. It must not be thought that this esoteric work was sporadic, without discipline, and just intended to experiment on the inner-planes. This was not true. The whole focus of Dion Fortune's work was centred around the inner-plane communications from the Masters, as she called them, and they gave very firm direction to the group about its development and future. Consequently suggestions and even dictates coming through from inner-plane sources would have inspired almost all the work described.

The last category of work applies to both types of members, but particularly to those who were permanently in the house. This was work involving trance. Any work involving trance means that the medium had to dissociate consciousness completely from the physical plane during the time of the trance. There was also a period of time after the trance when there was a degree of dissociation. The person would not be fit for normal human relations, or work in the world.

Those members who lived in permanently and who had been trained as mediums would, in addition to their other duties, be expected to undergo trance-training sessions for one or two periods each day. The preparation for trance and the length of time spent afterwards getting over the trance was almost as long as the period itself.

There was very little time left to pursue idle pleasures. Rules were laid down that everyone should take at least an hour off during the day and walk in Kensington Gardens, which was adjacent to Queensborough Terrace in order to get some fresh air and exercise. One period was set aside during the year when no occult work was to be done and this was devoted to a holiday. The permanent residents were more or less forcibly ejected from the house and sent away somewhere. But apart from that something like six-sevenths of their time within the house would have been spent on esoteric projects of one sort or another.

The esoteric work performed by people living within the enclosed order could be divided into three types. Quite a lot of the work was directed by the inner-plane advisors of the group. This work that they wanted would be either for the benefit of the group as a whole or for the particular development of the person concerned.

The next category would be work where the initiates were given a project, a subject, or a requirement, and then they were left to interpret it in their own way because they were in some way expert in that particular field. One might be told that it was necessary to do some work upon the forces behind the god Apollo, Solar forces that concern the cult of Apollo. Perhaps due to the inner constitution within the group or some past experience, one might specialise in this topic and one would be left to interpret the best way to work out this inner-plane requirement.

A great deal of the work was for personal regeneration. It must be remembered that the people in any group — no matter what grade — are far from perfect and therefore require continuous work upon themselves. They are always aiming towards the next higher stage. This is not done merely for their own personal benefit, but because they will be more useful members of the esoteric community and of more use to the inner-plane adepts. Some of the time was spent working on their own personal regeneration.

These are three types of esoteric work: work which the group was allowed to interpret, work which was personal for the individual regeneration, and work assigned by the inner-plane adepti probably through the Warden, for the good of the group or for the community in general.

All of this work occupied an enormous amount of total time and space. Some projects were going on in one room, some procedures or experiments were taking place in another room, and perhaps joint group rituals in the evening in which all the inner members were to participate. Then there were things like meals to fit in and a certain amount of personal time and exercise. Because of all this the practical constraints on those living within the community were considerable. It was frowned upon to make a noise in any corridor. It was improper to enter the room of a friend without knocking because it was quite likely that the friend was doing special work. A complicated sort of semaphore system was actually adopted where signs were put up near the doors of individual rooms indicating roughly what was going on inside so that it was possible to walk down a corridor and with a practised flick of the eyes, know whether or not it was permitted to sneeze, or whether there should be complete silence for the next half hour. Ordinary domestic activities had to go on in the house and these inevitably make noise — boilers have to be fuelled, meals have to be cooked, washing up has to be done. These were generally phased to occupy the minimum possible time or a time in the day when the esoteric activity of the household was taking place in the most remote room of the house.

To make all this fit together required a considerable amount of good will, and really amounted to learning a whole new code of etiquette. With people being so busy all the time with these very tiring and concentrated activities, it was important not to impinge upon other persons' privacy, upon their space, or upon their time, unless they agreed and required it. One developed a sort of sixth sense when meeting someone, knowing whether or not to talk to them or leave them alone. This perhaps is no more than a hyperdeveloped social sense but certainly was most necessary within the enclosed environment.

THE WAR YEARS

Hitler invaded Poland in 1939 and Great Britain became involved in the Second World War. Ordinary lodge work was curtailed and when the bombing blitz of London was in progress regular attendance was impossible for many members. *The Inner Light Magazine* was supplemented by a series of weekly letters intended to keep members, probationers and friends informed, and also to weld together an effective group-mind. The weekly letters rapidly became a remarkable institution, and Dion Fortune let down the barriers and included much information that would normally have been reserved for initiates only.

One of the features of the letters was a group-meditation in which all could join together in mind and spirit even on a worldwide basis. The meditation took two forms: (1) there was either a key phrase to meditate on, or (2) a guided meditation. London members and students who could manage to attend the Queensborough Terrace headquarters on a Sunday morning participated in the guided meditation under Dion Fortune's direction. Those throughout the world who could not attend in person participated remotely by using the same material at the same time. Letters were sent out well in advance but were not to be opened until the day the work was to be undertaken.

Careful instructions were prepared by Dion Fortune and sent out to all interested parties. These directions outlined the procedure for the meditation work, which she had divided into several stages. Stage 1, the student was to sit in a quiet, dimly lit room, free from outside interference, face toward London, with the feet together and the hands clasped to make a closed auric circuit, and then to study and think about the letter. The hands, the student was told, should rest on the weekly letter lying upon his or her lap, and the student was told that these letters were consecrated before being sent out in order that they could form a link. Then a slow, relaxed breathing was to be undertaken with a slight pause at the beginning and ending of each breath. It was stressed that the attitude should be poised, free from strain, and could be either sitting or lying. The position should be taken up a few minutes before the meditation was due to start so there would be time to settle into a posture of balanced relaxation and to stabilise the breathing. Once the meditation had begun, the student was to think no more about the mechanism of the breathing.

Stage 2, the meditation started. First by thinking about the subject allotted for the work of the week and attempting to realise its spiritual implications, but under no circumstances to consider its practical ones for it was believed that such thought would distract and cause the mind to wander. It was necessary to realise what ethical principles were involved and the student was advised that if there was knowledge of a Qabalistic method then the meditation should be aligned with the symbolism of the Tree of Life.

Stage 3, having thoroughly filled the mind with the ideas set for the meditation work, one pictured in the imagination a symbolic image, or a figure, or a scene, that symbolised that idea. Keeping this before the mind's eye, the thought processes were slowed down until there was feeling about the subject rather than reason. Trying to listen mentally, the mental stillness was not held for more than a few seconds, even if there were results. The student was told that this was a very potent method of mind working and it is not good to do it for too long at a time.

The real work started in the next phase, Stage 4. Here, it was necessary mentally to dedicate one's self in the name of the All-Good to the service of the One Life without distinction of friend or foe. Let the good that is to be invoked come through for all, relying upon the Cosmic Law to adapt it to the needs of healing.

In stage 5, the student thought of himself as a part of the group-soul of the culture. His life as a part of it's life, and it's life the basis of his life. Then, invoking the name of God, the mind was opened as a channel of the work of the Masters of the Wisdom.

Stage 6 was meditating again on the subject set for the work of the week.

Finally, Stage 7. At the conclusion say aloud: "It is finished." Imagine a pair of black velvet curtains being drawn across the scene built up in the imagination, as if it were on a stage. Let the curtains approach from either side until they meet in the middle, thus blocking out the scene. Then the student is to arise from his seat and stamp his foot firmly on the ground to affirm his return to normal consciousness.

The student was told to always be very careful to close down after meditation, otherwise he could find himself still tuned in and becoming over sensitive.

As to the work itself, the meditations on phrases were intended to consolidate the moral and spiritual integrity of the nation at a time of trial and peril, but they developed into more magical and symbolic work. The small London group, who met at the same time for the worldwide meditation, began to psychically pick up visual symbols. Patterns on the Tree of Life were developed and one particularly vivid and important configuration which built up over a matter of some weeks, was of a three-dimensional aspect of the Tree with the Christ seen in an ovoid of white light in Tiphareth, at the apex of a pyramid whose lower plane base corners were represented by a mounted sword bearing the figure of King Arthur in the red of Geburah; a seated figure of Merlin bearing a sceptre in the blue of Chesed; and in the purple of Yesod, was a figure of the Virgin Mary.

There was also other work connected with the boundaries of the country. In one notable guided meditation which was conducted mentally from the tower on the Tor at Glastonbury, there was a vision of a sort of angelic patrol about the boundaries of the country and the building of a centre of spiritual power in a cave at one of the great mystical centres.

It should be understood clearly that this work never descended onto the personality level, there was never an instance of 'God bless our cannons and damn the enemies'. The meditation on single phrases which form part of the work concerned principles: Truth, Justice, etc.

It is interesting that Dion Fortune initiated this work at that time under the stimulus of the War, because revelations of practical occult working of this kind were virtually unheard of then. Occult secrecy applied under sanctions of terrible oaths from the Golden Dawn days and covered all magical operations and only the abstract principles were allowed to filter through into books.

This work continued throughout the war. There is no doubt it constituted a powerful, magical presence within the group-soul of the British. The freedom of individual action caused by the unusual conditions of the war, undoubtedly removed many barriers and in the later work of the Society this principle of freedom of information surfaced again, but to a lesser degree, as part of the modern climate.

SEXUAL POLARITY

Sex meant a lot to Dion Fortune, not just the physical part but the vital magnetic and emotional flow between a man and a woman that makes for true relationship. Marie Stopes and other pioneers had been active in releasing women from the physical ignorance of the Victorian age, but of the subtle side of sexual interplay there was little appreciation. Occultists, like everyone else have to work within the society into which they are born, exploiting opportunity and overcoming constraints, and Dion Fortune was no exception.

In her novel *"The Sea Priestess"*, the central character, Lilith LeFay Morgan was trying to use the bewildered and sometimes unwilling Wilfred as one terminal in an experiment in magical polarity. The idea was for each partner to link-up with the cosmic principle of maleness or femaleness and then, by magical means, drive a channel through the twists and blockages of mind and emotions into the conscious personality. This was not being done for Wilfred's personal good alone but in an exemplary manner for the benefit of mankind. It is worth noting that the experiment, which forms the central theme of the book, did not culminate in physical sex; in fact it specifically excluded it because the experimental target was magnetic relationship rather than physical congress. Later, Wilfred was to repeat the work with his wife Molly in a rite that included physical union.

Following the philosophy of the Tree of Life, Dion Fortune considered all the parts of man as equally vital and holy. Each aspect formed a link in a chain that reached from spirit to body and the chain was as strong as its weakest link. Any element in the system could block the channel and inhibit the free movement of energy and inspiration. Weak links could break under the strain of magical practices where the flow of force is greatly increased, and blockages could colour and distort the clear light of mystical inspiration. The lower levels of man were the end-point of all operations and a vital link too often forgotten. Dion Fortune once said, regarding one of the more rabid biblical prophets, that the level of his rhetoric would have been greatly elevated had he had the use of an efficient laxative! In the same way she agreed with her fellow psychologists that effective sexual polarity was one of the keys to human fulfilment.

Dion Fortune was, above all, a pragmatist. Having once received an idea she would immediately try to put it into practice. She had accumulated a good deal of information on the subject of Atlantis through her own mediumship, some of it concerning experiments in emotional, magnetic and sexual polarity. In this legendary land, selected priests and priestesses were said to have been paired off for magical work of this type. The aims were, apparently, to correct personality faults, remedy deficiencies and extend the range of human capability. In short, to heal and to assist the evolutionary process.

The idea of putting this ancient priestly practice into a modern context probably originated shortly before the war of 1939-45. But there is no firm evidence as to when she first got the polarity work under way. Possibly the war delayed her, but there was no shortage of dedicated group members of both sexes to take part. No doubt many of her initiates had just the sort of development imbalances and blockages that she considered could be helped by this sort of operation. Dion Fortune restricted most of the work to the higher grades under strict conditions of secrecy. The majority of those involved lived at No.3 Queensborough Terrace or at number 21a, further up the road.

When the war broke out the life of the group had to be reorganised to cope with the new circumstances. Dion Fortune died shortly after the war and before the group had fully re-established itself, so there had been little opportunity to develop the work while she was still alive.

After her sudden death, this remarkable woman lost no time in re-establishing control of her Society, using mediumship as her channel and the High Priestess as her viceroy. Soon after Chichester became Warden of the Society, the polarity workings were reinstated under her direction from the inner-planes and continued until about 1949 when a major reorganisation of the group took place.

Two distinct levels of working were operated. In the first, the male and female partners functioned on inner levels only and no physical congress took place. Using techniques of *visualisation* and *composition of place*, an attempt was made to contact a particular wavelength of energy, a type of force usually associated with a god or other mythological figure. An example might be the force of Apollo for the male partner and perhaps Aphrodite for the woman. When both participants considered that they had made a satisfactory contact with the forces, the higher energies were channelled through the deliberately aroused feeling nature to form a circuit. In this method there was sometimes contact between the partners, by linking hands palm-to-palm, for example, but no overt sex. Dion Fortune gives a partial description (shorn of the higher aspects) in *"The Winged Bull"* when Ursula Brangwyn *magnetises* Ted Murchison.

In the second level of working, the same principles applied. Each initiate aimed to become a channel for the force invoked. In this case, however, the culmination was physical. The level of work would have been chosen on the basis of the apparent needs of the partners.

No initiate was ever forced to participate in this work, neither was there any enforced selection of partners. Suggestions were certainly made but there was no compulsion. The details of the working were left to the initiates concerned. There were none of the trappings of magical sex described in the more lurid occult novels. There were no naked priestesses draped over altars. The operation was controlled from inner levels by the active imagination.

Now, for control to be maintained over the astral images in conditions of considerable emotional tension (not to mention honest-to-god lust) is far from easy. There is little doubt that some failed to achieve the high purpose of the working. Just how much real benefit was gained is impossible to say.

About one thing there is no doubt; no matter how problematical the results, the intentions were of the very highest. This was no esoteric brothel with an inner-plane *Madame* in the wings. There was nothing that was sordid in either the idea or its implementation. Foolish it may have been, but in this chapter of its life, the Society of the Inner Light has nothing of which to be ashamed.

The Grave of Dion Fortune, Glastonbury.
Photo by Martin Staines, Glastonbury.

DEPARTURE

The war had seemed as if it would go on forever, but it was finally over. Both V-E Day and V-J Day had passed. The euphoria of victory was dispersing. Now people had to pick up the pieces, and Dion Fortune was no exception. Bombing had damaged the Queensborough Terrace house and reconstruction work needed supervising. A few members had been killed and some had moved away to other parts of the country, and there was a shortage of help as well.

The Glastonbury property was another problem. It was in need of care and attention and required reorganising to accommodate the new work that Dion Fortune envisaged. She had refused to take up residence there during the war, believing that her proper place was at the centre of things in London.

Amid all this uncertainty, depressing austerity and continued food rationing, Dion Fortune worked on. Lodge work was reduced but trance communications from the Inner Planes continued. She was writing, too. The current manuscript at that time was *"Moon Magic"*, the sequel to *"The Sea Priestess"*. The book was not proving easy to write. Several times she had torn up the copy in despair and started afresh. The figure of the priestess Lilith fascinated her and not until she let Lilith take over and dictate the book in the first person was the writing successful. As the novel developed, Dion Fortune became more and more bound up with her fictional moon priestess until her involvement developed into a mild form of obsession. Lilith embodied so many of Dion Fortune's qualities, not all of them regenerate, that she functioned as a schizoid aspect of Dion Fortune's Higher Self, in what is called a *magical body*.

Dion Fortune had always been a forceful personality. No one could have achieved what she had done without a very dynamic

CERTIFIED COPY OF AN ENTRY OF DEATH

Given at the GENERAL REGISTER OFFICE, LONDON.

Application Number 3427 A

REGISTRATION DISTRICT St. Marylebone

1946 DEATH in the Sub-district of All Souls in the Metropolitan Borough of St. Marylebone

No.	When and where died	Name and surname	Sex	Age	Occupation	Cause of death	Signature, description, and residence of informant	When registered	Signature of registrar
295	Eighth January 1946 Middlesex Hospital	Violet Mary Evans	Female	55 years	of 218 Queensborough Paddington W.2. divorced wife of Thomas Perry Evans, Medical Practitioner	1(a) Acute myeloid Leukaemia p.m. Certified by Cecil McIver MRCS	D. K. Cregg Causing the body to be buried 218 Queensborough Terrace W.2	Eighth January 1946	Frank Bethell Interim Registrar

CERTIFIED to be a true copy of an entry in the certified copy of a Register of Deaths in the District above mentioned.

Given at the GENERAL REGISTER OFFICE, LONDON, under the Seal of the said Office, the 17th day of July 1980.

DA 724076

Death Certificate: Violet Mary Evans, London, 8 January 1946.

approach to life. Everyone has faults and she was no exception. Sometimes she could be intolerant, overbearing or just plain bossy. People who knew her at this phase of her life noted that she appeared to be growing more dictatorial. Also a tendency toward flamboyance, usually kept well under control, was emerging. There is little doubt that unconscious elements in her psyche were making themselves known. In the words of an acquaintance, she was getting the bit between her teeth and Lilith LeFay Morgan was showing her scarlet claws.

All this is quite normal at a certain stage in an initiate's progress. It is blatantly obvious to everyone (except the subject) and is quickly dealt with. When the matter is confronted and seen for what it is, it can be equilibrated and eliminated. A valuable enhancement of the personality is the usual result. In Dion Fortune's case, there was no one available at the time with the required stature and authority to take the necessary steps. She should have been warned. Someone should have worked with her to clear the condition — or even joked her out of the state she was in. But there was no one. As a result, the condition developed. In retrospect, there is little doubt that her effectiveness and validity suffered from this uncorrected pathology and thus also her fitness to lead the group diminished.

"Uneasy lies the head that wears a crown". Leadership of an occult group is no sinecure — the Sword of Damocles always hangs above the head, and the thread is very thin. Group leaders are often so busy directing, inspiring and building, that they fail to correct their own faults or take the time to satisfy their own spiritual needs. The *office* of group leader is frequently confused with the human being who fills the title and the results are neither good for the leader nor the group itself.

Dion Fortune had returned from a trip to Glastonbury rather tired and complaining of a bad toothache. She was unable to contact her own dentist but a member of the group known as Uncle Robbie had been a practising dentist and offered to examine her. Whatever it was he saw certainly alarmed him and he recommended immediate treatment. She consulted her own dentist when he returned and was admitted to the Middlesex Hospital in London where she died in a few days. The Death Certificate gave the cause of death as acute myeloid leukaemia. She was 55 years old. Her body was taken to Glastonbury where it was buried.

The Mysteries teach that death is just a phase in the great quest. The group, operating on this precept, carried on as normal. A newly admitted member, being interviewed for the post of Secretary to the Society, recalls being told at the end of the interview, just as she was preparing to leave the room, "Oh, by the way, Dion Fortune is dead!"

"The King is dead; long live the King!" But there was no one to assume the mantle. Dion Fortune had failed to train a successor. The line was broken.

THE MAGICAL BODY

Each inner-plane adept is assigned a special type of work. In occult terminology he is on a special Ray and it is his destiny to work through his own tasks. Each inner-plane adept is especially interested in a particular phase of occult work with some specialising in one thing and some in another.

When communication is established with an inner-plane adept, and if the communication is effective in person-to-person interchange, then there is a strong sense of personality present which has been variously reported as feeling like you have just had a strong whiskey or received a kick in the pants, the touching of one strong personality and another.

What is not generally known is that in many cases where a communication is established in good faith with what seems to be an inner-plane communicator, the communicator is not in fact present at the time but is busy on other things. What happens is that a pool of ideas which are associated with the inner-plane adepti's Ray type and the work he is doing are attached to him, and when he is doing something else, this pool of ideas is contacted rather than the individual entity himself. In this case, the effect is that there is a very strong and continuous flow of ideas on a particular subject, but the significant thing is that the impact of one personality on another is missing. Therefore the idea is that contact is valid in the sense of making contact with part of the consciousness of the entity, but it is really the pool of ideas which is involved and not the entity itself.

The thought of the idea pool connected to an inner-plane adept is most unusual to any incarnate human being. The inner-plane adept is a very highly developed entity and the pool of ideas associated with him is uncontaminated by the confusions of the physical plane, so that the concepts which form this pool are very clear cut, very strong, very authentic, and not at all like the confused picture received from another human being. All of this is done telepathically.

When Dion Fortune died, there was not a missed step or a change in pace in her continuing to run all of the activities of the Society of the Inner Light. It was laughingly commented that she was *out-of-her-body* so much during her lifetime that she felt right at home *on the other side* after death.

She felt strongly that there was no reason why she should have died and left the physical plane so prematurely, without warning, and in a way that prevented her from training a successor — a procedure that is considered magically vital within any Western esoteric group. Therefore, she considered the best she could do was to continue governing the Society from the inner-planes through the mediumship of someone on the physical plane, and this she continued to do.

Even after Arthur Chichester took over the group Dion Fortune continued to run the Society through her trance mediums until he found his own esoteric feet and decided that the best thing to do both for the development of the Society of the Inner Light and more important in his view, for the development of Dion Fortune herself, was to cut all contacts between her and her magical body, and between her and the Society of the Inner Light. The decision made, he bade her: "Depart in peace," and declared that the work she had set about to do was logically completed because he had now become effectively her successor and the work of the Society was taking on new aspects and proceeding on altogether different and higher levels of work. This *departure ceremony* was carried out in a very formal and impressive manner.

Dion Fortune considered that at death the person was required to review the happenings of the previous life search for the essential message behind what had happened during life, and to learn from it. In other words the essence of the life was to be extracted from the detail of the life as it passed before the eyes of the newly dead person.

Undoubtedly certain experiences would be too painful for many people to confront — particularly in the case of a highly dynamic and magical personality whose life had been full of incidents and perhaps trauma. Therefore, in this period of post-mortem confrontation it is more or less axiomatic that certain parts of life would not have been reviewed adequately. This ignored part of the life acted as a sort of inner-plane complex, a magical body or entity, which the newly dead person carried with them into their next life when they reincarnated.

Dion Fortune's very vivid character in *"The Sea Priestess"*, Morgan LeFay or Miss LeFay Morgan, was undoubtedly a projection of an aspect of her own magical body, parts of herself that she had failed to assimilate at the end of past incarnations. This is a natural enough occurrence among initiates and is to be expected.

It is notable that by the time she wrote the book *"Moon Magic"* the form of her heroine, Lilith LeFay, had grown considerably stronger, much more authoritarian, and to any modern male worth his salt, quite insufferable. This undoubtedly was an aspect of Dion Fortune herself and the power of the figure in her writing is due to the fact that it does represent a living, if cut off part of herself.

After her death, Dion Fortune remained on the inner-planes, firmly convinced that she should remain in control of the Society of the Inner Light from which she considered physical death to have ejected her summarily. As a result, she was an essentially confused and deviated entity on the inner-planes still trying to carry on the earthwork.

The idea has occurred to many that Dion Fortune's death had been accelerated by the unnatural development of this magical body of hers, which manifested in her novels as Morgan LeFay. She became more and more closely identified with the Morgan LeFay magical body and it finally got so bad that Dion Fortune used to dress and walk and in every way appear to conform to the habits of her fictional figure Morgan LeFay. It makes compulsive reading and every decent novelist ought to have a magical body about because it makes the writing come alive.

When Dion Fortune died, she was in no way changed from the nature and names she knew in the flesh. She answered to many names: her own mundane name which was Mrs. Violet Evans; the inner magical name by which she was known in the Society of the Inner Light; her pen name of Dion Fortune; and by the name of her magical body with which she was very closely associated, Morgan LeFay or LeFay Morgan.

When the deceased Dion Fortune was dismissed from her control over the physical world in 1950, problems arose because many senior members who had known her intimately could not help invoking her presence, quoting her as how things used to be done and generally continued to hold her closely within their thoughts. Ten years or more after her death, a minor personality cult once again built up tending to contrast the way in which *the late Warden*, as she was then known, had organised things compared to the present incumbent of the office.

Therefore, at another special meeting, Arthur Chichester evoked her essential essence, her Essential Self, and in two moves gave her a clear picture of the progress the Group was making and the direction in which it was going and then bade her depart for her own good to regions where she could continue her own proper development. At that particular moment in time Dion Fortune began the assimilation of her magical body, the figure of Morgan LeFay, and withdrew from attempting to influence the day to day activities of the Society.

There have been communications from her at different times, through different people. Some of these are probably false and the communications quite spurious. But undoubtedly she has gone on with her development since that time and has opened new aspects within herself, which are considerably advanced on the status she had at the time of her death.

It is worth noting that experiments in telepathy produce inconsistencies when the receiving person is actually picking up ideas associated with the transmitter rather than the particular subject or symbol that the transmitter is supposed to be considering. In cases like this, the communication is passed as authentic, but very confusing because it appears to bear no relationship to the subject in hand but is a direct contact of consciousness with the transmitter.

An example of this was in a university experiment in telepathy where the Zener card symbols were used. The receiver got very strong but confused ideas about a love affair, a dog license, and some domestic worries. These he dutifully wrote down and of course, when it came to score the result he received a zero — no symbols whatsoever, just these strong ideas. When they were checked out, it was found that these thoughts were foremost in the mind of the transmitter. He was worrying over them and obviously they had been animated to the point where they were considerably stronger than the symbols he was looking at. In this case, they have to conclude that the experiment is valid but it produces no usable data.

Reference can be made here to the early twenties when Dion Fortune was being trained by the Order of the Golden Dawn or Stella Matutina, when she considered that they were providing her with inadequate instruction and she was forced to rely upon her own developing psychism to sort out the valid material from that which was entirely spurious.

It was about this time that she started to recover information about her own past and to the occultist this means past lives. You can imagine a person of her highly dynamic nature, not resting content with a small amount of information but pressing on. It is virtually certain that she recovered information about thousands of years of her previous incarnations in the course of a few weeks. What this meant in practice was that not only did she remember who she was, the personality she had had in a previous life, but she also recovered the capacities and the abilities of those lives, as well as the emotional problems and trauma. For a period of time, possibly several weeks or so, Dion Fortune was torn by the conflicting emotions she was forced to assimilate. The fact was that in certain lives she had been very strongly and almost offensively masculine, had occupied male bodies frequently in positions such as highwaymen, pirates, and flamboyant characters with criminal tendencies. On her questioning as to why these incarnations were so dubious, she was told that they were counter-balances that were necessary in order that she could get a lot of experience of the world in a very short time.

Be that as it may, she recovered information about her distant past and her associations with the priesthood. One must remember that she was a young woman brought up in a fairly sheltered middle class society in the early part of the twentieth century. She was in her early thirties when she was growing up in the occult and the impact of masses of information of this kind upon her must have been little short of shattering — the implications of the personal, the social life, and of the male incarnations she remembered, were all vividly recalled by her. It must have been quite a shock to an unmarried girl to discover the kind of things that she had been doing in the past.

The recovery of her past memory was considered necessary so that in a comparatively short space of time she would be in position to start a magical organisation of her own. It could be argued that it was premature and that she was exposed to too many stimuli in too short a time. Some of the problems she had later in relationships with people, women as well as men, could have stemmed from this experience. She ended up assimilating as well as could be expected the major details of the past incarnations and with the knowledge and reclaimed capabilities became a woman with considerable power and authority. It is possible that her personality would have been more rounded and more sympathetic if time had been allowed for her to accept and digest this enormous package of past information.

When memory is recovered the essence of the abilities connected with that incarnation is retrieved with it. The actual ability is not immediately restored, but the essence behind the ability is. Being Dion Fortune, she did not hang about, but immediately started to put her memories to practice and thus various psychic techniques, ritual techniques, and other magical techniques were developed by her in an extremely short time. Possibly it can be said about her and her system that she never really had time to develop these sympathetically, calmly and within context. She was, as it were, a young girl presented with an enormous set of very powerful and almost lethal tools and told to get on with it.

CHARLES ULRICH ARTHUR CHICHESTER

Arthur Chichester was tired of school and could not get along with his family, so at 18, he shipped off to Canada to be a lumberjack. This was the standard procedure in the 1920's and 30's for any young Englishman rebelling against the world. He had been a well-mannered and obedient youth but now that he had broken out of his shell, his family was relieved that he sought his freedom in the New World.

The Chichester family was aristocratic Irish, and Charles Ulrich Arthur Chichester's background was the sort one would expect. He was sent to Stonyhouse, an English Public School run by Jesuits for Catholic families. The school offered a highly authoritarian education, excellent on classics as well as other subjects. He had an intelligent, questing nature and essentially a mystical temperament. He found in the Catholic Church a great deal to which he could aspire and his natural mysticism carried him through because he enjoyed the power side taught by the Jesuits.

During adolescence, Arthur began to question many of the ideas that he had previously accepted as being axiomatic. He had some sympathetic understanding from his relations but not very much. They thought this was a natural reaction to be expected in a young man and his Jesuit advisors told him that the tendency to question would ultimately go away, but it did not. After some time, he cast himself off from the Catholic Church, was more or less expelled by his family before he went to Canada to be his own man.

In Canada, Chichester almost died from the cold but he quickly toughened up. He explored Western Canada through a number of jobs and then shipped out to the Far East where he got a job working for Shell Oil Company and spent most of his time in Malaya and

Singapore. He did have a good opportunity to travel throughout the whole area and enjoyed this phase of his work. With his interest in the spiritual he investigated the Eastern mystical theories and practices, and religion in general.

World War II came and he was back in England where he joined the services. Because of his specialised knowledge of the Far East, he was made an intelligence advisor on the psychology of the nations who were being subjected to the Japanese. Chichester's assignment was actually with the Royal Air Force in London and he remained in the intelligence branch throughout the war.

All of this time that he had been away from England he had been searching and had a very uneasy relationship with himself. At one time he even seriously considered that he would enter the priesthood. He had some confused ideas as to his future spiritual progress because his horizons had been restricted and limited by the Jesuits before he finally managed to break away. When he found that the world was a much bigger place than he had previously imagined, a lot of his ideas broke down, but the inner core of them remained. Once the Jesuits train you, they do not let go very easily.

This ruined his relationships with women as he had been trained to regard them as being manifestations of the Blessed Virgin, which indeed they are, but not entirely. Consequently he tended to idolise them and at one time told a story of how a beautiful girl was marooned with him in some bungalow during a tropical storm and how he never laid a finger on her, though she looked lustfully at him. He related the story rather wistfully, as something that he wished he had done something about — but at the time, it would have been an article of faith not to touch her in any way. So he had a very unhappy and mixed up life, a very honourable and intelligent man torn inwardly and seeking the mystical solution. Basically, it was the Holy Grail that he was after.

When a man is said to be searching for the Holy Grail within the mysteries, he is really looking for two things: his own spiritual essence and his own spiritual purpose. This in turn gives him the drive from his spiritual self, which is necessary to carry out his particular part of the divine plan. Strangely enough, in searching for this innermost spiritual reality within himself (it sounds like a rather egocentric exercise) he is actually finding the nature of God, because in practice the two cannot be divided.

Essentially the search for the Holy Grail is a search for the most intense, inner reality of the individual. When you are looking for the Holy Grail outside, you are having a *quest* or adventure, and you are really seeking the type of experience that the spiritual nature actually needs. So all quests for the Holy Grail put the objective in a position where people have to overcome their own deepest fear to get the vision of that which is sought. It always hits at the weakest point. In practice the search for the Grail is really the quest for the self carried beyond the normal dimensions, and in looking within and finding the self, one has to find God because the one is impossible without the other.

Chichester was in London during the war and early on heard of the public lectures being given by Dion Fortune at No.3 Queensborough Terrace. He attended one that was a popular introductory lecture on the general subject of the Western Esoteric Tradition. Toward the end of the lecture he came to the conclusion that the lecture had raised many more questions than it had answered. He accosted Dion Fortune after the meeting and said: "I asked you for bread and you gave me stones. A rather direct approach that she answered with what amounted to "Hang around a bit and I will show you the bread." He did and this got him interested in the system and he was subsequently initiated into the First Degree of the Society of the Inner Light.

Because of the unusual conditions of the war, many of the rigid barriers between the various grades were eased and as Arthur Chichester was an advanced soul in the Mysteries he rapidly progressed to a position nearer the centre than would have been possible under ordinary conditions.

The bombing of London was going on and Chichester was able to spend quite a lot of time with Dion Fortune in the basement of No.3 Queensborough Terrace talking about the Western Mysteries. She quickly realised that he was an extremely capable occultist and someone who would be important to the Group. There was no equivalent in the Group at the time, and she encouraged him to continue and expedite his training. It began to develop in her mind that he should be her successor, but she never committed this to paper or communicated the thought in any definite way.

Previously she had considered W. K. "Chris" Creasy, a merchant banker of some note in the city of London, as her successor. Creasy was a fine person and a good administrator but not as greatly advanced magically. Chichester was much younger, but she realised that he was a man with ability in the world and also of an advanced spiritual nature. Dion Fortune called Chichester *my young Sun Priest.* In actual fact he was of a much higher grade than that, but as *her Sun Priest* was how she came to consider him at that time.

Possibly, because of the fact that Creasy was always in her mind as the reasonable successor, she did not speak out her thoughts of Chichester. Then after Dion Fortune's death in 1946, she was in almost immediate communication with the physical plane, telling them that Chichester should take over. But again, she did not say so in any definite way. Strangely enough, when Chichester did take over in 1947 it was almost like a coup because by that time "Chris" Creasy was acting as the Deputy Warden and had to be moved to the side before Chichester could assume his new duties.

Creasy was a thoroughly delightful person and was accustomed to positions of authority and power. He had continued the Group in exactly the same way it had been, which is something of the temperament of a banker. Chichester was by nature a very shy and retiring person and by the time he came to realise that he must take over the leadership of the group, it was necessary to do so by force of will. The take over was not without bloodshed as there were a certain amount of ruffled feathers about the place, but subsequently, Creasy became totally convinced that the right thing had been done and he and Chichester became firm friends.

The take-over made very little difference at the time because Chichester still carried on in much the same way Creasy had. It was simply a leadership crisis, and Chichester must have been impelled much against his normal nature to say: "I am the rightful Warden of this Group." Chichester was impelled by strong inner urges and he pushed through his own leadership. He was finally accepted on the strength of the communications from Dion Fortune.

Dion Fortune recognised Arthur Chichester as a solar or Sun

Priest because she had only managed to bring the Society of the Inner Light up to the stages of the Outer Greater Mysteries which are essentially solar and at that time, she could not envisage a degree of development higher than that.

In the Mysteries there are three fundamental grades of the priesthood: the Lunar Priesthood; above them the Solar Priesthood; and the highest grade is the Stellar Priesthood — three distinct grades. Within those categories there are sub-grades but these are the three types of priests. The reference here is to the assumed civilisation of Atlantis, which is said to have had a dispersed Lunar Priesthood, the central Sun Temple where the Solar Priesthood operated, and the Withdrawn Temple which was at some distance from the Sun Temple and connected to it by an underground passage. The Withdrawn Temple was where the Stellar Priesthood operated. The Stellar Priesthood were the highest priests in the hierarchy and at that time were supposed to have direct access to what we would now call the inner-planes. If this priestly breakdown is correct, there probably were few distinctive sub-divisions among the Stellar Priests.

Dion Fortune knew about the existence of the Withdrawn Temple but she could not envisage raising the Group to that standard with the resources available at that particular time. The Golden Dawn had the equivalent of a Sun Temple that was the *Order of the Rose of Red upon the Cross of Gold,* the *R.R. et A.C.,* or in Latin the *Rosae Rubae et Aurae Crucis.*

Naturally, the highest accolade Dion Fortune could give to Chichester was to say he was her Sun Priest because the Sun Priests ruled Atlantis, with the shadowy figures of the Withdrawn Temple directing the Sun Priesthood, but few knew about that. Essentially the Moon Priests were concerned with fertility and natural processes — control of the sea, the weather, crops, animal mating and the process of human nature on the lower levels as well.

The Solar Priesthood were essentially a *power group.* Human development was different in Atlantis than it is now, but we would equate the Sun essentially with the logical mind. Having reached a grade where there is a degree of mind operating, they were in a very powerful position. They could use all the powers that they had in a logical manner, having the powers of decision, choice and so on, all of which are now considered normal in intelligent beings.

There were three grades of Solar Priests. There were the priests themselves, who taught, and there were the Scribes and Warriors. So there were three groups who lived within the Sun Temple area. The Scribes are the people associated, in the Egyptian sense, with mathematics, record keeping and so on. They were essentially the scholars. The Warriors were not necessarily engaged in actual warfare but would have been those who control military operations in general. They would be like Corp Generals almost like the Prussian Elite Military Corp. The Atlanteans traditionally waged a continuous war against wild animals and marauding tribes that were not at the Atlantean degree of evolution.

Atlantis actually existed as long as one understands what is meant by *existed*. It was a condition of human evolution for a very, very long time. It was not simply a place; it was an entire set of conditions that probably went on for at least ten thousand years. It was a whole *series of* civilisations — in both an area and a period of time. References to Atlantis sometimes mean something in that time period, and sometimes refer to a place.

The Stellar Priests are concerned with forces, which are universal and not limited to human considerations. Humanity is a specialised outcropping of intelligent life and there must be other forms of intelligent life in the Universe. The Stellar Priesthood is concerned with the fundamental forces of existence itself which underlie all forms of life, as well as all forms of intelligent life. They work outside of the confines of this human system. They deal with the fundamental energies that underlie everything.

Using Qabalistic analogy, the inner priesthood which is the Cosmic or Stellar Priesthood starts after the grade of Adeptus Major, on the Tree of Life, after the path from Geburah to Chesed has been assimilated. Remember that a grade cannot be claimed until initiation into the next higher one has been effectively consummated. From the viewpoint of the Tree, when the initiate or Adept has attained Chesed, the completed grade would be Geburah. The Sun Priesthood is centred in Tiphareth and the Lunar Priesthood is in Yesod.

The grade of Ipsissimus means the greatest attainment of

incarnation. If you were Ipsissimus you would be most intensely yourself. Ipsissimus reflects a state where the person is most totally his own true self. On the Tree it would be Kether or the Crown.

Arthur Chichester now had taken over the Group and was firmly in control as the group recognised his high degree of adepthood. In directing the activities, he came to realise that the Group could not be run by the deceased Dion Fortune from the inner-planes. He also realised that the High Priestess was not acting solely as a medium for the inner-plane government but was passing on some edicts which stemmed from her own personality, such as the high degree of detail she "brought through". This was something that no inner-plane entity would possibly be interested in — how to sweep the floor, how to cook the meals, etc. Something had gone wrong.

Chichester was a very quiet, withdrawn, shy, young man, but when that type of person summons up the courage to do something, he frequently acts with considerably more force than is normally called for. This was one of Chichester's problems, putting off doing something because he did not want to hurt people or even change things. When he finally would blow up, everyone would get a blast that was out of proportion. Consequently, when he realised that the operation of the High Priestess as a mouthpiece of Dion Fortune would have to cease, he moved like a tornado and blew the whole thing apart, removing the High Priestess and reorganising the Society in one major stroke.

Chichester acted with considerably more severity than the occasion called for and he undoubtedly alienated a large number of people in the Group. Realising that his action had shaken the foundations of the Group, he instituted a period of Severity in the Qabalistic sense — of formalism where all the Group's inner operations, from cooking to temple ceremonies, were very highly organised and every single operation that went on in the house including cleaning, was ritualised in some way or another. This kept everyone busy and took their minds off the major changes within the hierarchy.

Chichester laid out a framework that covered every form of operation and based it upon what he considered the esoteric principles behind it to be. For instance, operations in the kitchen were related back to some god-force which was roughly allied with culinary operations or with cooking, while the office and administration came under Hermes or something of that sort. There were guidelines laid out for everything. It was based, in his view, upon a set of principles, and there were procedures or rituals to follow. At seven-thirty of a certain day all laundry would be collected and ready for the cleaning action the following morning; all cupboards would be cleaned at a particular hour; all foodstuffs checked against a master list at another time — it ran exactly like clockwork. The object here is to set up a form that is a sort of vision of perfection. When you have the form running, you then take away the scaffolding. What Chichester had done, very wisely, was a very profound magical operation. He set up scaffolding but the important thing is to know when to remove it and he did know. After the phase had been running for perhaps a year, he removed the scaffolding. Although the discipline remained, it was by that time intrinsic and not external. As a result the place continued to run and everyone considered that certain operations would be carried out, probably best in certain ways. It worked very well because no one felt stifled and unable to express new ideas.

In 1949, Chichester decided to raise the Group consciousness to a higher level and he realised that all contact with exoteric or outside activities would have to be temporarily cut and the Society became *totally enclosed*. There were no public lectures and the only concession was the library, which was open to the public on Monday afternoons for an hour or two. Apart from that every other outside contact was cut — there was no advertising and the initiates were not permitted to lecture externally or have anything to do with any other form of organisation — it was totally enclosed. And within the framework that he built, the scaffolding that had been removed, the Group continued to grow.

A remarkable woman, Margaret Lumley-Browne had entered the Group during the war years and was living at No.3 Queensborough Terrace. She operated very largely as an extremely inefficient parlormaid doing the dusting and the routine cleaning until it was discovered that she was a natural psychic and a very powerful natural medium. She had been partly trained by Dion Fortune but her training had not been completed. Chichester

Above: Front view of 38 Steele's Road, London N.W.3
Photo by Donald Brooks, Enfield.

On Right: Rear view pf 38 Steele's Road, London N.W.3,
showing private garden and Temples of the Mysteries.
Photo by Donald Brooks, Enfield.

recognised her calibre, and when her training was completed, she turned into probably the finest medium that the Western Tradition has known. It became apparent to Chichester that the new Margaret Lumley-Browne was in an altogether different category from the other mediums. She was a highly educated woman, aristocratic and also very cultured. With Chichester's strongly developed mysticism and his restless nature, with the Quest for the Holy Grail foremost in his mind, with his tremendous force reaching out all the time, and now with Margaret Lumley-Browne with her mediumship and high capabilities — very rapid communications started coming through from the inner-planes. These messages were of an order far higher than anything that had ever been seen before and a remarkable amount of information on mythological subjects, psychology, cosmogony and so on, began to pour through. The new Lumley-Browne material that came through was coherent, highly intelligent, inspiring, and showed that a very strong personality was behind it. The messages were practical, frequently capable of being tested and proved immediately, except of course in theories like cosmogony. With the new inner-plane contacts through Margaret Lumley-Browne the Group started lifting to a higher level.

Chichester now brought in several new rituals of a higher level than previous ones and started thinking about the reorganisation of the Greater Mysteries from the new material. Dion Fortune finally got the Outer Greater Mysteries going and had reached a level equivalent to the Grade of the Portal, just prior to Tiphareth. This is basically approached with thinking on the Greater Mysteries, but she had not gone beyond that and all indications are that the people in that supposed grade were, in fact, not functional. The grade was more a thing of charter than a function. There is no doubt that the Greater Mysteries never effectively functioned under Dion Fortune except for a very small handful. It was opened, but not functional.

At this point Chichester demolished the entire structure that Dion Fortune had built up, returning everyone to the Lesser Mysteries and ultimately back to the first degree. He started the group up again, grade by grade through the Lesser Mysteries, and then pushed straight out and developed highly functional Greater Mysteries. Unfortunately, the standard of the Greater Mysteries was far higher than the candidates that could be found for it. So, he too was forced to accept candidates more by charter than by function.

At the time of Chichester's accession in 1946-47, the Society of the Inner Light had about fifty or sixty members. This was immediately after the War, and a number of the members were serving in the armed forces and had not returned. Later the membership did rise to as high a figure as one hundred and twenty at one time.

By 1960, the Society had outgrown its quarters and it was decided to move from No.3 Queensborough Terrace. Many members devoted their spare time to searching for new quarters and the Society was put on the books of a large number of estate agents. Nothing came up that was suitable even though many properties were inspected. The Society was not short of money but the property they wanted would have cost rather more than they thought they could afford at the time.

Then one of the members saw an obscure advertisement in the *London Times* offering a house for sale in North London. When Mr. Creasy and other members went to view the property, it was discovered that the owner was a man in deep mourning for his wife and he was in a rather pitiful, psychological state. His wife had just died after a long illness and he had been left with the family and really did not know what he was doing.

Mr. Creasy suggested coming back another day but the owner insisted that he wanted to go ahead. To Creasy's amazement the property was not only better than stated in the advertisement but there were also two enormous rooms in the back which would be ideal for ritual purposes. These were not even mentioned in the advertisement.

The price too, which had appeared reasonable was now obviously far too low for a house with this sort of accommodations and Mr. Creasy felt that he had to mention this to the owner. The owner simply shrugged it off and said "Thank you for being honest, I have plenty of money and if you will buy it you can have it." So the deal was completed almost at once and the Society came into the 38 Steeles' Road property that had more rooms than they would have believed possible, with the enormous benefit of the two vast studio rooms, a large private garden, and accommodations that could not be bought in that part of London for twice the price.

PERSONALITIES

Arthur O'Mulligan

In the early 1940s Arthur Chichester introduced Dion Fortune to a remarkable Irishman whose name was Arthur O'Mulligan.

O'Mulligan was so outstanding because he had a very profound contact with the Elemental Kingdoms and there is little doubt that his association with the Society led to a tremendous outpouring of creative work along the lines of the Celtic nature contact within the Society.

Art O'Mulligan was so advanced on the Elemental Ray of the esoteric that he was invited to attend ritual functions of the Society of the Inner Light even though he was never a member of the Society. As a further honour O'Mulligan was treated as a member of the Greater Mysteries, was robed appropriately and seated on the dais in the East. All of this was completely unprecedented.

O'Mulligan lived near Dublin with his daughter. Their life was conditioned with hardship caused by extreme poverty, but this was his choice as he was a well-educated and cultured man. It is thought that he studied at Trinity University, Dublin, as he was closely associated with them later as one of the great authorities on the *"Book of Kells"*.

He and his daughter lived in these conditions because it gave him an enormous amount of freedom to roam the countryside of Ireland for weeks or months at a time, sleeping out where and when necessary. Then, when he needed money for essentials, he could do some specialist work on Celtic texts in the libraries and universities of Dublin and make the necessary money in a few days work to pay for his next extended leave of absence.

The Society paid for him to visit London on several occasions and there is little doubt that they helped financially in other ways.

Arthur O'Mulligan's mundane speciality was as an artist illustrating the fine coffee table books of Celtic traditions or expanding into the field of ancient ecclesiastical and mythological paintings. These were all original illustrations for new works. He also painted impressionistic type works of nature where "his friends the elementals" were always appearing and disappearing in the landscape.

After Dion Fortune's death in 1946, Arthur Chichester further developed the relationship between himself and O'Mulligan. Chichester felt that from this contact he gained a great deal as Chichester's path was that of a devotional mystic while that of O'Mulligan's was a nature mystic. Their friendship was probably very good for the state of both their souls.

Unfortunately, Art O'Mulligan's association with the Society was limited to a few years as by 1949, or shortly thereafter, Arthur O'Mulligan was dead.

Colonel Seymour

Montgomery, Brooke, and Slim, some of Britain's top generals, may appear to be odd companions for an accomplished occultist, but nevertheless, Colonel Charles Richard Foster Seymour numbered them among his former pupils.

It was in the early 1930s that this remarkable man appeared upon the scene of the Society. He was ten years older than Dion Fortune and was much travelled. He was quite a rare figure for an army man, at that time. A senior Army officer, an intellectual, a man of many languages and one who specialised in Russian. He was a man frequently assigned to diplomatic missions.

This was Colonel Seymour, an ex-army Colonel back from India, very military in conduct and bearing. A man who did not suffer fools gladly, with no time for *can't do* or *self-glorification,* with a considerable academic as well as military background and an acquaintanceship with ritual gained through Freemasonry. In fact, it was his Masonic friends who recommended him to the Society of the Inner Light and, no sooner had he met the remarkable Mrs.

Penry Evans that he through in his lot with her and for a considerable number of years worked within the Society.

Dion Fortune rapidly saw his considerable potential. She liked capable people and she wanted to strengthen the intellectual side of the Group. Very quickly he brought his considerable skills to bear upon all sides of Group activities. He was a man with hindsight, there is little doubt. A man with profound pagan contacts on the power side of things, like Dr. Evans, he was moved through the grade system of the Society with far too much haste. But, one has to bear in mind that Dion Fortune was frantically building up the structure and therefore she thought it was expedient and probably was right at the time, to cut a few corners. Seymour certainly had splendid talents. He wrote a great deal and some excellent communication came through him, which was published in *"The Inner Light Magazine"*.

One tribute to his considerable intellect was that here was a man who could appreciate the subtleties of the *"Cosmic Doctrine"* and this, of course, endeared him to Dion Fortune because it was a work fundamental to the Society and very dear to her heart. It also formed an insuperable barrier to many students of the Society at that time.

In no time at all, Colonel Seymour was deep in the work of the Society, writing articles for the magazine, helping to run the organisation, and playing an increasing part in magic, of a degree to which he would not normally have access at that time in his esoteric career. Had he followed the normal degree structure, taking at least a year for each of the three grades of the Lesser Mysteries, then it would have been some time before he could have participated in the Greater Mysteries. Once again, Dion Fortune had cut corners on the lower grades and progressed him too quickly.

Colonel Seymour was very interested in the Hermetic work, but deeply concerned with the Elemental Ray, the Green Ray workings. Some of the articles he wrote in *"The Inner Light Magazine"*, which have been republished several times, have considerable beauty and power. There is no doubt at all, that had he received a more thorough training in the lower grades of the Society, he could have risen to great heights. As it was, like Tom Penry Evans, he had an inadequate foundation on which to rest his subsequent magical practice.

Some of his best material was undoubtedly the result of an inner-plane contact with which he was much concerned at one time. He would work, very often in a triangular manner, frequently with two priestesses, where some of this material came through. Certainly Dion Fortune considered that she knew him well and declared that one of his previous incarnations had been in Egypt where she had known him as a priest of Ptah. Later, she said she had known him at Avebury where their sexes had been reversed and she had, so she declared, sacrificed him at that time. He was, apparently, a young, willing, female sacrifice and she allowed the blood to flow into the sacred cup. If this is true, then sacrifice makes a very strong link between the victim, the sacrificial priest, and the group in which he was a member at the time. This would account for certain subtle love-hate elements in their relationship.

Dion Fortune loved men. She liked capable men, she liked able men, she liked determined men, she liked handsome men — as far as appearance was concerned he was fairly medium height, slight in build, dark skinned, dark hair brushed back over the forehead, and the description agrees with that of Brangwyn, who was the adept in her novel "The Winged Bull". Those who knew him say that, although he was not a large man physically, and outwardly modest and unassuming, he had something inside him that was utterly powerful.

Later, the Colonel joined in the Isis Rites and both he and Dr. Evans were involved in this type of work, in those years. The Society was based upon the triple concept of power, love and wisdom. The Elemental or Green Ray, the Devotional, and the Hermetic.

When Dion Fortune married Penry Evans in 1927, Dr. Evans was the ideal candidate to mediate the power side. That wonderful character, Thomas Loveday, took the devotional or love aspect, and Dion Fortune completed the structure, representing wisdom. When Colonel Seymour arrived, there was another candidate for the power side of things and Seymour was a more balanced example of an occultist than Dr. Evans was.

This was a period of enormous growth in the Society.

Christine Campbell Thomson

Christine Campbell Thomson, later known by the pen-name Christine Hartley, had a considerable amount to do with the marketing and editing of Dion Fortune's occult novels, as well as certain other works that Dion Fortune wrote which were kept a dark secret, and were, in fact, detective romances which she wrote to make money for the Society funds.

There were those within the Society who saw Christine Campbell Thomson as Dion Fortune's heir. But in view of the degree of esoteric development that she had at the time, it is doubtful whether she could have filled the bill. She was a competent hermetic worker and also had a deep sympathy with the Elemental Ray but lacked depth. The deep purpose, which was behind the Group, was a closed book to her. She was a competent lieutenant but would not have made a leader.

Christine Campbell Thomson did a considerable amount of work with Colonel Seymour and with one or two others who formed a small group within the Group itself and devoted a great deal of time to elemental workings. They also did some hermetic work together.

It has been said that Colonel Seymour, Dr. Penry Evans and Christine Campbell Thomson had taken over the reins of the Society as the 30s wore on, and that Dion Fortune was something of a spent force. This is a popular view but it is not an accurate one. Anyone who knew the sort of forces with which Dion Fortune worked, and who appreciated something of her character, would have realised that she would be quite willing to stand aside up to a point, and allow individualism to flourish. But, at no time, was there any danger of her loosing her control of the organisation.

Colonel Seymour, Christine Campbell Thomson, and even her husband, Penry Evans, functioned within a structure set-up and administered by Dion Fortune. Through Dion Fortune came most of the inner-plane direction of the Group. Despite what might have been thought individually, there is no doubt that Dion Fortune was still very thoroughly in charge.

Neither Colonel Seymour nor Christine Campbell Thomson actually wanted to create internal rivalries within the Society. The

competitive air seemed to be the result of the way they operated —
three triangles, instead of three facets of a perfect form.

One could level the accusation at Dion Fortune that she was too
busy trying to keep the organisation moving forward to give enough
attention to what was actually happening.

Despite what various commentators have said about Dion
Fortune being a spent force, the fact is that late in the 30s, at the
beginning of the war, it was Dion Fortune who remained firmly in
control and Colonel Seymour and Christine Campbell Thomson
and Penry Evans who went.

To some extent the situation changed and solved itself because
Colonel Seymour found himself another magical partner by 1938,
and worked a lot with her outside of the Inner Light organisation.
Also, Tom Penry Evans, perhaps received a strong attack of occult
indigestion and, for a variety of reasons, many of which are not too
clear, left Dion Fortune and resumed his medical career, particularly
his strong interest in nutritional problems. The work was, in any
case, moving into a new phase.

Margaret Lumley-Browne

Margaret Lumley-Browne was probably the finest medium and
psychic of this century, although the public never knew her. She
raised the arts of psychism and mediumship to an entirely new level
and the high quality of communication that came through her has
not been equalled.

She was a woman of many different facets. Her mother died
when she and her sister were still babies and they had been brought
up by a father who had rather strange beliefs and habits. In his
view, the Victorian and Edwardian way of educating young ladies
was a lot of modern nonsense. He believed that the Georgian system
was far superior. Hence both Margaret and her sister, who were
very close, were brought up to learn Latin and Greek, almost in
their cradles. They also were taught the rules of etiquette that their
father considered the normal in polite society.

This was a strange and somewhat claustrophobic childhood, and
the young Margaret and her sister were both keen individuals. Quite
soon, therefore, they wanted to break away.

They had many ideas, including those we would now consider coming under the province of Women's Liberation. She saw the plight of women, particularly poor women, and got herself involved with Marie Stopes and her campaign for proper birth control facilities for women, sex education for the lower classes, and the whole concept of the education of working women and the emancipation of women generally. After a while she became Marie Stope's secretary and was one of the leaders of the movement.

After they left home, she and her sister led a bohemian existence in London on so little money that sometimes they almost starved.

Before she met Dion Fortune and joined the Society of the Inner Light, Margaret Lumley-Browne's natural psychism had come to the surface. It first manifested while she was walking in the park as a series of voices, and then in particular one voice. She did not know how to handle it or how to interpret it and it got out of control. After a while she began to have other strange and very alarming psychic experiences that culminated in, what amounted to, a full-scale poltergeist attack. Articles in the room would fly about, the clothes on the bed would heap themselves up into strange shapes, dressing gowns would billow out as if they were filled with an invisible body and sail around the room, and there were bangs, cracks and terrible smells.

Far worse than this was the continuous stream of psychic impressions — sometimes visual, sometimes in the form of voices — that invaded her head. She almost broke down under this unwanted psychism and, had it not been for a Theosophical Society friend at the time who was able to help her to get back on an even keel, she might have been permanently deranged.

Her capacity had obviously been developed to a high degree in previous lives and, arising as it did without proper training in this life, being in other words atavistic, was not under her own control.

After some time Lumley-Browne joined the Society of the Inner Light because she had been attracted to Dion Fortune's teaching. She entered the group very quietly under Dion Fortune, and for some considerable time, was occupied in cleaning and dusting and occasionally helping with the cooking. She was not very good at these things, but as part of the natural development of a neophyte, she was forced to do them.

It was not until the mid 1940s, not too long before Dion Fortune's death, that she became fully recognised as an excellent psychic and a natural medium, and her formal training commenced.

After Dion Fortune died, she continued her training under Arthur Chichester, the new Warden. When her training was completed, she was responsible for bringing through some of the highest level communications from the inner-planes that occurred in the history of the Society of the Inner Light.

Mediums are many types and there is no doubt that the communication brought through a medium depends to a large extent upon the capacity of the medium to act as a suitable channel. There are two aspects to this: One is the grade of the medium, which reflects the medium's own evolutionary development; and the other is the degree of education and general culture of a medium. If a medium is not so ill educated and has few symbols available for the mind, then the inner-plane communicator can only work with what he has. Consequently, the adept has a poor selection of words and images to use to express himself. Someone has described the process of an inner-plane communicator trying to work through a poor medium as being analogous to Michaelangelo, trying to build his famous statue, David, out of tins of soup. If there are a limited number of symbols then one gets a poor result and a very inadequate expression of the inner-plane communication.

Margaret Lumley-Browne, after being trained, possessed both the grade necessary to allow a high level communicator to work through her and also possessed a highly educated and cultured mind, well stocked with imagery, facts, and an excellent vocabulary.

When she was fully trained under Arthur Chichester, her work was not sporadic, but highly disciplined. She would have certain times of the day when particular inner-plane communications were made and she was also available as an occult telephone, at any hour of the day or night. Normally she operated at about ten o'clock in the morning, when she would contact one of the leading inner-plane adepti interested in the Society of the Inner Light and she would frequently also act in the evening as well.

However, time without number, she was awakened in the middle of the night by an inner-plane communicator who wished to put an idea through or give some instruction to the group, and she always kept a pen and paper by her bedside. She covered page after page in black ink writing, in a beautifully formed hand.

She was the official medium of the Order, under Arthur Chichester. This meant that, quite apart from the duties which we have already mentioned, at certain meetings when the entire Fraternity was gathered, she would act as a medium and operate in the manner of a loudspeaker system. A communicator, at a certain part in the ritual, would make contact with her and, through her, with the Group. He would give public teaching and inspiration to the Group, at large. These communications recorded at the time in shorthand by a scribe, became some of the valued teaching material of the Society.

Margaret Lumley-Browne was a very remarkable woman and the one thing that anyone would have said of her, on meeting her, was that she was very feminine, extremely attractive, even in her old age. She was keenly interested in clothes and fashion, and was always seeking to find out what was going on in the world. She was a broadly cultured woman of many capabilities, she had many talents. She was interested in the emancipation of women. A considerable historian among other things, she was quite an expert on wine. She was always very willing to help those who were junior to herself. Her possible weakness was that she was fairly untidy and could be somewhat absent minded. She was a very, very warm and human person.

In her youth she had had innumerable emotional affairs which themselves were rather strange in that day and age. She had known almost everyone in the artistic and literary world who was worth knowing. It was even said that she had known the public hangman.

She grew to be a very old lady before she died. One day, when she was very old, a member of the Group who had not seen her for some time, met her outside the British Museum. It was Spring, and she said: "What a lovely day. I have decided to buy a new hat. I have to redecorate my flat, do a lot more writing, and may have to go to Africa — so, I will not have time to die until next year, at the very earliest." This remarkable lady was in her eighties at the time.

She was always known within the household of the Society, as MLB, the initials of her name.

Basil Wilby using the pen name Gareth Knight

Gareth Knight was closely associated with the Society of the Inner Light for a number of years. He joined the Society some time around 1956 and rapidly proved himself an able and enterprising neophyte. He passed through the preliminary grades of the Group and moved up the established ladder in the usual way until he encountered the philosophy of existentialism, which he investigated with enthusiasm. The new viewpoint made an impression upon him and he left the Society to get his thoughts in order, but after a short interval he rejoined and resumed an active role.

He never knew Dion Fortune in the flesh, having entered the group after her death, but he was associated with several of its leading members in the fifties and sixties, including Arthur Chichester.

While acting as librarian to the Society, he prepared his two-volume work *"A Practical Guide to Qabalistic Symbolism"*, a highly respected work in this field.

Shortly after this he resigned from the Society again, believing that he had a contribution to make to a freer, more Aquarian occultism. One of his earlier ventures was to launch a home study course, which became the highly respected Servants of the Light course. He has since written a number of books, produced and edited several magazines and done a good deal of lecturing.

Basil Wilby had been interested in writing for some time and had aspirations toward becoming a playwright.

While still a member of the Society, he married a delightful young lady called Roma, produced a family and took his place in the world of work.

He has always maintained a strong interest in Dion Fortune and her occult purpose and, over the years, the group with which he works has apparently been in communication with her on various occasions.

There is little doubt that Gareth Knight has some inner affinity with Dion Fortune. A number of people have remarked upon striking similarities in facial characteristics; one going so far as to say that, allowing for the age difference in the photographs he was studying, the two might have been twin brother and sister. Be that as it may, Gareth Knight would confirm that he feels that he is continuing the work she set out to accomplish.

W.E. "Ernie" Butler

Ernie Butler's first contact with Dion Fortune was quite early in the development of the Society. Butler had studied with the Liberal Catholic Church and various other organisations as well. He had been attracted to Dion Fortune's new Society of the Inner Light because of the clarity of her teaching, her no-nonsense approach to occultism and her impressive dynamism.

His association with her was much closer than would have been possible in the Society's later years for a person of his grade. The group was smaller and more intimate and the higher level work was not so confined to the upper grades. He was active in the Hermetic work but was notable for his participation in the development of the *Guild of the Master Jesus:* he was one of its first Lectors. Butler's activities moved him away from the Society for a long period during which time he wrote a number of books on occult subjects. He always acknowledged a debt of gratitude to Dion Fortune for whom he had a great regard. In preparing one of the later titles published in this period, *"Magic and the Qabalah"*, he briefly corresponded with the current Warden, Arthur Chichester, and received permission to include certain new material.

Shortly after this, Butler re-joined the Society. He remained for a comparatively short time, attending some Lodge meetings but playing little part in the other work of the organisation. It is quite possible that he was disappointed in the way the Society was going. At any rate, he left the group for the second time and became active with Gareth Knight in the formulation of the *Servants of the Light* organisation. He was an able, modest and likeable man with many friends.

S. L. MacGregor Mathers

Dion Fortune never knew the founder of the Order of the Golden Dawn. As she remarks in *"The Mystical Qabalah"*, she had at one time been a member of the organisation founded by him but had never known him personally, he having died before she joined his group. She certainly knew his widow, Moina Mathers, and the acquaintanceship was far from amicable; but she never knew Mathers. It is interesting to speculate on what their relationship might have been had they come together. Both were unusually strong personalities.

Aleister Crowley

At the time that *"The Mystical Qabalah"* was published Dion Fortune had never met Crowley, but they did meet later. Crowley's A.A. and O.T.O. activities never impinged upon the Society of the Inner Light. The two leaders did come together on at least one occasion where they met briefly at a public lecture at "The Belfry", a house used as the prototype of the church in *"Moon Magic"*. Apparently, Dion Fortune entered the room with some of her friends to find Crowley already seated there in the company of two of his *scarlet women*. He got up (an uncharacteristic gesture) and bowed to her. She replied with a curt British bow and passed on to her seat. That seemed to have been the beginning of mutual acknowledgement. Subsequently, they exchanged a number of letters and Crowley called her his Moon Priestess, apparently believing that she epitomised the role.

Although she had used the less desirable characteristics of Crowley as a basis for Hugo Astley in *"The Winged Bull"*, she was never really antagonistic toward him. In fact, in many oblique ways she gave credit to the work he had done, such as the publication of "777". She also cautiously recommended his books — though not for the beginner because they were "full of traps for the unwary She always called him "Mr. Crowley".

Crowley gained notoriety by flaunting his interest in sex magic. But there was little similarity between his promiscuous perversions and Dion Fortune's rites of polarity. Probably the best way to sum it up is to say that Crowley did not seem to know the difference between a whore and a priestess; and undoubtedly, Dion Fortune did.

OCCULT WRITINGS OF DION FORTUNE

Dion Fortune's occult writings fall into two categories: fiction and non-fiction. The first of her non-fiction books was *"Sane Occultism"*, which belonged to the early phase of her life when she was still being trained by the Golden Dawn organisation, the Stella Matutina. The book is a collection of articles that she wrote for the Occult Review and which were subsequently put together and published in hard cover at that time. She was attempting to provide some basis for an ethical system of occultism. The essays all go to support that end. She exposes vice, malpractice and far more important perhaps, sheer stupidity, in the occult movement.

Another of her non-fiction works is *"Through the Gates of Death"*. Dion Fortune was associated with a number of people at the time whose only contact with the esoteric had been through the spiritualist movement and who had in fact, left that movement because of general dissatisfaction with the shallowness of its aims. Dion Fortune wrote *"Through the Gates of Death"* for two reasons. One was to provide the general public with some sort of certainty about the idea of post-mortem conditions and as an antidote to the increasingly sentimental forms of spiritualism that were being promulgated by the spiritualist movement in Europe. A number of her followers of course, had come to her through this spiritualist movement and therefore this book acted as a bridge between the two activities. Secondly, she wanted to point out the dangers of spiritualist contact and at the same time the similarities between some of the techniques and those of established doctrine. Originally intended as a fairly light-weight work, the book sold a great number of copies because of the interest of the spiritualist movement.

"Mystical Meditations on the Collects" came from Dion Fortune's Christian contact. One of the profound influences on her life was the contact with the devotional aspect of the Great Work. During one of her dreams, she apparently ascended through the Theosophical Society library onto some higher level. The influence of the Master Jesus contact thrust her into Christian literature, which she considered in the light of a practising occultist. *"Mystical Meditations on the Collects"*, partly written in London and partly at Glastonbury, was a series of occult commentaries upon the collects of the established Church of England. The book had modest success, although it was castigated by the Church and not fully accepted by the esoteric movement.

"The Esoteric Philosophy of Love and Marriage" seen in the light of the 20th Century seems a huge joke and many people recommend its purchase as a source of amusement. In fact, at the time, the book was the only way she thought she could get across to the masses certain occult principles relating to polarity. She saw that the work of Marie Stopes was doing a very great deal to alleviate hardship, particularly among the working class and the lower middle class population of women. She hoped that the publication of this book would give some of the inner keys to an effective, emotional and sexual relationship. It is very likely that she failed almost totally. The publication of the book was restricted to several thousand copies, which were almost entirely bought up by the occult fraternity — who read into it more than they should have.

"Avalon of the Heart" is an interesting book because Dion Fortune and the Society of the Inner Light had been associated with Glastonbury, whose mystical name is Avalon, since developing a working esoteric community there. *"Avalon of the Heart"* represents a sort of mixture of Christian and nature mysticism with occult interests. She held the idea that the natural development in the United Kingdom of a church would have been best achieved through the Celtic form of the Christian Church. That is, an amalgamation of the Sun and the Son of God, and of the two together which would have made a liberated form of Christianity. This would have been emotionally rewarding as well as devotionally effective. She viewed the intrusion of the Roman Catholic Church into the community of

Glastonbury or Avalon in very early, pre-medieval days as a disaster and believed in fact, that the natural development would have been by way of the solar Christianity. *"Avalon of the Heart"* is in fact an expression of a series of meditations actually conducted in Glastonbury at the time her philosophy was being experienced. It had a larger circulation because it contains much that is of very real interest.

"Psychic Self-Defence" is possibly her most popular book. As she had suffered very greatly at the hands of a grey-black occultist who was the directoress of the commercial college that she had attended, Dion Fortune wished to warn people of the abuses of occultism and to use *"Psychic Self-Defence"* as a sort of compendium of cases concerned with occult pathology that had come to her notice over the years. It was a praiseworthy book that contains a great deal of interesting and useful material. It tended to become a focus for the sensation seeking and many people's view of the Western Esoteric Tradition has been derived entirely through the rather gory pages of *"Psychic Self-Defence"*, rather than through sound study. Nevertheless, this book is a book that everyone should read.

"The Esoteric Orders and Their Work", and *"The Training and Work of an Initiate"* are books of a rather higher order. Both of these books are of a much higher standard than the preceding works. In these two works she attempted to show serious enquirers the way in which a modern esoteric group would function with a purpose, its aims, what happened to a person who entered it, what the qualifications were for entering, and the modus operandi or its function. This was very nicely done and she was successful. Sales were not very great originally, but the books have been continuing sellers over the last fifteen to twenty years. Thousands of copies have been sold. They suffer unfortunately from the fact that like everything else, they are out-of-date. The significant thing about these publications is that they give the feeling of the Western Esoteric Tradition even though the facts make them out-dated. It is the feeling side that acts as a magnet to pull people into the field and therefore into these works. *"The Training and Work of an Initiate"* is simply a later, up-dated edition of *"The Esoteric Orders and Their Work"*. So the two have to be considered as a unit.

Another interesting book is *"Practical Occultism in Daily Life"*. Like quite a few of her works, this particular book was serialised in the pages of *"The Inner Light Magazine"*, over the course of about a year. It was supposed to provide a simple introduction for people new to the subject, on the one hand, and on the other to provide information for people who could not in the normal run of things hope to enter an esoteric work group, due to their family or personal commitments. It was supposed to give enough techniques that a person interested could use for his own betterment, to ease his own condition, and to help the condition of the human race, without having to enter into formal commitment with an esoteric group. Again the work suffers from being out-of-date but its general precepts are still stimulating and inspiring.

The two great works for which Dion Fortune will be remembered are *"The Cosmic Doctrine"* and *"The Mystical Qabalah"*. Taking *"The Cosmic Doctrine"* first, this was originally a secret manuscript reserved for inner initiates of the community and Society of the Inner Light in its early days when it was focussed largely upon Glastonbury. It was received entirely mediumistically at Glastonbury through Dion Fortune and in the presence of a small number of the inner order. The information that actually came through on the work *"The Cosmic Doctrine"* was reported to come from a very high arcane source. So high in fact, that the information had to be relayed twice before it reached the mediumship of Dion Fortune. Essentially *"The Cosmic Doctrine"* is a cosmogony and a high-powered spiritualist psychology relating to man and his place in the universe around him. It is very abstract and stresses that fact that its concepts are intended *to train the mind rather than inform it.* If read as a textbook, it is almost totally incomprehensible and useless. It has to be regarded as a series of meditations and taken simply a paragraph or idea at a time in order that the idea can be allowed to sink into the soul and produce its own food. The title is unfortunate, *"The Cosmic Doctrine"*; the title was probably a take-off from the Blavatsky's *"Secret Doctrine"*. Dion Fortune thought she would do better by producing a small, extremely powerful book, and she did.

Her other great book is *"The Mystical Qabalah"*. When Dion Fortune was involved in the Order of the Golden Dawn she was dissatisfied with many of the explanations on the Qabalah and was in fact given instructions that she did not feel were correct and she surely did not understand. At that time she was not in the grade that would penetrate the so-called secrets of the outer reaches of Qabalah, so she used her own psychism to work out a form of the mystical Qabalah and a system for the Tree of Life that was in her view, modern, effective and simpler. The writings originally appeared in a series of articles in *"The Inner Light Magazine"*. Later they were collected and then published by Rider, a publisher in England. *"The Mystical Qabalah"* was, and still is, the best single book on the subject of the Qabalah.

The other group of occult writings that Dion Fortune produced was occult fiction. These stories were taken from real life and most had to be toned down from reality. In some stories, two or three side stories would be combined. Her heroes and heroines were based on associates with whom she had worked.

"The Secrets of Dr. Taverner" is a collection of eleven short stories originally written for *The Royal Magazine* in the 20's. The central figure of Dr. Taverner is modelled on one of Dion Fortune's early teachers, Dr. Moriarty. Although the details of Hampshire nursing home may have been fictitious, many of Dr. Taverner's cases were not. In fact, they were "cleaned up" to make them acceptable to the publishers and readers of that time.

In the course of the stories Taverner treats cases of vampirism, retarded development, elemental obsession, and various shades of black magic. Woven into the fabric of the stories is a great deal of clearly presented information about the occult.

The cases, that form the source material for the stories in the book, were not fictional and were not glamorised. Taverner is presented as a man who was unconventional ethically, and who gave merely lip service to many of the laws of the land. He would take abrupt and sometimes violent action if he considered that black magic or occult malpractice threatened one of his patients.

The picture drawn by the illustrator for *The Royal Magazine*, shows Taverner as a remarkably good likeness to Dr. Moriarty, properly dressed in the fashion of the day.

"The Demon Lover" develops its plot against the background of an imaginary occult group, an organisation partly modelled on her experiences in the Golden Dawn.

The book is noted for its feminist theme with Veronica Mainwairing, the heroine, coming out of her shell and becoming a powerful occultist. Veronica finds herself penniless and alone on the death of her parents and is employed by a Mr. Lucas, the secretary of an occult fraternity. Lucas selected her for her latent psychic abilities and wanted to use her to spy out the secrets of the fraternity. She is detected during one of her nightly astral missions and the leaders of the group, jealous of their secrets, determine to destroy her. *"The Demon Lover"* is an interesting occult thriller and contains a lot of core information about occult beliefs and attitudes.

The novel, *"The Winged Bull"*, starts very evocatively with Ted Murchison, an unemployed World War I veteran entering the British Museum on a foggy winter's day in the depression years of the 30's.

His wanderings in the museum bring him into a strange contact with one of the giant Assyrian winged bulls and as he leaves the museum considerably agitated he invokes the great god Pan. His invocation is answered and Murchison is offered a job with Colonel Brangwyn who is apparently engaged upon research involving ancient religions. Murchison soon learns that his true role is to replace a corrupt occultist and to help heal Brangwyn s niece.

The feminist viewpoint is developed. Magnetic polarity between a man and a woman is stressed as a pre-requisite for effective relationship and this theme is continuously expounded in the later novels. Some of the characters are drawn from life. Brangwyn is clearly Colonel Seymour, a magical colleague of Dion Fortune in the 30s.

In *"The Winged Bull"*, boy was poor and girl was rich. However, in *"The Goat Foot God"* the reverse is the case. Hugh Paston is a wealthy and aimless young man whose adulterous wife dies with her lover in a car crash. Hugh roams the back streets of London trying to get to grips with his predicament and meets an old antiquarian bookseller who befriends him and puts him up for a few days. The old man is an amateur philosopher who introduces Hugh to occultism in an attempt to show him that there is a purpose in life and that his troubles are not merely random blows of fate. Hugh's facile interest is soon caught up in his new pursuit and he wants to buy a large house and devote it to the pursuit of the old gods, Pan in particular.

He hires Mona Wilton to find a suitable house for his project and she comes upon Monk's Farm, an original monastic house which is allegedly haunted by its former prior, Ambrosius. Hugh realises that he is a reincarnation of Ambrosius and that Mona and he share dreams of a previous life in Greece.

The book ends with a successful invocation to the sun god Helios performed on their wedding night. There is a great deal of useful material in this work.

"The Sea Priestess" is certainly Dion Fortune's best novel. In it, her developing powers of descriptive writing reach their peak and the generation of atmosphere surpasses that in all her previous writings. In this book, she comes right out into the open with her ideas about psychological and magnetic relationships between men and women.

Wilfred, a small town estate agent, is hired to find and prepare quotes for a new client. His frustration produces an acute attack of asthma, and when he is given a drug, he finds that it alters his consciousness and opens up the inner worlds to him. This is the beginning of a series of abrupt and sometimes violent changes in his life, culminating in his meeting with the Sea Priestess.

She is a strange creature, a client of his firm, who has lived most of her life abroad and ought, by all the records, to be at least ninety years old. However, when Wilfred meets her he finds her young and attractive and keen to get to work on the worship of the sea and the moon.

Wilfred finds a suitable property and converts it into a sea temple for his priestess and the remainder of the first part of the book is taken up with her training him and teaching him the ancient mysteries. The culmination is a ritual, essentially a ceremonial preparation of a magnetic link between man and woman, an archetype from which subsequent generations can benefit.

"Moon Magic" is the last of the books that Dion Fortune wrote. It stands on its own feet, but is actually a continuation of "The Sea

Priestess". Both the theme, and the central character, Morgan LeFay, are common to both.

The male lead is one Dr. Rupert Malcolm, a leading consultant in neurology. He is a withdrawn, repressed and horribly ethical man with an invalid wife and a strong Calvinistic sense of justice and duty. He comes over as a bad tempered genius with a heart of gold.

The Sea Priestess, Lilith LeFay Morgan as she now calls herself has finished her magical experiment with Wilfred and has withdrawn from his circle leaving the forces she has invoked to work out in his life. She is now starting a new phase in her work. Searching for a suitable London property to house her temple, she buys an old disused church, has it converted for her purposes, and takes up residence.

The first half of the book is taken up with the story of how she and the formidable Rupert Malcolm come together. Then when she finds her priest, she still has to train him and Dr. Malcolm's difficult psychology presents a lot of obstacles. In time, the terrible Rupert Malcolm comes under her tutelage and is changed beyond belief. A successful magical working marks the end of the book. A great amount of very useful information is given out, things that would never have appeared in the more uncompromising pages of a textbook.

Dion Fortune died before completing *"Moon Magic"* and the last two chapters were dictated by her from the beyond to one of the Society's mediums.

Despite much criticism Dion Fortune's books have guided many seekers to the door of the mysteries. Some of her fiction is now more than fifty years old but there is no doubt that it will continue to fulfil its function for years to come.

CONCLUSION

To encapsulate within the narrow confines of a book anyone's life, no matter how humdrum, is impossible, and the life of Dion Fortune was in no way simple or ordinary. Therefore we make no claim for completeness. There can be no "Full Story of Dion Fortune" because even in-depth interviews with the subject herself would have left many gaps, inconsistencies and inadequate explanations. Dion Fortune is dead and so are most of those who knew her and worked with her. Of those few remaining, some are unwilling to be quoted. In time, perhaps, more detail will become available.

The purpose of this book has been to examine this remarkable woman against the background of the Society she created and to disclose some of the motivating forces that governed her actions. Therefore we have known her by her works rather than by the details of her daily life. Surely this is no bad thing for, in the final analysis, it is the works that count.

It is difficult for those who have not lived and worked within a functioning group of the Mysteries to understand the attitudes and motivations of its members. The viewpoint is so different and the priorities so changed that they may appear incomprehensible to those without similar experience. So the reader may have had to extend his outlook and enlarge his comprehension to appreciate the special qualities of this woman and the significance of her work.

The Mysteries incarnate in occult groups in the same way as we incarnate in physical bodies. We are immortal, but our bodies pass away. The same is true for occult groups. Occultists and the groups they form are simply channels through which the love, wisdom and power of the invisible reality can flow into the mind of man. Dion Fortune would have been the first to emphasise this fact.

Occultists claim to represent the vanguard of evolution. The Mysteries evolve and their teaching extends and deepens as time goes on. Dion Fortune herself had scant respect for the dead letter of the law and continuously sought new techniques to manifest the Ancient Wisdom. The Great Work to which she devoted her life continues. It is incarnated in new Groups and expressed in fresh forms to serve the needs of modern Western Man. The principles are ageless, but the forms change. Dion Fortune lifted Western Occultism into the 20th Century. Let us continue the Great Work.

For behold we arise with the dawn of time
from the grey and misty sea,
And with the dusk we sink in the western ocean.

And the lives of a man are strung like pearls
on the thread of his spirit;
And never in all his journey goes he alone,
for that which is solitary is barren.

The Rite of Isis

INTERPRETATION OF THE
SOLAR CHART OF DION FORTUNE

As Violet Firth, Dion Fortune was born December 6th, 1890 in Llandudno, Wales. Her Sun is in the sign of Sagittarius and her Moon is in the sign of Libra.

Of her ten planets, counting the Sun and Moon as planets, all but one are in positive signs. From this, it is easy to see that she was quite positive, including a number of masculine qualities, particularly those related to the thinking process.

Her Sun in Sagittarius, along with Venus and Mercury in that sign, reveals a strong interest in religion, philosophy, dreams, and symbols — a high idealism regarding these matters is indicated — and much energy, both mental and physical, is shown. Saturn in Virgo, the sign that is analogous with ceremonial magic, squares these three planets. From this we can deduce much. Ambition, pride, a profound mind, belief in self, an exacting nature in regards to both self and others, and a bit of arrogance, all had their sway with her. Dion Fortune had a marked ability to create her own opportunities, then to take full advantage of them. Her capacity for controlling others, either through her personal charm or through her cold manipulation, is marked. And, mind you, she could be as attractive and pleasing as she chose to be. She was truly a sensitive and sympathetic person as long as her purposes were being fulfilled.

Saturn in Virgo gave her immense capacity to absorb and deal with detail; whereas her entire solar chart reveals a marked awareness of the large view.

Both Uranus, which relates to the occult, and Neptune, which is associated with the inspirational and the mystical, are powerfully aspected.

The overall pattern of Dion Fortune's chart reveals her as a leader of thought and action, although with great struggle and difficulty throughout her lifetime.

The Solar Chart represents only the inner self and motivations. It is not event oriented.

DION FORTUNE
(Violet Firth)

DECEMBER 6, 1890
LAUDUDNO, WALES
3 W 45 53 N 15

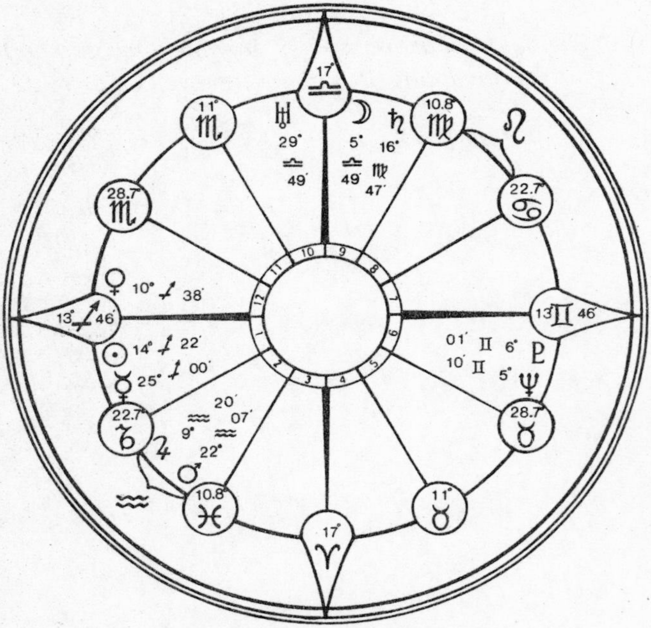

SOLAR CHART
(NOON PLANETS)

Aspects

☌ CONJUNCTION ♀☌☉ ♆☌♇

△ TRINE ☽△♃ ☽△♆ ☽△♇ ♂△♅ ♃△♆

□ SQUARE ♀□♄ ☉□♄ ☿□♄

✳ SEXTILE ☽✳☉ ☽✳♀ ☿✳♅ ☿✳♂ ☉✳♂ ☉✳♃ ☉✳♃

☍ OPPOSITION ♀☍♆ ☉☍♆

CARDINAL ☽ ♅
FIXED ♂ ♃
MUTABLE ☉ ☿ ♀ ♆ ♇ ♃

△ FIRE ☉ ☿ ♀
△ EARTH ♄
▽ AIR ♂ ♃ ♆ ♇
▽ WATER ☽ ♅

APPENDIX

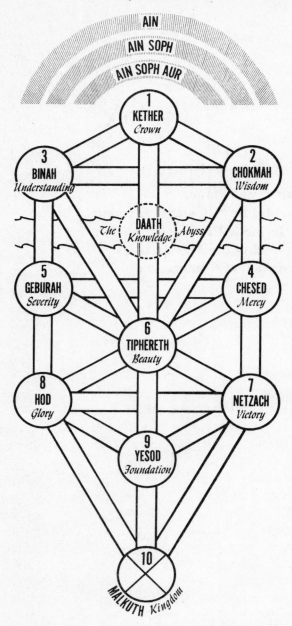

Tree of Life, symbolic diagram of the Qabalah

RISING ON THE PLANES

by **DION FORTUNE**

Students of the Qabalah will find the following experience of interest, for it illustrates the method of using the Tree of Life as a meditation symbol in order to secure astral projection.

Some minor details have had to be eliminated from the record, as they concern technical details of occult method, which must be reserved behind the veil of secrecy. * Enough remains, however, to convey a clear impression of the experience and enable an estimate to be made of its significance.

I should like to draw attention to the steadiness of the working, the absence of 'breaks', and the fact that even a dogfight under my window was not able to disturb the concentration. The record indicates clearly the device employed to prevent the disturbance from ending the vision. It was, as it were, taken up and made part of the vision, thus preventing me from being drawn out of the higher sphere. This is a useful device, for in the struggle between sensory consciousness and astral consciousness, the sensory consciousness has a great advantage.

It is interesting to note the different result obtained when the force was merely projected by a gesture, and when it was projected with one of the traditional *signs of power.* I had a similar experience some years ago, when a party of Carol Singers started to serenade us during an occult experiment. Force was projected onto them, the carol stopped in the middle of a line, and we heard the sounds of running feet departing into the distance. What exactly happened, we never knew. At anyrate, the Carol Singers could not have been

---

*At the end of this article detailed instructions are given concerning the techniques, signs and symbols used.

seriously damaged or they could never have run so fast.

The reader will observe that the method of projection is closely akin to the Jesuit meditation method of the *composition of place*. Definite symbols are used to determine the type of vision it is desired to induce, but these cannot be given here.

As far as the entry into the astral temple and taking up the meditation posture, the pictorial imagination was at work, formulating the scenes; after that, vision begins and continues unbroken until I was disturbed by the dog-fight. I then resort to fantasy again in order to keep the higher consciousness from closing down owing to the waking of the physical senses.

FROM THE MAGICAL DIARY OF DION FORTUNE
June 1st. 1930. Sunday. 8.20 to 8.45 a.m.

Seated in Egyptian god-attitude, facing southeast. Commenced meditation by drawing astral circle. Drew it rapidly and easily and with power. Turning with almost imperceptible quickness to unwind the usual kink of the silver cord in the northeast. Projected astral body to centre of circle, faced it to the east, and invoked names of god of Central Pillar. Clear projection. Consciousness very definitely centred in astral body.

Formulated path to a certain astral temple. Bright sunshine. Astral body appeared nude. Moved with rapid sweeping dancing motion up path and entered robing-room. Refused to robe in usual black robe, so compromised on a white robe with striped headdress. Astral body swooping and soaring like a bird, very full of vitality.

Outside on path again. Sunshine very bright. Astral body sweeping onwards in strong flight. Bright sunshine on green grass. Gray walls warm with the sun. Self in astral body enters temple. Takes seat on stone block, facing east. Did not experience any of the usual difficulty in turning. Consciousness very definitely located in astral body. All sense of physical body lost.

Experienced the sensation of rising in the air while seated on stone block. Went through the roof of the building into bright sunlight. Continued to rise rapidly, passing clouds, then saw a sea of clouds below me, bathed in sunlight.

Sky began to darken to indigo. Saw crescent moon, very large and bright. Knew I was entering the sphere of Yesod. Determined to push on, as the going seemed to be exceptionally good. Saw the Sun of Tiphareth in an area of deep golden-buff sky, like the drop-scene of a theatre, whereas the Moon of Yesod had been real.

Continued to rise on the Central Pillar, with no sense of strain but a feeling of breathless rapidity, wondering where I was going next. Borne on, as it were, not flying by will power. Passed over it, but not through it, making for Kether, as the going still seemed good. Saw Daath below me.

Passed through a sphere in which I saw shadowy angel-forms with the traditional harps sitting on clouds all around me. Very misty. Heard snatches of a great choir chanting. Entered a sphere of blinding white light, which I believed to be Kether. Could not see anything or feel anything. Had not even got an astral form. Just a point of consciousness without qualities, bathed in the white light. Had sense of the retention of individuality as a single spark of essential life. No memories, no qualities, thoughts or aims. Managed to hold to the idea of the experiment, however.

Saw the veils of Negative Existence behind Kether as the darkness of a starless night, stretching to infinity.

Was suddenly turned about, facing the opposite way to which I had been facing. Previously I had looked towards the Tree, as if gazing at a picture of it, so that Geburah was on my left. Now I found myself backed into the Tree as it were, and expanded to an enormous size, a towering cosmic figure. Nude, hermaphrodite, very powerful, of a golden-buff colour. This figure was the full size of the Tree. Its feet were planted on the globe of the Earth which appeared bluish, seen through dun-coloured clouds. The three supernal Sephiroth were about the head, but not actually in it. Geburah was in the right shoulder and Chesed in the left. The hands gripped Hod and Netzach. Tiphareth was not clearly formulated. Yesod was distinct as a semi-lune.

Had a tremendous sense of size and power, rising right up through the cosmos, not only the solar system. Felt like a great angelic being. There seemed to be an all-pervading undertone of music and a swinging of spheres in their orbits about me.

Reabsorbed down into Malkuth and re-entered the temple through the roof, and found myself seated on the stone block, robed in black, wearing the headdress and of normal size.

A disturbance in the street distracted my attention, which so far had not had the vestige of a break. Boys shouting and dogs barking under window, very loud. Was able to maintain vision, nevertheless. The great figure, though reduced to more moderate dimensions, was overshadowing the temple. I had now got this cosmic figure with my consciousness in it, and also a normal sized astral figure fully robed, with consciousness in it, and they could look at each other. The smaller figure ordered the greater one to stop the noise in the street. The greater one stretched one hand over the disturbing persons, but without effect. Then it projected force in the Sign of... Noise faded away and ceased.

Consciousness now centred again in the large figure. I did not quite know what to do with it, as I had never expected such a manifestation and did not know its possibilities. Decided to use it to project force onto...which it did most effectually. The force was projected in the Sign of.... and took the form of a downpouring of golden light.

Terrific force pouring like water from a hydrant, full of diamond sparkles of light, out of my hands, from the palms, not the fingertips. Soon force began to come from the solar plexus also, this entered into the base of the altar. Then force began to come from the forehead, this rained upon the altar like a light spray. All the time the force from the hands continued to pour out like a hydrant.

The altar appeared as a hollow stone tank, which the force was filling. Presently it appeared full to the brim and the force ceased to flow. I had the definite impression that altar and chair ought to be of granite, as this was the best material for holding magnetism.

Spontaneously assumed the dress of an Egyptian priest with Uraeus headdress and brightly coloured Horus wings.

Had a sense that time was up. Looked at my watch, and found it within a minute and a half of the appointed time. Noticed that breathing was very slow and shallow. Waited for it to become normal, and then returned to waking consciousness in the Sign of..., reaffirming entrance into the sphere of earth with a strong stamp of the foot. Had no difficulty in returning to full normal waking consciousness.

There remained, however, a sense of a scarlet triangle over the root of the nose, full of tingling. It seemed as if the skull had been cut away here, exposing the brain.

Editor's Note:

The operation described in this article uses certain techniques and a number of selected symbols and a Sign of Power, which will need explanation. Occult techniques are, in essence, very simple. Most of them depend upon capacities that can be developed by any intelligent man or woman providing that enough time and effort can be expended. The training is very hard work and can take a long time. Some have a natural aptitude; others have considerable difficulty in developing the necessary skills.

The techniques themselves are based upon three fundamental abilities: visualisation, concentration and creative imagination.

Visualisation is the ability to create a mental picture and to hold it steady in the mind for a reasonable time. The picture should be clear, life-like and in full colour. In appropriate cases, scent, sound and touch should also be clearly imagined. A simple exercise might be to visualise in your mind an orange, clearly seeing its shape, colour and texture. Then, when success has been attained, imagination of the characteristic scent should be added. Next, the texture is imagined, as if the fingers were passing lightly over the surface of the fruit. Finally, the orange is tasted in imagination. This is a simple enough exercise but by no means easy.

Concentration is the art of holding an idea in the mind without wavering or mind wandering until it fills the whole of the attention. Try this with the idea (not the picture) of, say, metal. Flood your consciousness with metal - metallic, metal-ness, and maintain your total concentration for just five minutes.

The third technique is the use of the creative imagination, which relies upon the ability to imagine a scene or a journey in three-dimension and colour with sounds, scent and touch. The operator enters into the scene he has built, or travels on the journey, with such a degree of realism that he is totally absorbed and quite unaware of the ordinary world around him.

These three methods are simply ways of changing the focus of attention, from the physical world to the realms of the unconscious. Like the psychologists, occultists believe that the real powers and motivations of a man lie in his inner world, not normally available except in dreams. Dion Fortune and her fellow occultists used the techniques described to gain entrance into the unconscious in a deliberate and willed manner. They believed that these methods made it possible to bring through to the conscious mind the wealth and experience of the inner man, thus enriching consciousness, increasing the abilities, broadening the mind and enhancing livingness. Repeated use of these and similar techniques would, they believed, build pathways between inner and outer worlds and make available all the hidden powers of man.

Rising on the Planes is really a controlled journey into the inner core where lies the true nature of human beingness. Certain symbols are used for visualisation, which have specific meanings to the occultist. Some of them are very old and can be found in the anthropology of many past cultures. These are the symbols that Jungian psychology calls Archetypes. The occultist uses them as gateways to different levels (or Planes) of the inner worlds.

The structure within which Dion Fortune and the other members of her group worked is called the Tree of Life (see illustration). This is a Qabalistic diagram in which ten spheres are arranged in three triangles with the tenth sphere offset by itself at the bottom. The spheres are used to represent the Universe or the Soul of Man. The spheres in the central column of the Tree represent human consciousness from the brain at the bottom to the spirit at the top.

Astrological symbolism places the Earth in the bottom sphere, No. 10; the Moon, symbolising the emotional world of images and feelings is assigned to sphere No. 9; the Sun on sphere No. 6, halfway up the central pillar of the Tree, represents the abstract mental world of pure ideas; while Spirit, the true core of man, is located in the No. 1 sphere.

Hebrew names are given to the ten spheres of the Tree, but only those mentioned by Dion Fortune in the article are relevant here.

The 10th sphere is called Malkuth, the kingdom. The 9th sphere, the next up the central column of the Tree, is called Yesod and is the foundation. The 6th, halfway up, is called Tiphareth and represents beauty and harmony; and the top sphere No.1; representing Spirit, is named Kether. There is also a mention of Daath, another condition representing a very abstract aspect of the mind, and this is located halfway between Tiphareth and Kether.

It is important to note that, when Dion Fortune, Rising on the Planes, reaches No.9 Yesod, she has actually gone 'inward' into the world of the unconscious mind. When she mentions Tiphareth she is talking about the world of abstract ideas and human ideals, such as truth, justice, wisdom and so on. The first Sphere, Kether, depicts pure spirit — simple, formless, powerful, hyper-conscious beingness — 'I am'.

The actual technique used by Dion Fortune to enter the inner worlds or 'Rise on the Planes', as she would have called it, was simple enough. Each of the spheres on the Tree is assigned a symbol. Initiates are trained to consider these symbols as representing states of consciousness. Rising on the Planes consists in concentrating on each symbol in turn, focussing consciousness on particular aspects of the inner worlds to the exclusion of everything else. Each sphere is also associated with a particular Temple, an imaginary but highly organised inner world location whose symbolic shape and furnishings epitomise the character of a particular sphere on the Tree. Malkuth, the 10th sphere, representing the physical world, might have its temple with rock walls, a double-cube altar with ten faces, and be furnished in black and sombre colours to symbolise the ponderousness and weight of physical matter.

The temple of Yesod, the Moon sphere, could be a construction of crystal, illuminated by soft, shifting moonlight. The colour violet would predominate. The altar would have nine sides and the lunar metal, silver, would appear in the symbolism. This construction would represent the strange inner world of the unconscious. Tiphareth is expressed with solar symbolism dominated by the number 6 and the colours gold and yellow. The temple of Kether, the 1st sphere, symbolising the spiritual essence of Man, would be a formless realm of blinding white light.

Rising on the Planes implies visualisation of each of the Temples in turn, moving from one to the next along an imaginary 'path'. Training, together with the archetypal nature of the symbolism, means that each temple tends to tune consciousness in a specific way so that the journeyer is led deeper and deeper into the inner kingdoms. For this process to be effective, very intense concentration is necessary, so complete as to cause total loss of awareness of the everyday world. This is the reason for the need of arduous training in concentration and visualisation.

In the description of the trip, Dion Fortune mentions the use of certain signs. These are special gestures in the use of which the initiate is trained. The first one, used to project force, is often called the Sign of the Enterer. In it, the two hands are placed at the sides of the head and then quickly moved out in front of you, palms inward and parallel to each other to make an imaginary channel for force projected from the eyes onto a particular object. The energy is imagined as leaving the eyes and travelling between the parallel outstretched arms as if down the barrel of a gun, and hence to its destination.

The other referred to sign was the Sign of Silence, associated with the god Harpocrates. It is a gesture that affirms the central and co-ordinating control of the Spirit over the lower bodies of Man. To make this sign, the person sits upright and the mind is stilled. Then the first two fingers of the right hand are placed together and laid upon the closed lips while the other two fingers and the thumb are curled into the palm of the hand.

It is as well to remember that all these techniques of symbols, temples, and paths are simply mental tools. They have no value in themselves, but like any tools, enable things to be done that would otherwise be difficult, or even impossible. Any occult system of the West is simply an instruction book and a box of tools with which the individual can work upon the inner realities of man and nature.

The term Rising on the Planes is one that was popularised by Dion Fortune, although Aleister Crowley had previously mentioned it. It is included because it has value as an exercise quite apart from its natural interest.

The procedure uses the glyph, the compound symbol of the Tree of Life, as a ground plan from which the initiate can find his position on the inner-planes and by using the symbols associated with the Tree can extend his consciousness upwards, hence the term rising.

The value of this exercise is that it teaches an initiate to move about within his own inner worlds, exercise control and maintain consciousness within those inner worlds, and learn to change the level of consciousness at will. This is a remarkable revelation to the many people who have no awareness of consciousness other than the physical world itself.

Dion Fortune often gave the impression that the exercise of Rising on the Planes would itself extend consciousness beyond the level to which the person, by virtue of his own development, had natural access. This is not true. If an initiate had developed to the stage where the Yesod consciousness was active, or in psychological terms he had become integrated to the point where he could consciously make contact with his own unconscious down to a certain level, then no amount of travelling on the planes, rising or falling, would in fact, increase his Yesod consciousness. The value of the exercise lies in its introducing the candidate to conscious mobility within his own sphere and not extending his natural limits. The limits are set by a person's natural development and only life experience, initiation, and sometimes considerable trauma, can extend them. No amount of Rising on the Planes will do that.

If we look at this text, part of the magical diary of Dion Fortune, we find that when she arrives at the sphere of the Tree known as Tiphareth which is a central position on the Tree and associated with the sun, she sees the symbol of Tiphareth, a great sun, as if it were painted on a theatrical backdrop. Whereas the moon associated with Yesod, which was the sphere further down the central pillar on the Tree, had been real and had in fact, made a considerable impact on her. This is interesting because at the time of these diary notes (1930) Dion Fortune had not extended herself as far as the solar forces associated with Tiphareth. She did achieve this later, but now when she sees the symbols of Tiphareth in her vision, she describes them as being fiat and two-dimensional, where the Yesodic symbolism of the moon (which she has exceeded in initiation) is real and actual and carries a considerable punch.

Other associations are worth noting as well. She mentions seeing cherubim sitting on clouds, playing traditional harps. This of course is nonsense and she is simply seeing the projected content of part of her own unconscious, her own childish imaginings about the possible symbolism of that level. She is not in fact, experiencing at all — she is just projecting her own picture idea of what it might be like.

In addition to these side remarks, the article is valuable as it shows how Rising on the Planes can be done and to some extent gives an impression of how it feels to do it.

One last note, Dion Fortune trained herself to become a psychic. She always maintained that she was not a natural psychic, and therefore, everything she talks about in her experiences on the inner-planes is in terms of past-thought psychism, she sees things.

Many people do not have a natural psychic ability and they have never attempted to acquire one. Their impressions of the inner world may be quite different from those of Dion Fortune and could possibly be more associated with feeling than with imagery, or even with words in the head rather than pictures seen in the mind.

Dion Fortune never made this clear and it is important in reading the article to realise that her impressions of this process are those which she gained through her own visual type of psychism.

THE ELEMENTAL RAY

by **F.P.D.**
(Col. C.R.F. Seymour)

Editor's Note:

This article by Colonel Seymour has to be understood in the light of the thinking within the Society of the Inner Light at the time.

One of the poets that greatly influenced Dion Fortune was Swinburne whose ideas were considered rather daring at that time. Associated with Swinburne was the philosophy of Nitzsche who emphasised that man by utilising his unconscious powers could become as a superman. Swinburne regretted the passing of the pagan gods saying that in turning away from them, Western man had lost the use of half of his faculties, was cut off from his unconscious powers, that the sparkle had gone out of life and that the dreary hymns of the Christians were no substitutes for the glorious, passionate, invocations of the gods.

Dion Fortune took this idea up because it obviously coincided with her philosophy. She spoke of it and incorporated it in several of her novels. With Swinburne she believed that it was possible to have an enlightened Christianity alongside a form of paganism; if combined, these would involve a whole man, rather then just a part of him. She saw Christianity as a great corrective to the excesses to the pagan era but she believed that both should be incorporated in this phase dedicated to the total involvement and completeness of man.

Seymour entered the scene with a natural ability to sympathise with the world of the Elemental Kingdoms, the world of fairy, and he had done a considerable amount of writing on the subject prior to joining Dion Fortune's Group.

What he is trying to do in this article is to introduce the reader to the Celtic representation of the inner world —basically the Celtic idea of the old gods and the Celtic appreciation of the powers of the unconscious mind. It was Seymour's contention, backed up by Dion Fortune, that much of the Celtic inspiration in painting, sculpture, poetry and music came about by virtue of man's natural free access to his own inner forces because of the racial-mind background of the old Celtic or pagan religions.

In this article, Seymour is taking the reader upon a journey into the symbolism of the Celtic fairy world. He brings the reader into contact with pictorial imagery and will induce in the sympathic reader some idea of the inner world of the Celts and help him to develop his own inner world channel between his unconscious and the conscious world in which he lives.

Seymour maintained that a group of two or three people working together, or even an individual reading the material and brooding over it on his own, could produce a great release of energy that is tied up within the soul of the average Westerner. This in turn would make a considerable difference to the amount of positive force available to him for creativity in his life.

I do not think there is anyone who has read these exercises and that has not noted some effect, but for the best results one should be able to be alone for a period of time, quiet, and relaxed, and then read the material slowly, building up the scene before the mind's eye, as the narrative proceeds.

INTRODUCTION

What follows is a study in imagery. It has been written around the results of experiments in group meditation using ancient pagan symbols. These experiments had for their objective the linking up of memories dormant in the unconscious minds of the members that still live in the unconscious mind of the Great Mother of all that exists on this planet.

Most of the members of these groups have, in the past, served at the altars of pagan religions and have met, face to face, the *shining ones* of the forests and the mountains, of the lakes and the seas.

Such memories never die either *here* or *yonder,* and they live because of their power, or shall it be said, their vital energy. They are *within* mans memory, as well as *without* him in the memory of our Great Mother, who is called the Lady of Nature, the Bona Dea, the Magna Mater, Isis.

In the course of these experiments it was discovered that if any one of the members of a group had in the past a strong contact with a particular cult at a certain period, that individual could communicate these memories to others, and could link them with the cult memories that still lie within the Earth memories of Isis as the Lady of Nature.

At first difficulties, contradictions and disappointments were many. It was almost impossible to distinguish between fancy and the results obtained by the imagination trained magically. Then, as the result of years of work carefully recorded, a system of cross-checking grew up, and in the experimental work of these groups a reasonable degree of probability was obtained. One discovery was made that cleared up many contradictions. Religions change their status. Bergson's philosophical concept of life as an ever-becoming applies to religions, to the Gods, both great and small, as well as to an individual man. Also every man's concept of a God is an ever-becoming, even when that man proclaims that his God is Being or the very Essence of Being. Man creates his own Gods.

From this conception of religions as changing gradually grew the idea of the religions of the high roads and the religions of the by-roads, an interesting theme that will be developed in more detail. It will be sufficient to point out here that most great religions start in their youth as religions of the by-road. Yet strange as this statement may sound, it is in the cults of the by-ways that power (not material power however) is greatest.

The members taking part in these experiments have in the past incarnations served at the altars of these cults of the by-ways. And again and again, life after life there comes the necessity for making the choice between the popular religion of the high road, and the religion of the by-road, which is despised and rejected by worldly men.

A study of the history of religion shows that the way of heresy usually is the way of the by-road, and, history tells us that cults and religions often changed their status. For example at one time the cults of Isis and Osiris were religions of the high road. Times changed and the cult of Isis became the cult of the simpler folk living in the villages and the country. To use a modern term the religion of Isis became pagan, that is the religion of the pagans or the country folk. Still later Isis-worship once again became fashionable and she developed into the divine ruler of most of the modern cult of the Virgin Mother of God, rightly beloved by certain sections of Christianity.

The feminine cults or Woman's Mysteries when working with the ancient moon symbolism are, even today in so-called Christian England, exceedingly potent as a means for obtaining and using the energies of the inner worlds on what the Qabalists call the level of Yesod. But this aspect of life is, and usually remains, a *terra incognita* so far as the rich, the prosperous, and the happy are concerned. Isis was, and still is, the divine consolatrix. The powers of Isis are often to be found manifesting through the old hag in the hut — they are not very often given to the fashionable woman in her town house.

It is more easy to get in touch with the Isis power by tapping the memories that pertain to a period when the Isis cult belonged to the religions of the by-way, when it was neglected by the wealthy, the educated and the hierarchical classes who lived in or near the great Egyptian towns. This too is a theme that will be developed later when dealing with the old conflict between patriarchy and matriarchy. For it is the woman that holds the keys of the inner planes for a man. If you want to pass the Cumaean Gates you must become as a little child and a woman must lead you. You must find your Deiphobe, you must turn up the by-way that leads over the wild heather-clad heaths, you must pass through the forests, you must sacrifice to the Goddess of Three Ways, if you would reach the Cave in the Mountains.

"Cherchez la femme!" has a hidden meaning which is known only to the initiate who understands the significance of Omar Khayam's lament: —

"There was a door to which I had no key,
There was a veil past which I could not see."

It was Deiphobe, daughter of Glaucus, priestess of Phoebus, and of the Goddess of Three Ways who, for King Aeneas, opened the keyless door and drew the veil that hides life from death, and death from Life.

THE CAVE IN THE MOUNTAIN

Another way went Aeneas the true, to the towering fastness where Apollo reigns, and, near, that monstrous cavern, dread Sibyl's seclusion; where he of Delos, he the prophet, breathes into her spirit's visionary might, revealing things to come. Now they came near the woods of the goddess of Three Ways and near that house of gold.

"Cumaean Gates," by W.F.J. Knight, pages XIV and XV.

Those who today seek to leave the broad highways of the orthodox world religions and to adventure along the various by-paths that lead to the Cave in the Mountain have served at altars belonging to Woman's Mysteries. The key to these mysteries is only to be found in the dark cave that lies in a wooded ravine just beneath a tree-crowned summit.

Nevertheless it is freely admitted that the great religions of the high roads have their part to play in civilisation, and a very important one it is. For not only do they shepherd their sheep along a broad and safe track, but they also are naturally conservative and so are a guard against spiritual anarchy. Organised religions make excellent ballast!

From the psychological point of view as taught in the Mystery Schools the conscious mind of man is considered to be predominantly male while the unconscious mind is usually considered to be largely female. The unconscious mind is, as is well known, a storehouse of emotional power. It is the source of that energy which drives a man into action. It might almost be called the human powerhouse. In the same way the generating station for the power that animates the group soul of any nation lies in its unconscious. If the argument

that has been put forward is historically and actually sound then
the driving-power of the English people lies in the Celtic potentialities
of its group soul.

Today, if woman is to regain in religion the honoured place she
once so worthily held, she must turn up the by-way that leads through
the woods, over the wild heaths, to the Cave in the Mountain. There
and there only will she gain the freedom that once was hers. There,
through learning the wisdom that is taught in the Cave in the
Mountain will she regain her ancient power, her religious freedom,
and the spiritual prestige which is hers because she is spiritually the
stronger and intuitively the wiser sex.

Man creates theologies; Woman is religion. In the realms of
religion man, if left to himself, is only too often content to remain in
a bog that is named psychical research. Deiphobe, daughter of
Glaucus, put the matter very neatly to King Aeneas when she said
impatiently: "Non hoc ista sibi tempus spectacula poscit." (Now is
no time that commands staring at sights, as you stare.)

If a man wishes to pass the Cumaean Gates he must first leave
the highways of religion and seek the by-ways that run steeply
upwards through the woods of the Goddess of Three Ways. But let
him not forget as he enters her woods that a woman must lead him
if he wishes to pass through the Cumaean Gates; for Cumae is for
us a western land of death and re-birth. The Druids taught this in
the story of Connla and the Lady of the Sidhe. Jung explains it in
his preface to the *"Secret of the Golden Flower"*. Practical
experience in group meditation confirms its truth.

It takes two, a positive and a negative, to make an efficiently
functioning psychic unit.

As Dr. Harding has so clearly pointed out in *"Woman's
Mysteries"* the worship of the Moon Goddess was an education of
the emotional life by means of a series of initiations. An initiation
ceremony may be acted upon the physical stage in a dramatised
myth, but initiation *per se* is an education of the emotions and its
field of experience is in the unconscious mind. Its culmination (which
the ancients called the summons of the God or Goddess) takes place,
sometimes before, sometimes not until long after the physical plane
ceremonies have ended. For these latter are only intended to stir the

heart of the man, that is, his unconscious mind. Initiation is not a ceremony, it is the *beginning* of a new way of using the mind.

This study in moon symbols is intended to show the reader a way of initiation. If studied with care it will enable a self-initiation into the symbolism of the moon cult to take place. For by means of a system for the training of the image-making faculty, unconscious memories that have been gradually accumulated over a long series of lives are stirred up and brought into consciousness.

As a study in imagery, in order to practice *composition of place* as described by Ignatius Loyola, build in detail the following word pictures as if you were preparing them in your mind before setting them out on the stage of a theatre. Picture clearly each of the characters in the various scenes and then try to live yourself into these scenes *as if* you were one of the principal characters, and taking in the first place the character that most of all appeals to you.

This study is meant as an exercise in practical meditation upon the information that has so far been given you. Invent as pleases you little turns and twists to make the scenes and the characters live more clearly. But at the same time it must be remembered that, as mental and emotional training, this type of meditation is potent for good or ill. It embodies much of the practical technique that is used in Mystery Schools, and if persevered in, it will bring the student out of the highway and on to the by-way that rightly is his.

Let it never be forgotten that a man is what *unconsciously* he pictures himself to be. For as Coue discovered, the unconscious wish is more potent than the conscious intention.

Exercise I.

THE BY-ROAD TO THE CAVE IN THE MOUNTAIN

Along the border of a wide, green and fertile plain rises a range of high hills with many steep jungle-covered spurs that are separated by deep ravines which run far up into a mountainous country that lies to the North. Picture range after range rising between you and the perpetual snows that glisten and sparkle upon the far distant northern horizon. Vivid green are the lower slopes that come down into this rich and well watered plain. Brown and russet are the bare crags. Blue is the sky that overhangs the peaks, their ridges, and the rivers to which they give rise. Bright are the colours of this hidden land that abuts on silver and purple Yesod.

Across this plain and up the widest of these blue-misted valleys runs a broad road built carefully to a very gentle slope. The eye cannot see whence it comes; whither it goes is also unknown. Its beginning and ending are incomprehensible for they are lost in that illusion which the conscious mind calls time and space. And the reason why you and the rest of humanity have to travel this road is beyond human understanding while still in the flesh. All that any one can surmise is that having climbed those far-off snow-clad heights, man sheds his humanity and prepares to take upon himself Divinity. Even now potentially man is as the Elohim, and we know not what we shall be then.

Having carefully constructed in the mind's eye this brightly coloured picture, continue for several days to build and rebuild it until as soon as you turn your attention upon it as a completed picture it will spring into being within you. Next proceed to elaborate this

picture; then analyse your reactions to it and to the pictures that
rise from your unconscious mind as you think upon it and noting
most particularly the colours in which the latter show themselves.
These latter as your own personal contribution to the process are
very important for your mental *tone* will colour them brightly or
otherwise.

*The road itself is crowded with a long serpent-like column
that slowly moves northward towards those distant snows.
This column is composed of men, women and children. It is
humanity seeking experience in the process of evolution,
usually, as the Buddha taught, through self-inflicted
suffering.*

*The Great Mother has children other than humans. And
winding up other valleys that lie to the right and the left of
that up, which climbs humanity, are yet other roads. These
too are broad and gentle of slope. Up them, in a manner
similar to humanity, toil "your brethren of the other
evolutions". They are hidden from sight by steep jungle-
clad ridges and humanity, as a whole knows nothing of them.*

*There are however individuals who have left the main
column on the high road and have climbed up the
mountainside to the white temple of Diana of the Three Ways.
These individuals on that sacred tree-clad mountaintop have,
in the House of Gold, received from the priestess of Phoebus
the gift of clear vision. It is however a vision which is not
just mere seeing; for it is a gift which enables the one who
has received it worthily to become aware of many non-human
aspects of the One Divine Life of the Many Breasted One.
For she too is seeking experience by means of an ever-
becoming. Nothing in that divine life which ever flows from
the sacred black and white breasts is stable. Everything that
has life and can reflect upon itself can ascertain this one
thing for itself - "Je change sans cesse". Her life is change,
and with cessation of change her life comes out of the yonder,
disappears, and its form fades out from our view here.*

Now picture yourself as moving upon that road, a unit of

*that column. Imagine clearly what you can see and feel.
Next try to catch hold of the thoughts that would fill your
mind as suddenly and upon an impulse you step out of the
caravan on to the grassy edge and watch it roll slowly past
you. You are now a spectator but they are busy living each
their own life in that column. It may come as a shock to you
to notice that you are now outside the herd. You are alone,
and it is said that the lone wolf away from the pack, as a
rule, perishes quickly.*

*Is that to be your fate? That sudden impulse which made
you, at a certain spot, step out from the main column is the
stirring of old memories. And it is well to pause and realise
this stage with the utmost thoroughness for it is here that
the soul takes up once again the path. It is here that it is
necessary to learn to be alone yet not lonely. It is here that
one surmises that for each one of us life holds a special type
of experience, something has to be done but no one else can
do it for one. It is here that people begin to look askance at
the one who watches the herd from outside the line of its
march. Then there are the guardians of the caravan, to whom
the caravan pays reverence, calling them its priests. These
guardians look at you uneasily. The unwise guardian seeks
to head you back into the column, the wise guardian watches
to see that you do not seduce others who are in his charge.*

*See yourself watching and waiting expectantly. Then a
little later feel yourself wanting to rejoin the column and
wondering what all the bother is about —for nothing happens
—just yet.*

*Loneliness and boredom are always the primary
experiences of the path, and it is well to be prepared for
them. As you gaze about you wondering why you obeyed
that sudden impulse, you see a narrow path leading up the
hillside. There is a notice at its entrance — "No Road.
Trespassers will be Persecuted". This path is forbidden, and
immediately a dark-clad guardian warns you that travel by
this road means madness, disgrace, perdition, hell forever
and ever.*

Now if you believe him you had better hurry back to the main body. You may not attempt that by-road in safety until you realise clearly and fully that each man is his own saviour. You are your own priest; no one, except yourself, can stand between you and your own divinity. Potentially you are divine, but actually you are as yet only human. This is the Age of Aquarius; the age of the free man who carrying his own burdens on his own shoulders strides manfully across the sky. The Age of Aquarius is to be the age that will free man from the bogies of any outworn superstitions.

If free from these superstitions, then press boldly up the path until a plateau forming a halting place that overlooks the main road is reached. This plateau, the first stage leading to The Path, is occupied by an arguing crowd that disputes vigorously, and its members are as dogmatic and fanatical over their particular doctrines as the guardians of the highway. For they have not yet discovered that the quarrelsome are not really on The Path that leads to an inner freedom.

There is a steep track leading up the hill from this plateau and it is closed by a gate. Its Guardian asks you what you know. He does not want your beliefs. He wants to know your knowledge, if you have any — and until you can distinguish between belief and knowledge you may not pass him.

You will also be asked your motive for seeking this particular by-path. And the only answer that will open the gate is:

"I desire to know in order to serve".

Any other motive is considered to be impure for only the pure in unconscious intention (this the ancients called the heart) can, with safety, invoke the powers of the Bona Dea who was and still is the Celtic Goddess Anu or Annis,Dana: Isis of many names.

Having passed the first gate a long and steep climb leads to another plateau, which appears to be empty, except for a small bench which is just long enough to seat two. Sitting

on this bench one can see the column far below; its advance
guard is beyond view and its rear guard is not within view.

"All will reach their destination — in time," says a voice.
And then a stranger draws attention to a notice-board
marked with an arrow that points straight up the mountain
and bearing the inscription: "To the Cave on the Mountain".

If questioned the stranger will say that in this cave is to
be found Wisdom: the Wisdom of the Cave in the Mountain.
He will also explain that this path is called the path of death
in life. In any case he will point out that this hill cannot be
climbed alone; the Wisdom of the Cave in the Mountain is
not for any man who is a solitary: "for that which is solitary
is barren".

This stranger will tell you to return to the high road and
to get a woman, who if she is the woman of your choice and
you are the man of her choice may be an unknowing Eve or
a very knowing Lilith. It matters not in actual practice which
she is, for women are intuitive and adaptable, and usually
take to the routine of The Path more quickly, though perhaps
less thoroughly, than a man.

But back to the high-road you must go until you have
found what is, in truth, your better half, for Anima and
Animus must be mated, so that the One becomes the Two
and the Two are Four.

THE WATCHER AT THE FORD OF THE MOON

At the end of each day when he goes to bed a would-be Magus, as
a symbolic action should wipe his brow with the back of his hand
and say to himself: "Has my brow this day been wet with mental
sweat?" This little rite has value not only as a reminder of the Great
Work that has been undertaken, but also as a mental and emotional
catharsis, for it has been truly said that the chief temptation of any
would-be Magus is creation without mental toil.

Now these exercises although they are elementary involve an
intensive and somewhat unusual mental effort. Their object is, by
the use of symbols and imagery, to enable the reader to deduce from

the content of his own unconscious mind much that has hitherto lain fallow. A technique is set forth first by giving the principles upon which it is based, and then by showing in an actual meditation how such a technique is to be used. The result should be that by visualising each exercise carefully and accurately, a freeing of the unconscious mind takes place. The dark prison in which the frustrated emotions are shut up is opened, the life-force flows out with greater freedom, and mental energy is thus released

This technique has been used for some years. The records of its successes and its failures cover thousands of pages, and they represent many hours of both group and solitary meditation, for the students who have taken part in them can be counted by the score. It is advisable, at first, to stick closely to the methods as given here, but later on when more proficient, each student should work out for himself the technique that suits him best, for Moon Mysteries have widely varying stories to tell to the many different kinds of souls that seek their initiation in Yesod, the sphere of the Moon, where the Moon Goddesses are each of triple figure — dark and destructive in waning, bright and constructive in waxing, integrating and perfective at the full. And this is true psychologically as well as cosmically.

Meditation in Moon Mysteries may be defined briefly as the pursuit of inner active objectives. And in some of the quieter moments of deep meditation, which is an inner process that is not externalised, one becomes at times very strongly aware of an observer. He (or it) almost seems to be something or someone that is external to oneself. Some authorities consider this to be an entity external to that unity that is *a man*. Others consider the observer to be the Higher Self that forever dwells in the most secret recesses of a man's being. Really it is the conscious finding of this *hidden one* that is important, the labelling is actually of little value, and it does not matter if he be *you* or *not-you*.

We think of Man as a unity which consists of a Cosmic Atom that is unmanifest and has its home in spheres that are utterly beyond all human conception. This Cosmic Atom or Monad, as some name it, has no beginning and no ending as limited human reason conceives of these two things. It sends forth from its own essential being what is called a Higher Self or Genius, an individuality, which is an ever-changing entity that evolves through the immensely long period that a man has to spend in the bosom of the Great Mother in order to gain his full quota of experience as a unit of the human race.

This Individuality or Genius in its turn sends forth from itself a portion of its own substance which is called the Lower Self, and this latter is that natural phenomenon which is known during earth life as Mr. Jones or Miss Smith. And let it be said (you can disagree if you like for no proof is possible) that as Mr. Jones and Miss Smith you incarnate. But Miss Smith and Mr. Jones only *incarnate*. They never reincarnate. It is the *Higher Self* of each one of us that seeks re-incarnation by incarnating a little bit at a time. And the non-incarnating portion of Miss Smith and Mr. Jones is the Observer, the Guardian at the Gate, etc.

The older, wiser and more perfectly human a soul seems to be, the greater is the extent to which the Higher Self is able to shine through its temporarily incarnated Personality. Man is an integral unity, though there are some that would deny this statement, but for the purpose of empirical instruction it is customary to think of him in this threefold fashion.

First, the Personality is the unit of evolution for the period of a single incarnation on the material planet Earth. It is the Miss Smith or Mr. Jones of everyday waking conscious life. Second, the Individuality is the unit of evolution for that immensely long period which the Hindus and Theosophists call a Manvantara, or in terms of the Western tradition, *a Day of the Gods*. It, the Individuality or Higher Self, is our Virgin Mother, the immeasurably ancient, very wise, infinitely patient Watcher at the Gates of the Unseen; the Judge who has to be faced at Death. Third, the Cosmic Atom or Monad is the unit of a period of evolution so immense and of such divine, supra-human potentialities that we call it unmanifest, and label is indescribable.

The above is a simple and convenient empirical system for beginners. There is no need for the student to believe in it. It may be, perhaps, 1% accurate, and it is almost certainly 99% inadequate, but if used intelligently as a convenient working hypothesis, it will enable the student to co-operate with his own far wiser "Watcher at the Threshold".

To learn how to use this system is the first step that has to be taken when on the path of the Moon Mysteries that leads to An-na-Rea — The Ford of the Lord of the Moon according to the Celtic Mystery teaching.

After meditation — but not during it — when analysing and comparing, and during the process of recording results, watch carefully for *The Observer* and the part that he has played. Also watch the inside of your own soul and see who has been there.

Now having studied these brief and elementary points with regard to the art of meditation, it is necessary for the student to think very carefully about the relationship between the Watcher and that which is called the *Collective Unconsciousness*.

Behind the physical body that each of us inhabits during this our earthly life is a purposive Entity that may in some far distant aeon transcend the limitations of human intelligence and begin a new stage of evolution as a Divine Intelligence.

In the unconscious depths of the human mind lie hidden all the experiences of humanity, for there is the unconsciousness of humanity as well as the unconscious of a human being. Man is an integral part of that greater whole which is called the human race, and the theory that there is racial unconscious common to all humanity is fairly generally accepted because it explains much that is not easy otherwise to understand.

Behind this physical earth that we and other evolutions inhabit during physical existence, is a purposive Entity that is divine: a non-human Entity that is intelligent and evolves through the expression of its own essential nature. As man evolves through an ever-becoming, so also this Entity, which we call the Great Mother, Great Isis, Dana, and by many other names, evolves by means of an "ever-becoming". The Law of Ceaseless Change is the law of her being just as it is the law of that much smaller Entity—Man.

This does not mean that the divine functions according to limitations that are set by human reason. The functions are analogous, which is not the same as identical.

"As above, so below," is a very ancient maxim which in effect means that man is a microcosm of the universe or macrocosm. Man's

mind is an integral portion of that larger whole which is called the Universal Mind: man's unconsciousness is an integral portion of a much greater collective unconscious; man's memory is an integral part of a much wider universal memory in exactly the same way that man's life in an integral and indivisible part of the Universal Life, and man's material body is an integral and indivisible part of the material body of the Earth Entity.

This as a method of description is pure anthropomorphism, and quite rightly it should be condemned as such, for anthropomorphism as an unreflecting way of thinking is deplorable. But in meditation, especially in its deeper levels, anthropomorphism works most successfully. And until you have found empirically some other and better method of working, you will have to be content with this anthropomorphic method if you wish to have life and power in your work. If meditation subjects are purely abstract ideas or just ethical, this question will not arise, because imagination is not being exercised.

Nevertheless, practical experience, which has been carefully recorded immediately, will soon teach that any real depth of communion with the Great Mother, with Isis as Nature, is only possible on the condition that one works with Her as if she were like unto Man, though of course without mankind's all too obvious, mental, emotional, and spiritual limitations.

Many years of experience has taught that if you want to meditate in a manner that will spiritualise and intensify as well as recreate your mental life you will have, in actual practical work, to make use of the two following maxims as if they were true.

i) *"There is a Principle of Life which is universal; it fills all space and it is immanent in all forms. The substance of this Principle of Life is Mind."*
ii) *"Man's mind is an integral portion of this Universal Mind."*

If these two maxims are true, and practical experience seems to show that they work as if they were natural laws, then all idea of mental separateness is an illusion. All minds are joined together as integral parts of a complete whole. They are parts of the Universal

Mind as waves are parts of the sea.

When a man is meditating with power, his mind is in action and affects its surroundings in this sea of universal mind-stuff in much the same way that the propellers of a ship churns the ocean through which it is passing. Steam sets the propellers working. Imagination fired by desire drives the human mind into purposive mental action. Imagination driven by desire is almost always stronger than mere reason; as Ignatius taught: *"Act as if..."*

It is well to remember that just as a man's mind is an integral part of the mind of Nature, i.e. of Isis as Mother Earth, so, in turn, Her mind is part of a still greater mind that is in its own degree universal, and so on ad infinitum. Be spacious in your outlook on infinity, remembering that the cosmic outlook of an earthworm is probably but little less narrow than is a man's outlook when compared with the cosmic consciousness of such a Divine Being as the Great Mother. After all, it is true that all knowledge is purely relative.

When contemplating the gifts of the Great Mother that are to be obtained through meditation it must be kept in mind once and for ever that one's meditation is not done for one's own personal benefit. This life force must not be drawn upon selfishly, but only to enable the life of the Great Mother to flow more freely, to manifest more strongly. The object should be for each in his own small way *to enable the Great Goddess to live more perfectly the experience she needs for her own development.*

There is no need to accept these hypotheses as true, but better results are to be got in one's practical work if they be accepted and used as if they were true.

Exercise II.

AT THE FORD OF THE MOON

The man found his woman. As a modern Adam and Eve going back to THE GARDEN of the Great Mother they left the second plateau above the High-way by a path that ran through a steep cleft in the hills and up on to a spur covered with rocks and dark juniper and small green thorn trees. There, taking breath, they looked about them.

In front, but some little distance away, is open country, a wild broken heath-land basking in a sunset glow of green and gold. Its shallow valleys are filled with a light mist of turquoise blue. Its heather-covered spurs slope gradually upward to the crescent-shaped ridge of Drum-na-Rea, the Ridge of the Moon.

Behind them no portion of the broad High road is to be seen, no sound of the tramping of weary feet upon its hard surface breaks the fairy-like silence of this green, grassy by-way. The alchemical operation of SOLVE has been carried out. A new land has been entered. The frontiers of the country of the Highway have gently closed behind them, and strange by-roads lead down into the greater freedom of— 'the Oldest Land'.

Below them is a shallow valley filled with green beech and oak woods that are slightly veiled in a faintly violet mist. The path turns down suddenly and steeply into this valley which it apparently crosses, for the narrow ribbon of the green by-way can be seen winding up the heath towards the centre of the ridge of Drum-na-Rea.

After a pause the man and the woman he has chosen to be his guide leave the spur and turn down the path that enters the wood. Once within that warm, moist atmosphere it feels as if one had gone into another dimension of soft, green, translucent spaces, spaces that are very still and windless, yet they seem to reflect something that is vividly alive. One gets the impression of looking into the green and pale blue depths of a woodland pond that is reflecting the sky and the aliveness of the green leaves above its surface. This is the Fairy Greenwood that surrounds An-na-Rea, the Ford of the Moon. It is lit by an inner light of brilliant fairy gold and green in which phantom-like forms appear only to disappear once attention is consciously directed upon them.

Actually nothing is heard, nothing is seen, but it feels as if many unseen Presences, hoping for recognition, are waiting just behind this veil of green stillness to greet these wanderers from the broad highway of everyday experience.

In spite of the utter absence of any visible form of movement, the wood appears to be pulsating with life. The trees are motionless in the early evening stillness, yet the tree folk children of Dana, the Great Mother, are holding their evening revel. One is never quite sure, until it vanishes when one stares hard, whether a tree is really a so-called inanimate thing of wood and soft green leaves, or a vast, tenuous, brightly coloured living Elemental with an almost humanlike form that seems to slip in and out of the imprisoning bark.

Laughing Dryads, if not watched too intently, seem to peep and peer with the curiosity and shyness of wild things from behind the thick boles of beech and oak; the ferns and bracken are alive with the smaller fairy folk all waiting for their play-time. Fauns with tiny knob-like horns people these green spaces that seem to close in upon one as if a wall of transparent, tenuous, very still water was preparing slowly and gently to pour through this wood which is now a fairy wood that is coloured with the greenish starlight of Netzach, the sphere of the Elemental Gods who are the Shining Ones that wear emerald green robes.

The note of this wood is that of friendliness, for all its dimly seen inhabitants are glad that this man and woman have come away from the hard glare of the great white highway into the softly shining greenness of the Celtic Twilight. All around are the "Children of Other Evolutions" ready to greet these accredited newcomers as their Brethren. For, have not they also for their Divine Parent, the Great Mother, the Green Isis, ruler of the still, transparent, shadowy green woods and all that therein dwell!

"Give to these children, new from the world,
Silence and love;
And the long dew-dropping hours of the night,
And the stars above..."

sings W.B. Yeats in "A Faery Song" sung by people of faery over Diarmid and Grania in their bridal sleep under a cromlech.

On the short sward some little distance away stands Caoilte (pronounced Kilte), a royal figure with hair burning as if touched by a last golden ray of sunlight. He is clad in green and gold with a spear in his hand and a rounded shield slung on his left arm. As Lord of the fairy wood he gives greeting, and then turns to the West. He passes down the wood, saluted by all, for is he not the Prince of the Sidhe! (Shee) He halts in a wide, open glade through which a deep stream glides silently and without ripple. In the brown of this clear bog-water is reflected the still sun-lit evening sky as well as a great golden harvest moon. For this is the season when the moonlight and the twilight of early Autumn strive for mastery, the fairy time when "The Host is rushing 'twixt night and day".

This glade is called An-na-Rea, the Ford of the Moon. Caoilte points with his spear into the dark, shining depths and bids the pair of humans look therein. The man, his thoughts bent on climbing the distant hill whereon is the temple of the Goddess of Three Ways, sees but a long dark ridge mirrored in the still water, and the shimmering silver-

shining rays of the round golden-silvery moon that is Her symbol. But the woman, more open to the fiery fairy magnetism that flows from the golden leader of the Host that is in Knock-na-Rea, has seen in its deeps the glitter of the green and golden palaces of the Sidhe.

In a flash, without breaking the still surface by even a single ripple, she has dived deep into the fairy pool and down, far down, into that fifth dimensional world which the Irish Celts call Tir-na-mbeo, the Land of the Ever-Youthful.

"Your guide has proved more clear of sight than you," explains Caoilte. "Yet look not behind you, but cross by the moon-bridge if you can."

A white moon-mist gathers upon the water; it swirls up into an arch and forms the moon-bridge over An-na-Rea. Alone the crossing is made and the western bank is reached.

Caoilte too has gone, but in his place is a woman of the Sidhe holding a branch of silver-like blossoms.

THE WATCHER, HIS SYMBOLS AND SYMBOL SYSTEM

The process through which is developed an awareness of the Watcher Within is meditation.

The tools that are used in this process are symbols and symbol systems. These are usually borrowed from active existing systems or from the so-called dead religious systems of the childhood of man. These ancient systems however are not dead. They are merely quiescent in so far as the ordinary man is concerned. For those who make a comparative study of the psychology of myth they are dormant like the sleeping princess in a fairy tale; but they can be awakened into an intense spiritual, mental and emotional activity when the right stimulus is given at the right time.

Jung in the chapters on the "Symbolism of the Mother and of Rebirth" and "The Song of the Moth" in his valuable and suggestive book, *"The Psychology of the Unconscious"* has set forth an almost inexhaustible supply of ideas that will repay careful and open-minded reflection in the quiet moments of meditation.

Conditioning is the first and the most important process in the art of using symbols. Unless you are conditioned to a symbol and can react to it either in an orthodox or unorthodox manner (it matters not which) it is not for you a symbol. A symbol must bring to mind active qualities. It is not just a portrait.

A symbol may have many meanings and these may vary in different persons. Take the symbol ♀ which is but a circle above a cross. For the zoologist this means a female as opposed to ♂ a male. For the poet ♀ means a pleasant form of restlessness that usually attacks a young man in the early Spring of each year. Astronomers and astrologers use it for the planet Venus, but each gives to it a different content. The astronomer thinks of ♀ as a bright body in the sky. For the astrologer ♀ denotes certain tidal energies in an ever-flowing cosmic life stream that comes from the Unmanifest source of all life.

It may be just as well to point out here, for it is an important point that is often forgotten that the educated astrologers know well that the planet ♀ no more causes these cosmic tides than the Roman numeral I on the face of the clock in the dining-room, causes lunch! The immediate cause of lunch is the cook, who remains, so far as the dining-room clock is concerned, in a state of unmanifestation in another dimension — the kitchen!

If this idea were extended to other symbols and groups of symbols it soon becomes evident that the importance of a symbol lies in what you learn about it. You can learn much from reading books, but you can learn a great deal more by turning over in quiet and regular meditation the knowledge you have already acquired from sources external to yourself.

Meditation in its early stages is training in the art of using symbols. And the details of the examples and exercises which are given at the end of each section should be repeatedly studied with care for many days in succession for they are exercises that have been used with good results in both solitary and group meditation. Never forget that if you want to become familiar with a symbol you must meditate upon it again and again and again.

Follow the example of Napoleon who said: "Read and re-read." His method of reading was really, as he himself has told us, a system for training his visualising imagination, and his re-reading took the form of a visualising meditation. A symbol is meant to be incubated over a considerable period if it is to be hatched out into action.

In pursuit of these inner active objectives it can be said truly that in most cases (i.e. for the ordinary individual) it is better to work strictly to a daily timetable, as well as to sit in a comfortable chair where the body is forgotten. Ten minutes daily methodical work done thus in consciously directed exercise is usually worth ten times as many hours done without method when the whim to meditate is felt.

These visualising exercises seek to present the internal activities of the meditative life, and their repercussions upon the physical make-up of the student, with a reasonable clarity and in such a way that he can understand with ease what is being done. Making a clear presentation to another or even to oneself is not an easy thing to do, for the realities of the internal activities of meditation are not to be described by means of a language that is limited to objects in three dimensions. Such realities can only be described by means of analogy. For example the moon is often used for the group soul of women as a class: then the moon is dynamic. Materially speaking, the moon in the sky is a passive ball of rock, which as a cold dead sphere reflects the light of the sun. In the former case, though a three-dimensional language is used, one is not dealing with science nor with facts, but with delicate and all but intangible feelings and moods and yearnings that are peculiar to a group soul and to the individuals who make up that group entity.

One talks of woods and marshes, of fords and ridges, and of "horned moons", but it is the effect (upon the unconscious mind of the reader) that is produced by the inner substance or the essence of these material things as *holy places* that is being referred to here, and not just their three-dimensional externals that are so fully and carefully outlined. The outer symbol is described with what may seem to many as unnecessary wealth of detail, which is often repeated with intention, because it is by these means that unconscious feeling and emotion are stirred up. This deliberate repetition is an important part of the process and it should be studied carefully, for the unconscious always works in terms of picture consciousness and it is the representations of colours and sounds and smells that tug most effectively at the strings of its memory.

The symbol of the physical moon and certain colour effects are described again and again. Not however in careless repetition, but deliberately, in order to stir up the energies of the sphere of Yesod that dwells in the soul of man as a microcosm of the macrocosm. The object is to call into activity the immensely dynamic and purposive inner nature of both these spheres of sensation, for one is subjective and the other objective in a meditation. Here is the same idea as that of shattering a glass by the repeated sounding of its note. For the sphere of the moon within the sphere of sensation (subjective) of the soul of a man is directly linked to the moon sphere that is within the soul (objective) of the Planetary Spirit of this earth, and the physical moon is thus but the symbol of that cosmic tide which then acts upon man's unconscious moonsphere. The rise of the tide in the North Sea will fill a London Dock that is many miles away from the coast but still in connection with the sea. And so it happens when the soul of a man is linked *consciously* with the soul of our Great Mother — Nature — Her tidal flow becomes our tidal flow — Her life is consciously felt in our life.

Once you have thoroughly mastered this system you can begin to build these images in your own way, and thus put the stamp of your own individuality into all your work. For if this is not done you can never become a true Magus and nothing that is real can be achieved by you, for you are working mechanically and without inspiration. Inspiration is the result of repeated efforts, and with it you create magically a *something* that will work quite independent of your volition. This something is what the priests of the Old Religion sought deliberately to create for use in their rites, rituals, and meditations. It is the link between the Magus and the cosmic energy he seeks to use. In the Old Religion the object of the priest or priestess was to work with inspiration, that is, with the inbreathing of a cosmic energy which was deliberately visualised and intentionally invoked.

Let the motto of a would-be-Magus be: *Labor omnia vincit.* Act and react to these inner representations until you have lost all sense of the *how,* the *when* and the *where* in the feelings spontaneously created within you by these visions which have been so often built up mechanically by daily mental toil. When this happens a representation is no longer just your subjective mental picture. It has become (for you) an entity, which is not only objective but also vibrant with life, and it is real upon its own plane of being, though that is not this material plane of physical sensation.

When this happens you have taken the first long step that leads to self-mastery as a true Magus: that is, as a person who has trained his unconscious mind to create by means of the ancient technique of the Western Mystery Tradition; a technique that is, in its own way, as sound for us as is that of Eastern Yoga for the peoples of Asia.

With the flowering of the powers of the subconscious mind comes inspiration, and then the Magus pours into the visions that he is creating ALL the energies of his own soul. Read Ezekiel's vision of The Valley of Dry Bones. (Ezekiel, Chap. 37.) Then very carefully visualise it, for you have in it, barely hidden behind a transparent veil of commonplace words, a practical magical technique with each step described in detail and the final result clearly indicated. There is much magical lore in the seemingly strange tales of the Hebrew Bible.

Working in this way, the would-be-Magus is developing in a perfectly safe manner his own inner life. With steady development character is being rounded off and matured. This development will tend to show itself in his mundane activities.

Thus one gives life to one's visions by living them in meditation and in ritual with a desire that is made as strong as possible, even if in the early stages such desire may have to be stimulated artificially. The vision is lived by experiencing its appropriate feelings, and each time this is done with intention reinforced by desire more and more life is infused into the vision. Ignatius Loyola based his wonderful magical system of training on this fact.

Again, never build your visions if you are bored with them lest you undermine their vitality. Instead visualise another totally different but familiar symbol as a mental drill for a disobedient mind. Drill your mind during periods of "dryness" with the visualisation of the Tree of Life and vibrate gently its God-names. They are a potent cure for what some call "the Dark Night of the Soul".

It is a great help when building symbols in vision to feel that behind one is the life power of the Unmanifest waiting for any opportunity to find expression through forms that are created by a visualising imagination. Feel strongly that you have behind you and flowing through you the limitless energy and everlasting harmony of the Great Mother of All. Then by working *as if* this were so, one's natural abilities are transcended.

In working a moon ritual in group meditation, there are certain phenomena that practical work has brought to notice. Among these is the important fact that better results are to be got by working as a trinity. For example, the Hierophant if a man, will find that his powers are immensely enhanced if he will think out the implications of the following facts.

The Roman Church uses three priests for its High Mass. In the Vignettes of the "Pert em Hru", i.e. "Coming into the day", Osiris as the Hierophant is supported by Isis and Nephthys. *Hecate Triformis* is a combination of *Aphrodite-Selene-Hecate* and represents the Powers of Heaven, Earth and the Inner World. Sinn, the Babylonian Moon God, was also Triune in his inner nature. In the Islamic faith, the Three Daughters of Allah retain the ancient names of the three aspects of the Arabian Moon Goddess. They are Al-Ilat; Al-Uzzaz; and Manat. Again the three Celtic Bridgets are three aspects of the great Celtic Moon Mother, Anu, and so on.

There is much to be learned concerning the use that was made by the ancient initiated priesthoods of the fact that the gods and goddesses in the sphere of Yesod are three-aspected by watching with the inner eye what is done in group meditations by those Orders that have recovered something of these ancient methods from their own unpublished manuscripts as well as from the published works of Briffault and Frazer, and from Hastings' *"Encyclopaedia of Religion and Ethics"*.

Exercise III.

AT THE PILLARS OF AURD-NA-RAE: THE HIGH PLACE OF THE MOON.

In the place of Caoilte in a faint haze of golden light stood a smiling woman of the Sidhe (Shee) very soft and young and graceful, and the man wondered if this were Niamh of the Golden Hair. But seeing his perplexity at this sudden change of guide the woman laughed and said, "I am old, very old as you men count years, and yet I am ever-young, for unlike Eve I made not for myself a coat of skin. Your former partner Eve is now renewing her youth in Tir-fa-Thonn, the land beneath the waters. And now that you have passed safely over An-na-Rea by the Bridge of the Moon I will take you the long green way over the wide spaces to Aurd-na-Rea. There between the Pillars of the Whispered Truth you may learn of the Great Mother; for it is She whom we also serve who are of the Dedannans, the children of Dana. But first look once again in this deep brown pool of An-na-Rea and tell me what you see".

He gazed into the still dark water that now, seen from the West, reflected the trees of the fairy wood and the steep dark mountain beyond it. A faint mist rose and then cleared, and in the pool was a seemingly drowned land. A land of high towers, lofty trees, and bright colours where dwelt a people ever young, every happy, ever advancing in a wisdom that is not the result of human experience and suffering.

This is the land that some call the Summer land of the Astral Plane. Long ago it was called the Garden of Eden and Adam dwelt there with Lilith for his first wife. But because progress is slow in perfect happiness Adam was filled with a divine discontent. And so, when in deep sleep, he dreamed of Eve as the imperfection that should complete his own perfection. And when his dream exteriorised through intense desire he sought with her the golden wisdom that the sacred green all-wise snake would give him through failure. And so the two wandered from that golden land — "on the verge of the azure sea". For Adam was divorced from his first inner and subjective love when he sought for the objective as Eve.

Lilith remained in Tir-fa-Thonn, the bright land that is in the Astral Sea, until the Moon Mother who rules the rise and fall of Astral tides called her to her temple that is within Aurd-na-Rea, the High-place of the Moon. There it can still be seen, it is said, as O'Brasil: as long ago it was seen by Maildun - the Irish Seer, who saw it without the sight of his physical eyes by means of the two-petalled Lotus that is between them.

The vision vanished and the woman of the Aes-Shee moved up the green way through the heather, purple with its summer blossom and smelling like new honey, past golden furze bushes bright with yellow blooms. There was no sun nor were stars visible. Yet all details could be clearly seen in the green and faintly orange lights that cast the purple shadows of the sphere of Yesod where rules the Lord of the Moon who is the king of this Land of Life. He who is the first-born of the Great Mother Dana, the ruler of the non-human peoples of the Etheric and Astral planes of consciousness.

They stood before two great pillars. Beyond these pillars only faintly to be seen was a temple, and before it a throne — that of the Great Moon Mother who sat thereon.

The man stood alone before the Pillars of the Whispered Truth for his guide the Bean Sidhe (banshee) had vanished; and he sought to pass between them, but could not. Then he saw the sword of Life that flames red as blood between the Pillars of Life and Death, the Jachin and Boaz of the Temple of Solomon. He heard the right-hand pillar whisper — "Moy Mell is barred to you without Eve". The left pillar whispered also, "Moy Mell is barred to you without Lilith".

And then the blood-red sword whispered, "If you would pass while living, here is the Key of the Door that is barred by me, for I am the Sword of Azrael. Come again as Adam bringing your Eve and your Lilith".

The functional nature of the unit for leaving the Astral Garden is dual, for returning however it is Triune.

THE WATCHER AND THE TRIUNE DIVINITIES

In the Old Religion a snake symbolises the *inner wisdom* that is *intuition*. Also in vision it is a symbol for a Lord of the Moon sphere. Cernunnos is often shown with serpents as is Hermes, and so are other Wisdom gods.

Eve is the Moon. She is Woman, as the man of the Earth-sphere knows her. Lilith is Woman, as the Lords of the Moon-sphere know her. The Moon-sphere is positive and the Earth-sphere is negative, and both are contained within the etheric of that purposive entity which is called the Great Earth Mother, or the Great World Mother. She is a macrocosm and the human entity is a microcosm. The latter is also bi-polar. And the four poles of these two entities — the World Mother and the human being — can be linked so that the more potent will charge with life energy the less potent. The process by which the microcosm consciously charges itself from its immediate macrocosmic superior is the wisdom of the serpent according to the non-Semitic religions of pre-Christian times.

This process can be carried out by a single person working alone in meditation. It can also be carried out by two or three persons of opposite sexes in what may conveniently be called a ritual meditation. The most powerful training unit is either a man and two women, or a woman and two men. That is, Osiris supported by Isis and Nephthys, Adam with Eve and Lilith, or Isis supported by Osiris and Set, and Isis supported by Horus and Anubis.

A glance at the vignettes of the "Pert-em-hru", or a study of the wall paintings in the tombs and temples of Ancient Egypt will show

how the ancient priest or priestess invoked divine energy into a Temple Ritual.

For the Romans, Janus, who like the Qabalistic angel Azrael, sat at the Gates of the Inner World, is the personified guardian of this knowledge. And here it must be pointed out that knowledge (in such matters) is not the same thing as a belief, theory or speculation. Any one can speculate and theorise about the ancient teaching that is shadowed forth above, but something more than this is necessary in order consciously to pass the blood-red sword of the Angel of Death that guards the ever-open gate that is between the Pillars of the Here and the Yonder. But unlike the gates of the Roman temple of Janus Bifrons (two-headed) this gate is never closed (except to the living by the blood-red sword) for there is never peace between those twin brothers that are Life and Death, Osiris and Set, Vishnu and Shiva.

"On the day the Silver Cord is snapped and the Golden Lamp drops broken", you will, as it were in sleep, pass the sword of Azrael and the gates of Janus Bifrons, and you will then find that they are each of them the kindly helper who gives sleep to his beloved. But it is quite another matter to face the flaming sword that keeps the way through the Gate of Life and of Death (for they are not two things but one thing viewed from two aspects) and to consciously bring back to this earth tidings of that which in human language is said to be behind or beyond or within this ever-opened, yet closely guarded gate.

This conscious entry and return through the Gates of the West is the result of knowledge that can be gained by using this so-called Wisdom of the Serpents; however, the method itself can only be learned through the trial and error of practical experience.

In a certain sense Osiris on his bier is the candidate. But in another sense he is the officiating priest. Both have to take the way between the Western portals of night and day. Look closely at this scene, for Lilith, who is the Egyptian Nephthys, must come to the aid of Eve, who is Isis, the mysterious Sister, Mother, Wife of Osiris who may be either the candidate or the officiant at the double altar.

In certain of the mystery rituals Osiris is referred to as the child of two Mothers and the clue to this curious aphorism is to be found when and where the functioning priestly unit is triune. In the Old Religion the priest who stands at the altar as mediator between the Great World Mother and her devotees is also in his inner aspect a child of the two moon mothers. For he is the focussing-point for the consciously directed powers of Nephthys and Isis as energising negative and positive cosmic factors. Hints with regard to this point are given in the following quotations from the Litany of Nes-Amsu.

> *"Behold the lord Osiris ...*
>
> *Are not the two impersonators of the goddess, and Hunnu,* the beautiful, approaching to thy shrine at this moment?*
>
> *Lo! the Bull,* begotten of the two cows Isis and Nephthys!*
>
> *He, the progeny of the two cows Isis and Nephthys, the child surpassingly beautiful!*
>
> *He appeareth unto us in thy image, like the one beloved.*
> *Behold! He* cometh!"*

The proof of a pudding is said to be in the eating of it. It is equally true that the proof of the magical efficiency of a *unit* in any ritual technique is in the working thereof.

The priest with the mask of Osiris had at his left shoulder a priestess wearing as her headdress the throne of Isis. At his right was another wearing the cup of Nephthys. In other ceremonies Isis functions with Horus and Set as her supporters. In modern psychological terms, reason (Osiris) is the focal point for the powers of superconsciousness and unconsciousness. In ancient times space was conceived of as having Osiris for the horizon line which forever hides Isis. Osiris is the ever-moving present that divides Isis, as the past, from Nephthys, the dark and ever-hidden future.

Religious psychology has taught that a man has within his soul his Isis and his Nephthys; Adam carries in his bosom both Eve and

---

* *refers to Osiris*
    Quoted from Wisdom of the East - "The Burden of Isis",
    The Litany of Nes-Amsu.

Lilith. A woman, as the microcosm of the macrocosmic woman, the Moon, has within her soul Osiris and Set, those great and vastly ancient gods that are the twin sovereigns of the moon phases. "Hell," it is said, "knows no fury like a woman scorned," a saying easy to understand when Set as the Red Lord of the dark moon phases becomes the ruler of a woman's inner emotional life — for is not Set the slayer of Osiris?

Analytical psychology tells much about these secret moon aspects of the soul, but the habitual working of magical rituals not only tells but also brings into manifestation much more than can the former method.

Here is a list of triune divine manifestations that will repay study, provided the processes that have been described in the previous chapters have been brooded upon and used practically and with understanding in meditation.

TRIUNE DIVINE MANIFESTATIONS

(A)   *MALE*

Shiva	Vishnu	Brahman	
Set	Horus	Osiris	*(as Moon-Gods)*
Ptah	Sokar	Ausar	*(as the primitive*

creative power and darkness, the Dweller in the Secret Place).

Ptah	Seker	Temu	*(the Lord of the*

Hidden Place).

Balor	Bress	Tethra	*(the three aspects of*

Buar-Ainech who is Cernunnos as the wearer of the Horned Moon).

(B)   *FEMALE*

Hathor   Nephthys   The Green Isis *(Aspects of Isis).*
The Three Bridgets as aspects of Dana.
The Three Bridgets *(Bride)* as aspects of Anu.
Aphrodite   Persephone .   Hecate.

(C)   COMBINED

Ptah	Nefer-Tem	Sekhet *(Sekhmet)*
Horus	Set	Isis
Sinn	Merodach	Ningala
Nannar	Bel-enlil	Ishtar
Tammuz	Belit-Sheri	Ishtar
Tammuz	*(Eresh-Ki-gal)*	Ishtar *(Allatu)*
Osiris	Isis	Nephthys
Shiva	Kali	Durga
Adam	Eve	Lilith

The Master Jesus had a friendship with Martha and Mary, and you will not waste your time if you meditate upon the story of Jesus and the two Marys at the foot of his cross. One Mary is the Virgin, one is the Harlot, and the cross of Jesus is symbolic of the unfolded Black Altar of the Universe upon which the Divine Manifestor and Architect of the universe is always being sacrificed in an unceasing ever-becoming. "Je change sans cesse" is as true of the mind of the cosmos as it is of the mind of man. Again ponder on the fact that the first human being is Mary the Harlot, a very significant point for those who understand that Yesod is the PowerHouse of both the universes — the Macrocosmic and the Microcosmic. Why also did Jesus call Mary and Martha to him when he went to the tomb of Lazarus to perform a magical feat upon the dead?

These trinities have nothing to do with the father-mother-child combinations so delightfully explained by some students of comparative religion and folklore. There *are* divine forms for use in magical rituals. They are still potent and can be unpleasant and dangerous if used unskilfully by those who fail to balance wisdom and power in harmony.

As a method of training the mind to realise through visualised symbols these ideas, draw a large red triangle on a sheet of paper. Put Harmony at the apex, Wisdom at the left basal angle, and Power at the right basal angle.

Draw a blue triangle with its apex downwards and label it in the same way. Let the red triangle be considered as Tiphareth, Netzach and Hod and the blue triangle as Netzach, Hod and Yesod. Remember however that these two triangles are in different states of consciousness, or on different planes of being. Or again, consider the red triangle to be Fire (not physical but metaphysical fire), and the blue triangle to be Water (also not physical). Now the qualities named at the angles refer not only to cosmic manifestations of the divine Henads or gods, but also to analogous psychological factors in the Soul of Man.

Use the red triangle for the negative feminine goddesses. Then draw with its apex upwards a third triangle in green, the fairy colour, the sacred colour of those who work the moon magic in what the Celtic world calls Tir-nan-og. It too is in yet another dimension, as you will soon discover when successful practical work begins.

Use this green triangle as follows. If you have a trinity of two gods and a goddess, place the goddess at the apex. If two goddesses and a male god, then place him at the apex. In a ceremony at the altar this rule is observed by those that wear the priestly masks. Visualise the apex of each triangle as touching the altar, and watch your reactions to this picture when it is firmly built in the astral temple.

Again, in magic the woman is the equal of the man. In the Mysteries of Eleusis the Hierophantissa played a part equal to that of the Hierophant; one of the former was able to boast that she had initiated no less than three Roman Emperors. In the highest of the three grades that the Mystae ordinarily achieved, the roles of the Hierophant and the Hierophantissa were equal even as late as in the Christian era. So picture yourself in the role of your sex, and behind you the two who serve at the altar with you. Every woman has her right to face across the Black Altar the Divine Being that she and her assistants impersonate.

Sometimes the old memories return at such a moment very clearly; so visualise carefully and feel deeply.

Sit down in meditation, and as soon as the mind is quiet, visualise any temple sanctuary that appeals to you. In the centre is a black stone Altar, a double cube about four and a half feet high. On it is the Sacred Light. You as priest or priestess stand at the altar facing east. Before you, dimly seen in the darkness of the sanctuary in the

East, are the conventional forms of the three gods, or goddesses, or the mixed trinity you decide to use. Behind you are the two priests or two priestesses of the gods or goddesses that form the basal angles of the triangle.

Build that scene until it appears automatically the moment you are seated for your meditation. Now - as the *Watcher* - see what happens when the priestly figure that is you (as the Hierophant) invokes.

When the meditation is finished record the results (if any) and your emotional results (if any).

You may get a surprise the first time you try this method. But in all probability (as happened to the author) you will get nothing without many weeks of steady concentrated visualising with strong desire. So do not be discouraged — you value most that for which you have had to work hard.

Exercise IV.

THE HOSTING OF THE SIDHE

(A) As a part of this Exercise, and before continuing the vision of Tir-nan-og, visualise clearly with strong feeling this glorious piece of English rhyming verse.

CHORUS
Some Maidens

Will they ever come to me, ever again,
The long long dances,
On through the dark till the dim stars wane?
Shall I feel the dew on my throat, and the stream
Of wind in my hair? Shall our white feet gleam
In the dim expanses?
Oh, feet of a fawn to the green wood fled,
Alone in the grass and the loveliness;
Leap of the hunted, no more in dread,
Beyond the snares and the deadly press,
Yet a voice still in the distance sounds,
A voice and a fear and a haste of hounds;
0 wildly labouring, fiercely fleet,
Onward yet by river and glen...
Is it a Joy or terror, ye storm-swift feet?...
To the dear lone lands untroubled of men,
Where no voice sounds, and amid the shadowy green
The little things of the woodland live unseen.

Euripides, "The Bacchae," translation by Gilbert Murray.

(B) The Bean Sidhe (banshee) - fairy woman - led him back from the pillars to a spur of the heath lands, and they looked not back until she came to a low mound surrounded by silver-barked birch trees whose thick gnarled and twisted trunks showed their age.

Handing him the branch with the silver blossom, she ordered him to touch the root and trunk of the largest birch, which was in the centre of the path. As he did so the tree vanished and in its place was a temple-like portal across which was hung a heavy dark green curtain through which she entered and he followed.

They were inside and in the transparent brown earth; a great mountain stretched below them and they started to descend its rough, rock-strewn slopes by going further down into the deep. Swiftly they moved downwards in order to reach the top of the mountain upon which a brilliant city of gold and green appeared.

This world was indeed solid just as is that which is upon the surface of the earth, but one seemed to see the inside as well as the outside and the inside was outside the boundaries of the outside. One felt rather like Alice when through the looking-glass.

This city had walls of a semi-transparent green and gold, and it was made of stones that looked like a piece of glass that has been a long time on the sea-shore and has been marked by the grinding action of the stones and shells.

At the gate of the city were guards. Each was armed with a golden-headed spear and a round shield. They saluted the silver-like branch and allowed the Bean Sidhe and her companion to pass into a wide street which led to a tree-bordered square on the far side of which was a portal leading into a great palace, where a Prince of the fairy people met them.

"Your companion," he said, "had the right of entry, but you have to be vouched for by a guide. By what authority do you come?" The Bean Sidhe showed the silver-white branch of blossom, the symbol that in the ancient Celtic Mysteries

admits the would-be initiate in to the land that lies between the Here and the Yonder, and between the past and the present. It is the dimension that is between the outside and the inside, where consciousness is able to transcend the ever-passing present. Here the initiated, like Mohammed's coffin, seems to hang between heaven and earth. This is the Land of the Ever Young, because having no present there is no past and no future. Time as generally understood by man, is not, for with the Sidhe time is but a graduated scale for the measuring of joy. There is no sorrow, no suffering, only degrees of joy and degrees of beauty, and degrees of wisdom; here, however, wisdom is not just being well informed.

Yet they lack one thing which mankind has - suffering, and the joy that suffering ultimately brings. They live in an unending perfection, and because they are perfect, though in a way that man cannot even faintly comprehend, they can only remain in that state of perfection in which the great World Mother has placed them as they are the children of but one of her many forms of evolution.

Men are mortal because Adam took Eve with him when he left the Garden of Eden, which is fairyland, to seek mortality as an escape from the timeless, spaceless perfection of Tir-nan-og.

"Now that you will be shown Tir-na-mbeo - the Land of the Ever Youthful - will you have me as your guide, or do you prefer to have this woman?" the Fairy Prince asked his visitor.

There was something in the way that both looked upon him that made the man realise that much hung upon that apparently simple and courteously put question. He read in both their eyes something that was almost like anxiety, an anxiety to escape from perfection it seemed, and he felt an unspoken appeal from the dark fairy woman beside him.

He asked that she might remain with him, and with a sigh the Fairy Prince left him, and the fairy woman took him into a garden immense as a park.

She sat beside him holding his right hand in her left;

then she passed her right hand over his eyes and told him to watch the trees and flowers and to try to see how they manifested on the physical plane their real life which is the fairy world of the Moon-plane which some call the Astro-etheric.

The scenery had become just that of an ordinary earthly landscape in a rich, cultured man's private park. The fairy woman had grown dim to his sight, he no longer saw her form though he felt the energy pouring from her to him and he heard her anxious whisper "Concentrate or I am lost for you".

It was difficult to concentrate. Sight had grown abnormal; nothing was clear, and the wide landscape was dissolving in a seeming chaos of colour that lost itself in a mother-of-pearl-tinted haze. Only one form held - a beech tree, and in despair he compelled himself to see it as he knew it ought to be. A brief struggle, and then the tree and the park came once more into focus as a clear and beautiful astral garden.

"Now try to see the tree as a purposive intelligent entity," he was told, and he felt a hand placed on the nape of his neck.

As he watched, the green of the beech-leaves and the faint silver colour of the bole seemed to merge in a form that was not the tree, and yet it was like the tree. He was no longer seeing the tree with his eyes - he was feeling it. He was once again in his inner, subtler, Moon-body, and with it he saw and felt the Moon-body of the tree. Then appeared the tree spirit, the Deva, the Shining One who lives through the trunk and branches and leaves of the beech tree as a man lives through his torso, limbs and hair. That beech was very friendly and Moon-body to Moon-body they met, and as his Moon-body merged into that of the Lady of the Beech Tree the sensation of the nature of the seasons, of the caress of the sunlight, of the stimulation of the bright increase of the waxing moon, and of the sleep-time that comes with the decrease of the waning moon were his.

"You can merge thus into all life," he was told; and then

*he saw, as the fairy sees, the flowers, the waterfalls the rivers,
and the brightly coloured holy mountain of Derrybawn,
which means the home of the Shining Ones. He merged
himself into the roaring life that was at the summit of that
great and sacred mountain — and in so doing he took the
initiation of the Lady of Nature - the Green Isis - in her
temple on the heather-clad hill-top that is above the deep
ravine.*

*The fairy woman stood beside him on a small platform
that overhung an immense gorge the bottom of which was
almost lost in mists that rose from a dark, still lake.*

*She stretched her arms as if to dive and whispered, "I
dare you!" and was gone.*

*Next moment both were speeding on the wings of thought
downwards, and out from the blue mists below came the
galloping Host riding from Knock-na-Rea. A pair of riderless
horses sped beneath them like a flash. She took a gray horse
and he a black mare. And hand in hand, with the flanks of
the screaming gray stallion and the whinnying black mare
touching, they raced across starlit astral space in the wake
of the "Hosting of the Sidhe".*

Retrospect and Summary

THE SONG OF DIANA
The Goddess of the Old Religion in Italy.

"Endamone, Endamone, Endamone!
By the love I feel, which I
Shall ever feel until I die,
Three crosses on thy bed I make
And then three wild horse-chestnuts take;*
In that bed the nuts I hide,
And then the window open wide,
That the full moon may cast her light

---

*The three should come from one shell. Quoted from "Aradia" by Leland.

Upon a love so fair and bright,
And so I pray to her above
To give wild rapture to our love,
And cast her fire in either heart,
Which wildly loves to never part:
And one more thing I beg of Thee!
If anyone enamoured be,
And in my aid his love hath placed,
Unto his call I'll come in haste.

At the *Twin* doors of the objective Divine Unconscious (as is said to have been the case at the dual-doored Crypt of Ancient Eleusis), stand three vast figures. On the left is that of the Great Queen, the Soul of the World, who is personified as the All-Mother Saraswati, Aima, Ama, G'e, Demeter, the Heavenly Isis - the celestial light and source of life, Great Diana, and Ishtar.

On the right is a youthful Queen with the narcissus on her brow, the young and ever-virgin bride on the throne of the Under-World, ruler of the kingdoms of sleep and of dreams, She who is Death, and as such is also the Holder of the Secret of Life. Kore, Nephthys, Belit-Sheri, Aradia the daughter of Diana, are but some of her personifications.

Between these two doors and in the centre is the Lord of the Ivy Crown holding a winged thyrsus interlaced with two serpents. He is personified as Dionysos who is Life, Death and Resurrection, and as Osiris, the Risen Lord of Death.

It is wise today, as it was in the past, having passed and repassed this dual-doored gateway, to place finger upon lip, for talking about psychic experiences, except to the teacher, breaks their magical validity.

The initiated occultist, that is, he who has stood on the floor of the cave that symbolises the Beyond, is usually chiefly interested in three things.

First is the training of his earthly personality, both body and mind, so that it shall become as sound an instrument for the work he has to do, as he is capable of producing within the limitations of his Karma.

Then he spends much time and thought in meditation or in a potent type of ritual by means of which he, voyaging into other states of consciousness, endeavours to get into contact with the beings of other evolutions that are progressing along cosmic paths which are, so to speak, parallel to that taken by humanity.

And thirdly he aims at gaining conscious contact with entities that, being more evolved than himself, have for their sphere of operation realms of existence that are supraphysical. The occultist's early studies lie in the sphere of Yesod, which is that of the Machinery of this Universe as cosmic energy in action. In the past the initiated called these great beings, the Gods, and the Buddhists and Hindus today call them the Devas.

These three objectives were, and are, often pursued more or less simultaneously, though it is, as a rule, wiser to make some considerable progress with the first objective before the second and third are undertaken. All three methods seek to teach one *how to live in the Universal Soul consciously.*

Thus three levels of the mind are dealt with in the course of training: the conscious level, the unconscious level that is personal to each individual, and that still deeper and more primitive unconscious level that is common to all humanity and to all entities that are part of the evolving life of the Great Mother Isis, Ishtar, and Dark Diana of the many breasts.

The more materially-minded moderns think that man is the highest of God's creative acts. But in this matter they flatter themselves. In this physical world the human line of evolution may be higher than that of the pig, goat, bird or fish, but occultism is not concerned with the lines of evolution that have externalised completely into physical manifestation.

In this paper only the beings that belong to the Sphere of Yesod have been touched upon, and no attempt has been made to develop in the reader the contacts that give access to certain of the Great Devas that rule in Spheres of evolution that are other than human. Nevertheless some readers who are far advanced may have successfully touched certain of these great Beings that in the New Testament are called Powers, Principalities, Rulers, Elements or first principles. This leads up to the great truth that in the Mystery

schools the teacher is not so important as the personality of his
pupil — for all development must be self-development.

Masefield has written in one of his poems: —

"Fate, that is given to all men partly shaped,
Is ours to alter daily till we die."

And he has here put into modem English one of the famous and
secret maxims common to the Mystery training processes of all
times.

This word *secret,* however, is used here in a very particularised
sense. One great Master has talked of it as seed growing in secret,
the grain growing secretly in the dark black earth. Here reference is
made to what a certain type of teacher calls a *Seed thought,* which
is what this maxim is.

A Seed thought means that if you put with strong intention a
magical idea into your visualising imagination and build it clearly,
and then with intention consign it to the fructifying darkness of
your unconscious mind, it will begin to grow in energy. If you go on
repeating this process with strong intention every day even for but
a few short moments when rising from and also when going to bed,
this magical idea will in time come to energise your life and your
expression of life in matter.

Suppose you feel drawn to the Old Religion, to the Mysteries of
Diana in the sphere of Yesod. If your circumstances bar you from
participating in them, and if you are unable to change those
circumstances in the ordinary way, there is no need for you to sit
down and do nothing. By working upon your unconscious mind
you can change the nature of your relationship to your environment
— a thing that Omar Khayyam has hinted at, and Aradia taught in
the "Song of Diana" just quoted.

Build the Green Ray pictures that have been given you. Strive to
feel within yourself the joy that they are intended to produce in your
emotional nature. If you can work yourself up into ecstasy — that
is, to a state of consciousness that enables you to stand without
yourself — a few moments are all that are necessary — in time you

will so change that circumstances will cease to hinder, for you will have changed their relationship to yourself.

"When the student is ready the Master will come": for usually the teacher is more anxious to find the student than the looker is in locating the tutor. The first step is always preparation, and on its thoroughness depends the speed at which you will advance. So begin upon your own inner self — your first and last task in the Mysteries.

The Ancients used the Fire of the Wise to burn away the dross in their own personalities. The Fire of the Wise is the visualising imagination. As a man thinks in his heart, so is he. The modern rendering of that term heart is unconscious mind. And the psychological rendering of this saying should be — As a man's unconscious mind *sees* him to be, so he is. The unconscious mind is not the reasoning mind. It is something far more primitive and powerful which works in picture-images and not in words. Its guide is feeling, not reason. In it are hidden the memories of the past aeons. In it lie also the potentialities that will determine the future for the cosmic unconscious mind is Aradia, the ever-virgin daughter of the Dark Diana, the Cosmic Mother of the Old Religion.

In the imagery that has been given you here is hidden a method for doing two very different things: first for developing and maintaining an emotional drive that will enable you to get started on your task of finding the hidden wisdom that contains all the ancient wisdoms of the world, and secondly, the construction of a *form* which will enable you to link your varying states of consciousness to their appropriate type of subtle matter in the Soul of the Great Mother.

When this form is adequately functioning, and when it is filled with the appropriate type of energy, you have within yourself an *Ens Realissimum, which* is as the Philosopher's Stone. It is a magical personality and it is the key to symbolism used when worshipping great Diana, the Compassionate Mother.

So long as you remember and act upon the ancient proverb, "The Gods give their rewards only to those who sweat for them" you have, by virtue of this key, the power to function as a member of the priesthood of The Old Religion.

THE HERMETIC RAY

All occultists are concerned with the hidden forces in man and nature, the invisible realities that lie behind appearances. There are three basic ways in which man can contact these forces of life. These are through the three rays so often mentioned by Dion Fortune: the *Elemental Ray,* the *Devotional Ray,* and the *Hermetic Ray.*

The Elemental Ray is often called the Green Ray, and this conjures up in the mind the greenness of nature grass, trees, and plants. The Green Ray concerns the forces in man associated with the physical, instinctual and feeling life in nature — the part of a man that responds to the forces of growth in plants, the life force in animals, the wind in high places, the power of water and the moon, and the miracle of fire. This part of a man is primitive. So, you might ask, why should we concern ourselves with something that is in the past of man's evolution? The answer to this really lies in one word, pathology, because modern civilisation with its enormous stress, technological growth and the use of the mind in all parts of life has tended to starve western man of his roots, starve him of the emotional and instinctual food that animal man needs.

The Green Ray, for the modern Western man, is a compensation to put right what has been twisted or missed in his life. All parts of a man have to be known and experienced if he is to become a fully integrated being. It is the forces of the Elemental Ray working within a man that give him zest, passion, and a joy in living.

Contact with the nature forces is achieved by learning to feel at one with nature and to recognise one's self as a part of the natural world about him. Nevertheless, in its pure form, this ray belongs to the past of man's evolution.

The Devotional Ray on the other hand, appears to be opposite in every way to the Elemental Ray. The Elemental Ray is concerned with a natural, instinctual and animal life force, whereas the Devotional Ray operates on the level of the higher emotions — aspiration, devotion, and the spiritual life. Though these two rays appear to be opposite poles, they are similar in essence since both of them are concerned with forces: the Elemental Ray with the lower forces, and the Devotional Ray with the higher forces —the elemental with body and soul and the devotional with spirit.

The methods of contacting the Devotional Ray use the same principle as those for mediating the Elemental Ray —both achieve their results by getting into sympathic rapport by establishing a harmony, the only difference is the level on which it is done. In work on the Devotional Ray the target is the spirit of man, the inner self. We all know that the perfection of spirit has not yet manifested in earth, the kingdom has not yet come on earth as it is in heaven. Therefore the Devotional Ray, in its pure state, belongs to the future of mankind's evolution.

Between these two poles lies the Hermetic Ray. The name is derived from the mythical Hermes Trismegistus, as the Greeks called him, or Mercurius Ter Maximus, as the Romans knew him. This famous figure is traditionally a great teacher of mankind who introduced reason, logic, and philosophy into the search for the light.

The Elemental Ray speaks to the instincts and emotions, the Devotional Ray to the higher aspirations, and the Hermetic Ray addresses the mind of man. The Elemental Ray initiate may thrill to the call of wind and water, and the Devotional initiate may swoon in the embrace of the divine, but the Hermetic initiate thinks —he plans, designs, constructs, and uses structures in the mind — he builds bridges to span the gulf between the heavenly vision of the Devotional Ray and the hard realities of physical life. The initiate of the Hermetic Ray is a tool user. He uses his powers of mental organisation and image building as an engineer uses his tools to accomplish what otherwise could not be achieved.

The purely mystical approach whether on elemental or devotional levels, is to place one's self in harmony with the appropriate forces. This is essentially a passive approach, whereas the Hermetic method builds channels, constructs forms, and organises and directs the forces of life.

The Hermetic Ray is concerned with mind, and mind is very important esoterically because it is halfway between spirit and matter. At the moment the focus of consciousness in mankind at this stage of his evolution is mind. Therefore the Hermetic Ray *is* the present time of evolution.

Some people are naturally passive in their approach to the inner realities and others are basically active, but both methods should be possible in a properly balanced man. Because the Hermetic Ray is at the point of balance between spirit and matter, and because mind is the focus at this stage of man's evolution, the Hermetic Ray holds the key to practical occultism in the Western world.

We have spoken about the natural approach of the Devotional and Elemental Rays — the establishment of a sympathetic rapport with the spiritual and/or elemental forces. In practice a trained occultist in the West would rarely use this method. If a devotional level approach was being used, the hermetic tools of reason, logic and order would be employed to make a structure to convey the devotional experience to others. One good example of this is the church service of the Mass where the aim is devotional but the method uses the hermetic tools of ritual, form, and ceremony. The same applies in contacts with the Elemental Ray. No occultist in the West would normally think of mediating the forces of the Elemental Ray simply by *feeling with them*, because if he did he would become a tool of those forces. He would become a passive instrument and the forces would flow through his nature and he would have little or no control over them. One of the aims of the Hermetic method, which is the essence of Western occultism, is to exercise control at all times.

In working with the elemental forces and the Elemental Ray, there are two approaches, which are equally applicable. It is possible to contact a force such as the energy of the moon by passive mediation, trying to adjust one's inner rhythms to correspond to the basic rhythms of the moon and deliberately building up a sympathetic rapport with the lunar forces. The tidal movement can be emulated in a human being and by this means, if the person is patient long enough, he can contact the energies of the moon by stimulating the equivalent forces within himself. The problem is two-fold. The first is that many people do not have the ability to concentrate for a long enough period to get this sympathetic rapport developed. The second point is that assuming the experiment is successful, the initiate would have no control over the depth of the experience, very little control over the duration of the experience, and would in fact, be completely passive. It would be the astral equivalent of going on a drug trip.

One of the things stressed in Western occultism is the need to control exposure to forces of this type. Always the initiate is counselled to remain in control. The Plan of life does not permit one to indulge oneself and go on *trips*.

The Hermetic approach, which is taught in the Western Mysteries, is a quite different procedure in establishing contact with the moon. The Hermetic procedure for a moon contact would be to first select a suitable god-form or goddess form for the ceremony. This form may have been used for thousands of years as a focussing point for thinking about the moon and getting in contact with lunar type forces. Moon forces belong very much to the unconscious of man which has its tides and phases and responds strongly to a rhythmic motion like that of the moon. After selecting a suitable form, as for example the goddess Selene, this form would be carefully built up in the imagination in dress, action, pose and also with patience and concentration. At the same time the initiate would be getting his inner nature into sympathy with the lunar forces. The essence of the operation is that when rapport has been to some extent built and developed, the form - in this case the goddess Selene - would act as a channel for the forces. Because this god-form was built deliberately by the initiate and because it exists within his own consciousness, then as he made it, he can equally well unmake it. Therefore the operation can be carefully controlled and when considered time to end the experience, the form can simply be dissolved and the contact will be broken.

This method has many subtleties. Over the course of his evolution man has built up many forms to represent the natural forces to himself and all these natural forces have their equivalents within the soul of man. Therefore, the trained occultist can select a suitable god-form to represent and mediate exactly the right wavelength of the force he wishes to contact. In this way the objections to the passive method are entirely removed. Naturally there is more to it than simply selecting a suitable god or goddess from mythology and using it to contact a natural force. There has to be training and there has to be the ability to get into sympathy with the force.

Unless this self-starting technique is used, nothing is going to happen, but once a flow of force has commenced then it will flow through the channel appropriate to it. If the right god-form has been chosen it will pass through that form, the form will mediate it, filter it into consciousness, and the form remains under complete control of the initiate throughout.

Modern, urban, Western man is not in a position to devote his life to passive contemplation of the inner realities — he has a job to do and learns to live with the worries and stresses of the mundane plane. He has to be able to contact the forces rapidly, control them, and disperse them quickly so he can return to ordinary life in the physical world. In practice, the purely passive approach is rarely seen in the West.

In this connection it is interesting to note that the official stand of the Roman Catholic Church is to discourage spurious mysticism. Any monk or nun showing signs of spending hours in rapt devotion to Jesus or the deity is discouraged and given a scrubbing brush to occupy their time. The Roman Church is very loath to accept this form of uncontrolled mysticism because experiences taught that it could lead to a pathology. This experience has been gained the hard way over a period of hundreds of years.

The mystical vision, whether the vision is of Pan or of the Christ, vanishes like mists of the morning unless a channel can be built in the mind and emotions of man to convey the experience through to his normal consciousness. No matter how wonderful the vision, it is useless to help his fellow man unless he can bring it down into normal consciousness and let it spread out into the life of the people.

Man is a tool user. He makes tools and he uses them. The Hermetic occultist is no exception. Tools enable work to be done that could never be accomplished unaided. A soul may long for a drink of the Waters of Spirit — the initiate of the Hermetic Ray will provide the pump, the plumbing, and the cup, and the people will not go thirsty.

The Hermetic occultist is essentially a maker and user of tools. Basically the tools used are *concentration* and *visualisation*. Concentration just means keeping the mind on a particular subject for a period of time by excluding all other thoughts. Simple procedure but it has to be learned.

Visualisation or image building is constructing a picture in the inner imagination with as much detail and colour as possible, and then holding this mental image for a reasonable period of time. These things we do naturally, but to do them to order takes considerable practice.

Most people have experienced getting immersed in the pages of a book and being totally unaware of what is going on around them; this is concentration. Visualisation is commonly indulged in fantasy and daydreaming and can completely hold the individual's attention to the exclusion of all else. But again, when concentration or visualisation is done to order, it becomes more difficult to do and practice is necessary.

These are the two basic tools that are used but the way in which they are used is also important. Essentially, the Hermetic occultist uses symbols and one example has been a god or goddess form.

The god-form is built up in the mind. Because it is a picture rather than the thought, it belongs to that part of the mind, which in modern man is largely unconscious. It belongs to the picture consciousness, which gives us dreams and visions. If we build something up in that part of the mind then, as it is to act as a channel for forces, it will channel those forces into the unconscious part of the mind. If we take the example of the goddess Selene, then the lunar forces which the goddess is used to contact would pass through the goddess-form into the unconscious mind and would not directly be available to ordinary conscious life. While the initiate was in the experience when he built the god-form, he would be aware of the lunar forces flowing through the form, which would appear to be animated, and part of his unconscious nature would naturally respond in turn. There is a gap here between the unconscious level of the mind and the ordinary everyday world. We have managed to build a bridge but the bridge has only come part way.

In order to complete the Jacob's Ladder between the inner part of man and the outer, ritual is used. Ritual is simply an extension of the two power tools, the power of concentration and image building. In a ritual the actual, physical body of the initiate is deeply involved. Rituals use words, sometimes music, physical movement and gestures, and they also use visualisation.

A church service is an excellent example of ritual action and is an extension of the process of image building. In a Mass, whether it is Roman Catholic, Orthodox, or any Mass which uses colour, light, music, and so on, the *ritual extension* to the process of visualisation and concentration is being used.

In the Mass the actual priests or officers of the Mass have words to say, often in a foreign language, which are poetic in form. There is incense, there is the colour of the robes, the colour of the altar cloth, there are lights used to symbolise different things, and the congregation who participate in this experience, are led by the movement, by the sound, and by the images suggested to them — toward their own personal image building. But in the case of the ritual form, there is an extension to this in that the actual participants, the priests, are moving about in physical bodies and making gestures which actually ground the forces by giving them the level of the physical plane to operate on. When the priest raises the chalice, for example, he is making a gesture with his physical body and that movement is highly symbolic. The priest is not merely relating, he is not telling the congregation to visualise something which would put an image on the level of the unconscious mind — he is actually making a physical movement and bringing that inner image to life on the physical plane. The effect of this is to make a further connection between the image building of the unconscious mind and the physical world about us. Therefore, ritual is frequently used in Hermetic occultism because it provides the essential link between the inner worlds achieved by visualisation and the physical plane itself. Ritual is not just a further step. Ritual in its proper sense embraces concentration, image building, physical movement and symbology. All of this combines to increase the participation of the people themselves so that every part of their being is involved instead of the Mass being purely a mental or emotional experience.

If you ask the average man to visualise some simple object such as a brick or perhaps something geometrical like a triangle, the operation is essentially simple but like many simple things it is by no means easy. The Eastern schools of occultism have a saying: "The mind is like a monkey, you cannot keep it still." In teaching it is necessary to tell people practising these things to imagine the simple form they are to visualise against a moving background, because in some way this movement satisfies the mind. As long as there is something moving the mind seems to be happy.

An interesting side issue is that if it were possible for a student of these subjects to concentrate so perfectly upon a simple form such as a triangle without deviating in anyway from his clear image, he would immediately and totally lose all consciousness of the physical plane. Because all of his attention units would have been transferred to the image and because the mind was not allowed to get in there and have its part to play, the mind will simply shut-off. This is one of the techniques used in deliberately inducing a trance state. By long practice it is possible to visualise to the point where there is no movement and nothing else in the field of consciousness except the thing visualised. At this point physical consciousness shuts off and the mind becomes silent. This is extremely difficult to do.

Another Hermetic tool, which is widely used by Western occultism, is the technique known as *Path Working* or *Rising on the Planes*. Here the use of pictures in the mind includes symbols to represent the inner realities and act as gateways to control the flow. Here it is also possible to use a moving technique, which the mind greatly appreciates. Instead of sticking ourselves with a fixed set of symbols we go on an imaginary journey. The mind is very happy when it is moving. The technique is to compose a suitable journey consisting of a number of important symbols which are appropriate to the operations being undertaken and use these symbols in such a way that the mind is led from one state to another without having to concentrate upon a static image.

Taking, as an example, the desire to tune the consciousness away from the ordinary earth level onto the level represented by the unconscious mind of the moon. Instead of using a god-form like Selene it would be possible to construct an imaginary journey with symbols that gradually lead the mind away from the mundane plane toward the inner world of the moon. These roadways are called paths and the technique is called Path Working.

A simple example would be to design an imaginary path, starting with an image which represented the state that the initiate is currently in (in this case an ordinary, physical condition with the mundane world about him). He would chose an image to represent this state and then select a terminal image, an image to place at the end of the path to represent the state that he wanted to achieve. In between these two appropriately chosen symbols would be other symbols placed along the Path and those which would gradually transform the mind's functioning from the first state to the desire state. It would appear that the initiate was building up in his mind an *Alice in Wonderland* like journey where there might be certain types of plants, certain types of animals, and a certain type of countryside in this imaginary journey. Every one of these animals and plants would have been carefully selected to symbolise some aspect of consciousness because they have been used by initiates for ages past to represent these phases of consciousness and are instilled in the deep unconscious, the Collective Unconscious in Jungian terms, even though the conscious mind does not change its focus when its attention is drawn to them. So a journey would be undertaken, starting with the first symbol of beginning and ending at the second symbol of the goal and in between passing through the stages of many subsidiary symbols which gradually change the focus of the mind and tuning it away from the physical and leading it on to the lunar condition that is designed.

This technique, properly employed, can be very effective and is considerably easier to use than the concentration method of the pure simple symbol.

The Qabalah, which of course was one of the subjects dear to Dion Fortune, is greatly concerned with the use of Path Workings to take the student from one state of consciousness to another. Basically however, one has to realise that this is simply a method, a trick if you like, of getting the mind to cooperate in moving from one condition to another. The Path Working does not produce the condition - the condition is inside the soul - it has always been there and it always will be. The question is getting at it because the inner levels of man have been so overlaid with modern civilisation and the demands upon the ordinary conscious mind.

If one realises clearly that this is simply a technique, another one of the Hermetic occultist's tools, then one can construct these journeys as movements from one state to another and satisfy any requirement as long as one has the necessary information and the basic ability.

RITUAL

In a *ritual* the man or the woman taking part should use every part of his nature that is available to him — his higher aspiration, his emotions, his mind, and his body. This makes it possible to consider ritual in a slightly different way.

It is part of the belief of Western occultist that there is purpose behind everything, and in the mind of God there is a plan for God's creation that embraces all of this phase of evolution and that man has a unique part to play within this plan, and this part is bound up with the mystery of free will. The Plan, held in the mind of God, is like a beautiful mosaic pattern, without the actual stones themselves being in position, it is an outline and Man is supposed to fill in the details. The twist to this is that Man being a creature with free will has the right to do what he pleases within very wide bounds within this creation. Therefore if each man has a part to play in the creation, and if he has free-will, then it is quite obvious that he is frequently going to act in a way that is contrary to the best interests of the Plan in general and of the other plans of his fellow men. Therefore, chaos, sin, disease, and so on result. It is hoped that as a result of man's improvement from his continuing evolution he becomes more into tune with the idea of the Plan and his part in it and better understands the part that his fellow human beings are to play. As time goes on, man becomes more and more attuned with the idea in the mind of God and his fellow men. Thus at the end, the Plan which was previously a beautiful outline now becomes an amazing jewel of many facets, each facet being the personal plan of a human being who has exercised his free-will in perfect freedom and harmony with his neighbours and the Plan in general. This advanced stage is what the Bible calls "the coming of the Kingdom on Earth."

Ritual, because it involves all of man, can be used to exemplify this Plan on a small scale. Suppose a number of people participated in a ritual with the object of the ritual to contact the forces of the Redeemer, the Christ force. Were the ritual successful, the result would be that the Christ force would flow into the consciousness of those present and through them, because they were human beings and part of the human race, into all the people of the world.

Another aspect, which also should be considered, is that a ritual is a tiny part of concentrated life and it uses symbols on all levels right down to the physical symbology of the human body, its movements, and its gestures. Therefore, were the ritual performed with a high degree of excellence, it would represent a tiny moment - perhaps an hour, perhaps less - of perfection where each member of the ritual team operated in complete accord and harmony with the other members of the team. Such a ritual would be a tiny replica of a perfect Plan, an example on a very small scale of total co-operation between completely individual human beings, all working together to produce an overall idea, an overall form of perfection. Thus the ritual would represent a tiny Plan in miniature.

The significance of this is simple. The effect of any action on the part of a human being or a group of human beings always interacts with the entire human race. As the poet said: "No man is an island." Each man is linked to every other man through the Collective Unconscious, as the Jungians would call it. Therefore, it is impossible to take an action without in some way affecting the whole though this may be subtle and not easily discovered. But in the case of a ritual where forces are being deliberately focussed for the effectiveness of that ritual, that moment of perfection, that small example of a perfect Plan would tend to pull into it the life of the world around it and to correct the deviations, the stresses, the strains, and the wrongnesses that abound. Also the ritual would tend to spread outward in a positive way so that the moment of perfection of this ritual would have an effect spreading through the group-mind, completely out of proportion to its time and importance.

Ritual has this second reward of representing perfect co-operation and a tiny replica of God's Plan of perfection as it will be at the end of evolution when man has completely fulfilled his destiny.

GUILD OF THE MASTER JESUS

Editor's Note:

Dion Fortune considered that by temperament she was suited to the Hermetic Ray and had considerable ability in it. In that she was right and at the time she was confused and somewhat resentful at having the Devotional Ray pushed so forcefully into her life. Her original dream experience at the Theosophical Society library involved a profound contact with the Master of Compassion, a form of the Christ force. However, meditation and a considerable amount of personal probing led her to understand that this was the right decision and that since she was so weak in the Devotional Ray she was unsuitable to lead a group until she had more experience with the devotional which would balance the strong tendency toward the intellectual that can sometimes occur with a hermetic type.

The Guild of the Master Jesus was really the result of a considerable amount of inner work, which she undertook, as well as the work of Thomas Loveday who bore the brunt of much of the organisation of the early Guild.

The devotional part of the Guild of the Master Jesus is a quest for the spirit, the innermost part of man, the point of his own greatest reality. However, this journey is often misrepresented, as it is sometimes made out as if it is a path straight up to the light from which there is no return and all problems are dissolved in the blinding light of the spirit.

This is not so to the Western man. The destiny of the Western culture is to conquer matter and to bring down the spirit into matter so that ultimately the kingdom comes on earth when the Plan is fully realised. The duty of the average Western man is with the spiritualisation of matter, not the escape from it. Hence, premature, deep involvement with the Devotional Ray can produce pathology rather than enlightenment. This can easily happen in young neophytes who have a natural ability through many past lives involved in devotional exercises, monastic communities, and so on. They feel this natural ability, they have little patience with what appear to be pointless procedures and forms, and they want to escape out of the light. Generally they are people who cannot manage the physical plane very well, and it is a welcome relief to them to leave promptly. When a person is allowed to become unbalanced on the Devotional it produces a degree of disruption which is even worse than that which can occur when an initiate is allowed to have his head on the Elemental Ray.

There is a second important point that should be noted, and that is when any real experience of the self or the Christ force within is achieved through the practices and disciplines of the Devotional Ray, there follows an inevitable reaction which has been described by many mystics including John of the Cross as the dark night of the soul. In this experience, the blinding white light of the heights is followed by the most profound suicidal depression and darkness when the pointlessness of everything becomes so strongly apparent. Very often neophytes have left an esoteric group through wrong exposure to this Devotional Ray and the reactions that followed it.

This always happens in devotional work and is of varying degrees of severity. It will only cease to happen when the regeneration, the integration of the individual, has reached such a point that there are no dark parts, no unknown parts in the soul. Then when the white light of the spirit illuminates the soul, there is only light reflected back, not darkness. This is an advanced stage.

Therefore it is seen that the Devotional Ray can be looked at in two ways like the Elemental Ray. It has validity in its own right at the proper stage of evolution. Just as the Elemental Ray was proper to the development of man at a more primitive level, so the Devotional Ray is proper to the development of an initiate who has passed beyond the normal level of the human race.

The secondary purpose of the Devotional Ray is like the Elemental Ray, in that it is a corrective. There are people who have been made cripples by life or by their own past misdeeds in previous incarnations. They have become perhaps warped or twisted, and sometimes the Devotional Ray with its stress upon the love of God and of the Christ can correct these pathologies. But, always remember, that anything that has any power, also has a bite as well. The Devotional Ray is dealing with the pure powers of the spirit itself and therefore the reactions can be equally violent.

It is noted that minor changes have been made to the original text material and certain Bible verses substituted in the Mass itself.

GUILD OF THE MASTER JESUS

By **DION FORTUNE**

INTRODUCTION

Esoteric science can give the only rational explanation of religion, but mystical devotion is the only valid key to the occult operations. We strive therefore to develop these two balancing aspects in order that the mystical temperament may be stabilised by a logical understanding of what it is experiencing, and the occult temperament may be illuminated by devotion.

Unless our nature is polarised, we shall have no stability. It is devotion, which polarises occultism, and it is esoteric knowledge that polarises mysticism. As an occult school, therefore, we must have a mystical and devotional aspect to our work or we shall turn out unbalanced pupils. The aim of initiation is the perfecting of man; but man cannot be perfected unless all seven levels of his nature are developed, purified and synthesised.

When we first began our work, we urged upon our students the need of devotional and religious practices as well as occult ones, and advised them to continue to worship in the churches in which they had been brought up. But this proved in many cases to be unsatisfactory. Very few places of worship meet the needs of the people who find themselves drawn to the study of esoteric science.

We therefore decided to organise divine worship on our own account, for there was an obvious need for something of the kind. We do not ask people who are content with their churches to abandon them; all we are trying to do is to meet the need of those who have not been able to find what they want in any church. We do not represent a new religion, but a different attitude towards the one and only religion, which is to "Love the Lord our God with all our heart and with all our mind and with all our strength, and our neighbour as ourself."

We have always maintained that theology is only man's attempt to understand God, not God's comments laid upon man's desire to believe, and is of relatively little importance to the spiritual life. The only thing that matters is the desire of the soul for God. If that desire is present, it will find a way:

> The path whereby thou seekest Me
> Is that whereon I welcome thee.
> For all the paths are Mine, that lead
> To love and pity for man's need.

Our aim, therefore, is not to create a doctrine but to make an atmosphere each Sunday morning in which souls may commune with their God. The aim of the service is to lead consciousness up through the different stages of realisation, and purification to the culmination of the Eucharist. To this end, and in order to avoid doctrinal questions, the service consists of a series of passages from Holy Scripture interspersed with certain simple prayers and invocations designed to sum up and express the soul's aspiration at each stage of its ascent. The form of Eucharist used is that made holy by tradition of the Church of England.

This form was chosen because it is esoterically sound, intrinsically beautiful, free from superstition and controversial elements, being expressly designed by those who compiled our Book of Common Prayer to meet the needs of the greatest number and to do violence to the conscience of none.

We have no doctrinal tests, nor do we make any inquiry concerning the spiritual condition of those who wish to join us in partaking of the bread and wine because we hold that the greater the spiritual problems they have to solve, the greater their need of God's grace, and if they shall find any measure of it in the Sacrament as we administer it, surely the last thing we should wish would be to deny it to them. All are welcome to attend our services and partake or not, just as they wish.

There is a short address each Sunday and different aspects of the Christian faith are interpreted from the esoteric and mystical

viewpoint. Ethical teaching is also given as well as the application
of the esoteric teachings to daily life being shown.

We make no claim to Apostolic Succession, but celebrate the
Eucharist as Our Lord bade us, as a means of contacting Him. We
take Him as our guide by the Way of the Cross. We look to Him as
our initiator and Master.

We seek to fathom the significance of the Holy Books of our
faith by means of the esoteric keys which open door after door of
revelation as consciousness expands in realisation.

It is our aim to study and practice the higher methods of prayer
as taught by the great saints of the Christian tradition, St. Theresa
of Avila, St.Francis of Assisi, Ignatius Loyola, St. Therese of
Lisieux, George Fox, Jacob Boehme, and many others, great souls
of many ways of thought and types of temperament who, each in
their different ways, were masters of the Inner Life.

We counsel all those who are following the Way of Initiation to
make use of the sacraments not less than three times a year, at
Christmas, Easter and Whitsuntide. It is immaterial to us in what
church they receive the Eucharist so long as the full rite is celebrated
and the bread and wine consecrated in the Name of Jesus Christ
and with the Sign of the Cross. Where this is not done, we do not
consider the rite to be valid or efficacious.

From these counsels we must except the members of the Jewish
race who, with us, share the Way of the Western Tradition. They
have their own sacramental method of contacting the One God in
the rites of their faith, and from these they receive the spiritual
protection which is so necessary to the soul that is seeking to
penetrate the Unseen. So long as they have no sense of antagonism
to Our Lord and are prepared to count Him among the prophets,
Jew and Gentile meet on the level upon the floor of the lodges of the
Western Esoteric Tradition.

APOSTOLIC SUCCESSION

When we decided to organise the Guild of the Master Jesus we gave
very serious thought to the question of Apostolic Succession. We
desired to use the Sacraments because of their intrinsic value. Had
we the right to do so? And if we did so, would they be efficacious?

Or would we be partaking unworthy and to our own damnation? Believing in the reality of spiritual things, these questions gave us much thought. In order to explain the conclusion at which we arrived, we must open up the whole question of the significance of ceremonial and touch upon the historical questions involved in the transmission of the Apostolic Succession.

In order to make the subject comprehensible, we will deal with it point by point.

Apostolic Succession is the line of consecration descending from archbishop to bishop and bishop to priest in a sequence of the laying on of hands in ordination. It traces its origin to the charge of Our Lord to Peter, "Thou art Peter", (Petros, a stone), "and on this rock will I build my church." The Roman Church maintains that her line of ordination descends from hands to head from this historic moment, and she makes this incident the keystone of her claims.

The reformers of the Christian faith, who from time to time have risen up to cry out against the abuses that inevitably develop in any great body of organised religion, have followed two paths. One section has declared that forms and ceremonies are of no value and that the powers of God works direct upon the soul of man when invoked by prayer. Of this path are the many forms of Protestant communions, of which the Quakers may be cited as an example of the most purely mystical type.

The other section declares that forms and ceremonies unquestionably have a value and should be retained. The spiritual heritage of Peter is important, but the material and disciplinary authority of his successor at the Vatican is not. Of this section the Anglo-Catholic movement within the Church of England and the Liberal Catholic Church are typical examples.

If we accept the doctrine of Apostolic Succession at its face value, there can be no question whatever that any church but that of Rome has more than a shadow of a claim to it. For if the absolute authority of Our Lord is vested in the Pope, as according to the principle of Apostolic Succession it must be, and the Pope says you have no part in the Apostolic Succession, then, *ipso facto*, you have no part in it, and there is an end of it. If Christ committed the keys of heaven and hell to Peter and by Peter to his successors in perpetuity, then what they bind is bound and what they loose is loosened, and it is useless to argue the matter. This, so far as we can see, is the only logical position to take up if one accepts the doctrine of Apostolic Succession at all. It is the position that Rome takes up, and her logic is indisputable if one grants her premises. But does one grant them? For our part, we do not.

If, however, you look upon the sacraments as a means of conveying the power of God to the soul of man, we say to you, "Come to one of our services and see whether or not our celebration of the Eucharist gives you a sense of spiritual power you seek." That is the only satisfactory test. It is equally important and potent in a church. The person who has what is called Apostolic Succession is one who has access to the group mind of that communion. For this purpose it is not enough that he should possess a good legal claim to have at some time been admitted to membership, he must also be in good standing, because if the collective mind of the group thinks of him as outside the pale, outside he will be for all practical purposes.

Every group mind dedicated to mystical practices gets in touch with mystical forces of different types and becomes a reservoir of these forces. Whosoever is in touch with this mind can draw upon them. Hence the value of Apostolic Succession and an undoubted value from an occult point of view and one by no means to be belittled. One has, however, to take into account the quality of the forces gathered in this reservoir; they may be waters of life, or they may be waters of *Lethe*. Who would care to contact the Roman group mind in the fifteenth century or the Anglican group-mind in the eighteenth?

It is not our policy to try to exalt ourselves by belittling our brethren. No one has ever added one cubit to his intrinsic stature by so doing, but when the validity of Apostolic Succession is argued in opposition to living spiritual contacts one can best reply by calling the evidence of history and pointing to the record of the Papacy during the Middle Ages. If that is the line by means of which succession to the legal rights of St. Peter must come down to us, one can only compare it to having lunatic and syphilitic ancestors in ones pedigree. Surely one is better off with honest red blood and no pretensions than such hues in one's veins? Who wants such contacts as those of the Borgia Pope with his two unholy children, Lucrezia and Cesare?

The members of other communions have frequently raised the question of our right to administer the Eucharist, and it is therefore felt to be desirable to offer the foregoing explanation of our attitude. Our answer to their strictures may be summarised as follows. If you believe Apostolic Succession to be essential to the administration of the Sacraments, we have not a title to validity. Nor have we ever claimed one, and in every invitation to receive the bread and wine our Ministrants explicitly say so, declaring that they celebrate the Eucharist, "not claiming Apostolic Succession, but as a means of contacting Our Lord".

CHURCH OF THE RISEN CHRIST

Most people think that the central point of Christianity is the Crucifixion. We, however, hold that the Crucifixion of Jesus of Nazareth would have had no more significance than that of His two companions upon Calvary, the two thieves between whom He was crucified, if it had not been for the Resurrection. It is this that gives the Crucifixion of Our Lord its importance among the innumerable crucifixions of offenders against the Roman law of that brutal period.

In the worship of the Church of the Initiates, which is what the Guild of the Master Jesus is designed to be, we invoke the Christ-force neither as the Good Shepherd nor as the Crucified Christ, but as the Risen Christ, 'the unseen companion of the heart'. This is the Christ that is known to the mystics in their inner experiences, and it is something quite different from the other two aspects, contact with which really constitutes two grades of Christian initiation.

Let us clearly realise, however, that we cannot hope to contact the Risen Christ until we ourselves have trodden the Way of the Cross, for there can be no resurrection without a crucifixion. It is out of the discipline of the Crucified Christ that we come to share in the glorious life of the Risen Christ. Let us remember, however, that though suffering is unquestionably the first stage on the Path, it is not the whole of the Path. We might, in fact, more justly regard the stage of suffering as the preliminary to the Path, the rough journey through the wilderness that the soul makes from the place whereat it awakes and says "I will arise and go to my Father", till it reaches the paved highway of the Path, made firm and clear by the treading of countless feet through the ages.

If we look upon goodness and affliction as identical, as well we may, if we listen to the teaching of most of these sects and observe the experience of their more advanced adherents, we can hardly be blamed if we turn away from religion in alarm as long as life is not unbearable, and that it is only when the blows of fate are so severe that we have nothing left to lose that we turn to God. But there is a great deal more in the spiritual life than suffering patiently borne for the love of God; there are also the times when all the sons of God shout for joy, and the morning stars sing together.

In addition to the image that rises spontaneously in the mind as the result of intense unconscious emotional tension, there is the image that we purposely build and objectify. In this process is much more power than is generally realised. All the New Thought movement is built upon the principle of the potency of the objectified image, but of this matter they have but rule of thumb knowledge, discovered by experience and with no philosophy behind it. For the adept, this image making is one of the chief instruments in his psychic laboratory, and he uses it according to definite and well-understood laws. These we must consider in order that we may understand what we are doing when we meditate upon the Master Jesus as the Risen Christ.

In such meditation we formulate a clear mental picture of Our Lord after His resurrection, bearing the stigmata, even as He appeared to the disciples on the banks of the Sea of Galilee. We picture Him as clearly as we can, using for the material of our image any sacred picture that appeals to us; and in particular we try and see the life and character in the eyes as we look into them. At the same time we invoke Him with a strong inward calling, trying to draw Him to us by our desire, and making the mind still and listening with the inner ear for His coming. If we are successful in our formulation, we shall experience an indescribable sense of His presence, of a spiritual power stirring our hearts and quickening our whole being.

In performing this operation we are under no delusions as to any objective evocation of the spirit of Our Lord to visible appearance; we know quite well that we are building an image in our own minds; yet that image can be made a channel of spiritual power if, with strong desire and great love for Him in our hearts, we call upon Him to project a ray of His consciousness to indwell it. We do not believe that Jesus himself appears to us when this image takes on the semblance of life to our subjective eyes, but we do most firmly believe that the influence He is for ever radiating out upon the world ensouls this image, and that by its means we gather this force into a ray and concentrate it as light is concentrated through a lens.

Whoever tries this experiment under the right conditions, and these include a real love of Our Lord and hunger for His presence, will find that something unquestionably does occur in his inner consciousness; power touches him and abides upon him; for the influence does not fade with the fading of the vision but remains with us, it may be for days and it may be for the rest of our lives. It is indeed a strange and marvellous experience of the Unseen when life looks out of the eyes at us and the image steadies and objectifies and becomes independent of our will and imagination: when it seems to us to take on objective life and its influence flows out upon us. It has become a channel for something more than our own desires and emotions. We get out of the operation more than we put into it.

Are we justified in such use of the image-making faculty of the mind? Its justification is to be found in its results. If, from such an operation we rise up with renewed hope and strength, if our faith is made a living thing and our lives are filled with spiritual power, surely the experiment is justified. It may have in it intrinsically no more than Coue's little bit of knotted string and his formula "Every day in every way I get better and better", and yet it is effectual because it is based upon certain fundamental properties of the human mind which, though little understood, are exceedingly potent and certain in their action. These powers of the mind are used empirically by all faith healers. They are also used by the hypochondriac for his own undoing.

Cosmic Images

But in these deliberately formulated cosmic images into which power is invoked, we have something much more potent than the mental pictures which students of the New Thought and kindred systems are taught to formulate; for the initiate does not formulate any arbitrary image of the fancy, but builds up a replica of what is called a *cosmic thought-form*, an image that has been constructed in the immemorial past and that lives on in the Akasha, the universal storehouse. It is this *Alcashic image* which is the prototype of his mental picture. In these Akashic images psychic force of many kinds and degrees is stored. This force ensouls the subjective image built by the imagination of the adept and causes it to take up an independent existence. It is rare for an image of the imagination to be externalised unless this is done, for to externalise the works of our private imaginations we have to project something of our own life into them, and this can only be done under great emotional pressure or by concentration of a degree rarely to be met with.

The knowledge of these cosmic prototypes and their formulation is among the secrets of occultism that are never revealed. Each Order has its own archetypes, and these are among its most important arcana. Among these are the gods of ancient times, and that potent occult method of the assumption of god-forms is based upon this principle.

But in the rites of the Master Jesus, we do not proceed to use the assumption of a god-form, for we hold that the power invoked by His name is too purely spiritual to find a channel through any human consciousness, however highly trained. There is much of the concept, however, to be traced in the Catholic conception of priesthood. It is enough for us if we obtain the exaltation of consciousness that this method gives. In this sense every man and woman is a priest, as Martin Luther said; each one brings through his quota of power and contributes it to the pooled emotion of the group mind of the congregation. This makes a very powerful psychological atmosphere, and in this atmosphere individual minds are temporarily exalted and are capable of realisations that would elude them in their ordinary state.

It may be asked, why do you thus reveal the modus operandi of your process and so rob it of its glamour? It is perfectly true that if we kept our own counsel and exhibited our results as a psychic marvel, or more effectual still, wove legends round them, we should no doubt have far more of a popular success. But would this popular success help or harm the souls that participated? To our way of thinking it would do as much harm as the sensational and emotional revival meeting which exploits mob passions as basely as any political demagogue would. The men and women who experience spiritual exaltation by such means are astray in the realm of illusion. No soul can experience lasting benefit from such methods; it is spiritual dram drinking. No words are hard enough for the popular preacher who relies upon the administration of repeated nips of psychic alcohol for his influence over audiences.

But if the psychological basis of this method be understood, if we realise that it is a method of handling the mind, a gymnastic of consciousness, we shall be able to use it without danger of abusing it, for we shall not be hallucinated by our own images, but able to use them as lenses to enable us to focus forces and bend them to our use.

If we utilised this method to make an image of Pan, we should get the odour of a goat; if we used it to make an image of Thoth, we should feel the wisdom of Egypt. When we use it to construct a mental picture of Our Lord, we feel, in precisely the same way, all that has gone to the making of the New Testament. In every truth we walk with Him in Galilee and feel His influence, and this influence can be so potent as to change our whole life and heal us of our infirmities. It can even produce the phenomenon of instantaneous conversion. Great powers are hidden in this method, both for good and for evil, and if we use it for unworthy ends, picturing the object of an unsanctified desire, we do undoubtedly work our own undoing; but used in the picturing of Our Lord, nothing but good can come to us, for in Him there is nothing but good, and that good so far transcends our realisation of the possibilities of good that if we allow it to do so, it will, by its subtle influence, extend our realisation and purify our natures as well as exalt our consciousness.

Those who are accustomed to the use of this method learn many things by experience. They soon find that if their mood is not Christ-like the image will not form, or that when it does form, if they are persistently unrepentant, it looks at them with reproach in its eyes; and however hard they may try to build a harmonic image, as long as they are unrepentant and will not right the wrong, the image will continue to gaze at them with sorrow and forbid them to draw near.

This image has been constructed by countless generations of devout Christians, and it has a life of its own and we cannot deal with it arbitrarily by any means.

Likewise in times of great stress those accustomed to its use may find that the image formulates itself with an extraordinary semblance of objectivity. Who shall say what takes place when this occurs? Is it some instinctive trick of the unconscious mind or is it some power from beyond reaching down through the accustomed channels, called forth by the invocation of the soul? We cannot tell. We only know that the method is effectual and therefore we use it. Nor have we ever known any harm or mental unbalance to come from its use for the formulation of the image of the Master Jesus so long as it is realised that we are not using a spiritual method, nor even a psychic method, but a psychological method, and that what we are evoking is a picture of our own making; yet nevertheless, the nature of the invisible universe being what it is, we have by this means laid our fingers upon the control levers of spiritual force and can call it down into our souls.

Mental Techniques

We have considered in this chapter both the psychological and psychic technique and rationale of the invocation of the Master, or in other words, the building up of the thought-form that is to be used as an astral matrix for the concentrating of the spiritual force employed in the ceremony of the Eucharist, because the whole ritual turns upon this point; all that goes before the tremendous words "This is my body", is but a preparation and a building up.

By understanding this technique we are at one and the same time saved from the pitfalls of superstition and enabled to avail ourselves of the tremendous potentialities of ritual used as a means to an end and not an end in itself.

Let us now consider the implication of the words "That which we are about to do may be potent in spiritual power". Having made his thought—form in the pictorial imagination to the best of his ability, having visualised the Master with the most graphic detail of representation that his imagination can supply, and having lifted up his heart in love and adoration to the Being whose representation that pictured image is designed to be, the Ministrant proceeds boldly with the ceremony *as if* that which he had invoked had actually come about and the Master Jesus were indeed pouring out upon him a ray of power as a definite shaft of light. It is this *as if* which is the critical point in any magical operation. If the operator proceeds in the same spirit as the reported last words of the atheist — "O God (if there is a god!), save my soul (if I have a soul!)" — he will never get very far with the practical operations of occultism. He must have the courage of his convictions, and give himself up boldly to be the instrument of the forces he has invoked, relying upon them to bring about the transition from fantasy to fact, which is the meaning of transubstantiation. If he proceeds to play the part he has assigned himself *as if* it were a reality, he will find, provided the force he has invoked is a genuine force and the pictorial image he has made is a suitable one, that imagination has become reality and that an influence is flowing into him, and emanating from him, which is a very real thing indeed, and that he himself will be permanently enriched by the experience and those in whose presence he is performing the operation will be aware, with varying degrees of clarity, of what is happening.

All Participate

In the celebration of the rites of the Master Jesus, the Ministrant invokes the Master Jesus audibly in order that the congregation may be aware of the point that has been reached in the ceremony and be prepared to play their part. As far as the actual invocation goes, the same results, depending upon the *faith* of the operator, could have been obtained if it had been done silently. But in group devotions it is essential that those present should participate, should enter into the spirit of the rite, if it is to be more than a vain observance.

At the conclusion of the invocation, therefore, there is a silence, and the congregation as well as the Ministrant should give themselves to the task of image-building in the pictorial imagination, the *composition of place*, as the Jesuits would call it, fantasying the vision of the Master until His very presence is felt as an objective reality. And out of the fantasying will come something that is not imagination as the ceremony goes on. To those employing this technique with faith, whether blind or comprehending, will almost invariably come a feeling of the peace and the power of God and the drawing near of the very Presence Itself.

With this invocation and its ensuing silence concludes the first portion of our service. The invocation has been made, and we proceed *as if* the power invoked had begun to flow into the sanctuary and was available for the work that is to follow.

CHRISTIAN INITIATION

In many of the ancient mystery-religions, the initiation ceremony was a dramatisation of the sacrificial death of the God for the salvation of His people, and the candidate was made to act out in his own person the drama of that death and resurrection. He played the part of the sacrificed God and in his turn rose into newness of life at the bidding of the initiator. In the great drama of the Passion we have just such an initiatory rite if we understand it in its mystical significance. It is not the historical Gethsemane and Calvary that make an initiation of the Passion, but the undergoing by the candidate of an experience of life which is their equivalent. We cannot enter into the joy of Our Lord unless we have shared in His achievement.

The key to the Mysteries is contained in the words engraved upon the Emerald Tablet of Hermes: "As above, so below". As it is with the Cosmic Christ, the Second Aspect of the Godhead, so it was with Jesus Christ Our Lord when He manifested the power of the Godhead upon the earth; and so it is with us when the Christ Within rises from its crucifixion in the senses. The process of the initiation of the soul corresponds exactly to the process of the evolution on a planet. As sleeping potential unfolds, life is withdrawn from outworn forms. It is this last which constitutes the Crucifixion, the lying down of the worn out life in order that a newer and higher concept may come to birth.

When we seek initiation through the Master Jesus we follow a path which is known to mystics as the Way of the Cross. The Christian initiation is not given in a lodge-room or temple, but is acted out upon a vaster stage, for it is an initiation of the soul into the degree of Redeemer, and it is an initiation of spiritual experience acted out against a cosmic background. "Take up thy cross and follow Me" says the Master of the Lodge, and it is this in truth that the candidate does.

The Christian Mysteries may be considered as having three degrees, and they are distinguished from each other by the aspect of Our Lord, which is the object of our meditation. For those of us who are in the First Degree, He is the Good Shepherd who carries the lambs in His bosom. To Him we go for comfort and protection and He never fails us. The loving heart of Jesus hears the cry of the lost soul out of the darkness, and He goes out into the wilderness to seek the last and least of His sheep, and will not rest until it is found. It is this aspect of our Master which is known to the younger souls, but even to the soul old in initiations He is still the Good Shepherd of patient compassion, and there are none of us so strong that we never have need to cry to Him to stretch out His crook to us when we have fallen into the pit. This is one of the glories of the Christian Path — that to our Master we are always children as well as pupils. Even Our Lord, approaching His supreme ordeal, was able to say, "O Father, let this cup pass from me," was able to reach out for comfort to Divine Love; and it is the memory of this experience which wrung from Him the cry, "My God, why hast Thou forsaken me?" which links Him so closely to our human frailness. No Gnostic Christ, any occult interpretation of Christianity will ever replace the Good Shepherd to His sheep.

The Second Degree of our Mysteries is the Degree of the Crucifixion. When we take this degree we say to our Initiator, "Thou hast been to me the Good Shepherd; Thou hast brought me through the wilderness and made me to lie down in green pastures of spiritual illumination and my strength is restored. Let me cease to be Thy sheep and become Thy sheep dog. Let me go out with Thee into the

wilderness and seek that which was lost, even as I was sought when
I had strayed."

And the Good Shepherd will answer us, "Canst thou drink of
the cup I drink of, and be baptised with the baptism I am baptised
with?" We need to ponder this question well, for the cup is the cup
of our own blood, shed for our brethren, and the baptism is the
baptism of the Holy Spirit and of fire. These things are not necessary
for our own salvation, for we who are of the First Degree of the
Christian Mysteries are already within the fold; the Second Degree
is the degree of the Redeemer, not of the redeemed. If we essay this
degree, it is in order that we may lift the burden of humanity, having
already laid our own burden upon Our Lord. Hence it is said that
the initiate must be karma-free. Instead of working out our own
karma, and escaping from bondage, we take up the burden of the
karma of the earth.

And the voice of the Christ says to us, "Ye shall indeed drink of
the cup I drink of, and be baptised with the baptism I am baptised
with. I will be to you the Master as well as the Shepherd. You shall
come out with Me from the fold into the dark and dangerous places
when I go to save that which is lost. When I open the gate of the
sheepfold and call, "Go seek", you shall be out on the trail of the
strays; and the cry of the lost sheep shall guide you, and you shall
mount guard over it till I come with the great Crook to draw it up.
You shall guard it from the wolves of the darkness, and this you can
do because there is in you something of the wolf. We do not set
sheep to guard sheep. The sheep dog is a wolf that has been won
from its wildness, the wolf that knows its master; the strength that
is dedicated to His service. But in order that you may serve Me
thus, you must be trained".

It is this training of the soul for service that is the Degree of
Crucifixion. The way of the Cross is not a way of joy, but of
redemption through sympathetic suffering in order that there may
be peace at eventide for the whole world. The deep lessons of the
soul have never been taught by joy. All the great ones have been
"Made perfect through suffering". It is only young souls that want
to be happy at their play; the older souls say, "Let me know in order
that I may serve. Let me taste of the cup". And the Master says,

"You must fill that cup with your heart's blood if it is to be for you the Grail". And they reply, "We will so fill it, if it may be, that we can give it as the chalice to those who thirst."

"This is my body, broken for you", said the Master when He consecrated the first bread. And we, when we enter upon the Degree of Redeemer, must say to those we gather around our table, "This is my life, broken for you", not otherwise can we feed the innermost hunger of the soul.

This is a hard saying, but thought will reveal its inevitable truth. Do we go in our sorrows to those who have only known the joy of life? Will souls come to us and trust us unless they feel instinctively that we too have known? It is the crucified soul that has risen again that draws all men to the feet of the Christ. Out of suffering comes power, for out of suffering comes realisation. Therefore we go by the Way of the Cross in order that we may be made fishers of men.

We shall always know when Gethsemane is nigh by one infallible sign; the populace will cast branches before us and cry, "Hosannah to the Highest" as we ride into their Holy City in triumph. The reply, which the candidate learns to make to that hailing, is — "Could ye not watch with me one hour?" Though there may be watchers at the foot of the Cross, for humanity has been sufficiently crucified to understand physical suffering, Gethsemane has to be gone through alone, for Gethsemane is the Garden of Decision. The Master could have gone quietly away from that Garden in the darkness and found safety in the wilderness as He had often found it before, but when His prayer for the passing of the cup was rejected by infinite compassion, He replied, "Not as I will, but as Thou wilt", and waited for the crowd to come with sticks and staves to take Him. To take counsel with the disciples would have been useless, for their consciousness could not have understood the issues. The solitude of the heights is part of the ordeal of the heights. I have always believed that the words, "Sleep on, and take your rest" must have cost the Master more than the words, "It is finished".

The next scene in the drama of initiation through which the soul goes on its path to power is represented by the coming of the crowd "as if to take a thief". The Judas-kiss is given and accepted. Did the Master fail to discern the spiritual status of Judas? We have little need to answer that question: He that knew that He would be betrayed would know His betrayer. The Master left Judas to be dealt with by his own conscience and the law of God. Judas' love for his Master re-asserted itself in the end, and he made what amendment was in his power. Had the Judas-kiss been rejected, that love would have been smothered by pride; but who that knows human nature can doubt that when the hour of realisation came, Judas would sooner that he had struck his Master than kissed Him?

The scene of the drama now moves between the palace of the high priest and the fortress of the Roman governor. In our experience of the Path of the Redeemer we shall find that we too will stand arraigned before human justice and spiritual authority, and we shall find that human justice is the fairer and more compassionate of the two. We shall realise for ourselves why it is that the justice of spiritual authority is a misnomer; there is no such thing. The only authority of the spirit is love. The only power of the spirit is service. Spiritual authority has shed more blood than greed or revenge, and today, as in Jerusalem, it is always the high priest of official religion who intrigues for the crucifixion after ordinary human justice has replied, "I find no fault in Him". There is no one so cruel or so treacherous as the high priest who has not his roots in God; he sees his system threatened, and not having sufficient faith to trust in God, descends to depths that the Roman soldier would scorn.

The drama of initiation by experience moves slowly on, and the neophyte soul sees the scattering of the disciples and the dividing of its garments among the soldiers by the throw of dice. The disciples scatter because they see only the man going to his doom; their inner eyes are not opened that they can behold the soul in its transcendent experience against a background of stars. They think that failure finished the work, that death ends all. They do not realise that unless the seed be cast into the ground the green blade will not spring. The garments are divided among the rough hands that can grasp them; his persecutors cast lots for that which the initiate has already achieved; nevertheless, the Master wore the seamless robe when He walked beside the sea.

Then comes the terrible march to Calvary, when the prisoner fell again and yet again under the burden of the Cross. Let us remember these falls when we ourselves go down under our tests, and learn to accept with gratitude the help of the kindly bystander who sees in us only a criminal being punished for his crime.

At last comes the hill of Calvary and the Cross set up between two thieves. There is deep significance in the mystery teaching concerning the criminals who were the companions of Our Lord in His death, and the prostitute who met Him on His resurrection. He knew the depths and He loved the dwellers of the depths and they loved Him; He never made any separation between them and Himself, He shared in their lives as a friend.

The cross of the soul is set up on high on the hill above the city and the neophyte hangs upon it. His eyes are darkened and he feels that God has forsaken him. It is a strange thought that there is no spiritual comfort at the time of the crucifixion; Our Lord suffered as a man, and in a man's strength did He endure, and here-in again He is linked to us.

But the tide is beginning to turn, for though He was not understood in Gethsemane, though He was left alone in the palace of the high priest, there are watchers at the Cross-foot. And who are these watchers? Not the disciples who said, "In Thy Name have we raised the dead and even the devils are subject unto us". Not the disciple whose spiritual insight enabled him to cry, "Thou are the Christ, the Son of the living God", but the women from the humble home at Bethany, the streetwalker of Jerusalem and "the disciple whom Jesus loved". There is a deep lesson for us in this. The women of Bethany may have wondered what they could have offered their beloved Master comparable with the feast of Simon the Pharisee but we can guess whom He wished to have near Him in His hour of trial. The more we see of the initiation of life, the more do we learn to put our trust in the simple love that is faithful over few things. It is only these beautiful souls who can endure the drudgery of the Master's service who can endure the watch on Calvary.

And the Master was mindful of them; He never forgot the need of the human soul for affection, and although He had said, "Who is my mother and who my brethren but they that do the will of My Father?". Although He did not call Mary, mother, yet did He provide for her human grief in His loss and gave her into the care of the

Beloved Disciple. It was not the disciple who drew the sword to defend his Master, but the one on whose breast He had leant who received the most sacred charge that Jesus has to give.

Then came the earthly end. The scene passes to the inner-planes, and we are told that the Master preached to the spirits in prison. Mystics know what those "spirits in prison" are. Let us note that the Master did not banish them with an exorcism, but descended into their hells and preached to them; He sought even the redemption of the devils; and when He returned from preaching to them, He was met by a prostitute, and the Master loved them all.

The Master never shrank from any souls on account of their dirt. His response was in proportion to their need, and the one who was the first to see the Risen Christ was the one who had needed Him most — the Magdalene, "from whom He cast seven devils out".

So we go by the Way of the Cross, knowing every experience that human nature can know, for not otherwise can we give the hand of a brother to those who are in the depths. So we go from our Gethsemane to our Calvary, and then — to our Easter Morning by the Sea of Galilee. For it is by the power generated on Calvary that we cause the hearts of those who speak with us unknowing to burn within them. From Calvary we pass to the great Third Degree, the Degree of the Risen Christ. Then, and then only, is the sorrow of the Crucified One turned into joy in the morning.

The face of the Risen Christ is calm; the fainting Christ of the road to Calvary has risen up on eagle's wings and passes before the disciples with the speed of the wind. Those who have attained are at peace. They have joy. They have strength. But it is the joy that comes out of sorrow, the peace after pain, and the strength that has risen up from weakness. So was He "tempted even as we are" so did He "take upon Him our infirmities". So may we hope to take upon us His strength for the redemption of our brethren if we tread in His footsteps.

If we go by the Way of the Cross we shall come to our resurrection and be with humanity for the lifting of its burden, even unto the end of the world. For the sheep dogs of the Good Shepherd do not enter the fold until every sheep is through the gate, and behind them all comes their Master. Not until the last soul is redeemed does He take His rest, and then the hounds of God lie down at His feet and are at peace.

CHURCH OF THE INITIATES

Our aim in forming the Guild of the Master Jesus was not only to make a centre of mystical worship, but to make what should be in reality the Church of the Initiates wherein the principles learnt in the Mysteries, the principles which are observed in all ceremonial, should be applied to that rite which is, in actuality, the Rite of the Mysteries of Jesus.

To anyone who understands the principles of ceremonial, it is obvious that the Eucharistic rite was formulated by those who were also familiar with these principles, who were accustomed to the rites of the Mysteries, which antedate Christianity by many thousands of years, and who modelled the ceremonial of the new system upon traditional lines. The present form of the Eucharist, as practised in both Anglican and Roman communions, is the result of the labours of many councils of learned Churchmen working upon existent tradition, for the traditional methods of celebrating the Sacrament existed long before any council codified them and established a canon.

The original rites were pure magic and understood as such by those who took part in them. They aimed, as all magic does, at building a thought-form on the astral plane, exalting the consciousness of the participants, and invoking the appropriate forces, in this case the forces that Our Lord incarnated in order to establish upon the plane of earth. Later generations of ecclesiastical authority, lacking the direct insight of the earlier generations, failed to distinguish between the symbolic actions that were essential to the validity of the ritual and that which was accidental and incidental. For instance, the maniple, the embroidered band that hangs over the left arm of the celebrant, was originally the receptacle for the priest's handkerchief. It has no ritual significance. Nevertheless, a blind and ignorant adherence to custom has made it a part of the celebrant's vestments, although the modern trouser-pocket has superseded it for all practical purposes.

But, on the other hand, equally ignorant attempts at the reform of a repetitious ritual have thrown away the baby with the bath-water, and discarded symbolic actions that have real esoteric significance and are essential to the magical validity of the ceremony.

In formulating the order of service of the Guild of the Master Jesus, we have aimed first and foremost at the utmost simplicity which is compatible with the retention of all that is essential to the ceremonial as ritual magic, which is what it really is. We have aimed at simplicity in order that the mystical elevation of the soul may have free play, uncluttered by the distraction of elaborate forms; but, at the same time, we have aimed at the retention of all that is vital to the ceremony as a magical formula, for otherwise it would be inert and ineffectual, neither calling down the powers of the higher planes nor exalting the consciousness of the participants.

It is essential that in a church such as ours, which is designed to be the Church of the Initiates, the congregation should be as well instructed as the priesthood, for upon their trained and intelligent co-operation, a great deal depends. It is for this reason that I propose to elaborate the teaching which has been given in the addresses which form part of our services, and set it out in such a form that all who take part in the work of the Guild may know the exact significance of our order of service and be able to co-operate intelligently in the performance of the ritual. A great deal more than is generally realised lies in the hands of the congregation.

Preparing For The Service

The aim of a service is to make an atmosphere in which certain spiritual experiences become more readily accessible. To certain souls, spiritual experiences come in the silence of their own hearts, but others are not so gifted; nevertheless, it is possible for those who themselves have access to these spiritual experiences to make, by means of organised worship, an atmosphere in which many who by themselves could not arrive at these experiences may have a temporary extension of consciousness which enables them to reach up and receive the spiritual. Out of such repeated temporary extensions of consciousness, it soon becomes possible to achieve a permanent enlargement of awareness.

Two factors enter into the building of this atmosphere:

(1) the mental attitude of the congregation; and
(2) the formation of certain channels of power in the subtler
planes of existence.

Spirit does not act direct upon matter; a channel must be made for
it; it must be, like electricity, passed through a transformer which
shall reduce it to a form in which it becomes operative on the physical
plane. The transformer is the mind. Spiritual force must be conceived
by the intuitive imagination and reduced to a form that the finite
mind can apprehend if it is to influence our normal consciousness.
It is not everyone who can grasp spiritual things by means of spiritual
intuition, but most people can grasp them if they are made to appeal
to the imagination and thereby touch the emotions. Of those who
can thus grasp them, however, many are confused unless their reason
is also satisfied; they cannot permit themselves to respond to an
emotion, even an idealistic one, and unless their reason gives consent.
It is to these that the work of the Guild is especially directed. The
link between spiritual emotion and logical reason is to be found in
the explanations of the psychology of superconsciousness. It is this
psychology that we teach, and it is this psychology in its practical
applications that we utilise in our ritual.

There is nothing to this method that is in itself spiritual, which
is the reason why many profoundly spiritual minds are alienated by
ritual; but the method can be used most effectively as the handmaid
of spirit, enabling those to obtain spiritual experiences who, unaided,
could never arrive at them. It is in this way that we use it. No-one
knows better than those who have experienced the reality of spiritual
things, that the spirit of man is independent of all accidental aids
and can see God face to face by its own Inner Light. As Whittier,
the Quaker poet, says:

> But as we rise
> the symbols disappear;
> The feast, but not the love,
> is past and gone;

The bread and wine remove,
but Thou art here.
Nearer than ever,
still are shield and sun.

Equally, however, until we rise in consciousness, the aids to realisation afforded by ritual can be of the greatest assistance to us; and if we remove the bread and wine too soon, blind eyes may not know where to look for their Lord.

RITUAL
Meditation Expressed in Action

In the services of the Guild of the Master Jesus we deliberately make use of ritual, not superstitiously, nor as a blind observance of which we have forgotten the significance, but as a means of raising consciousness to spiritual things. In brief, it is a psychological device, and we use it as such.

But its effect is not only upon the minds of the congregation. There are aspects of our ritual which are designed to produce certain changes in the inner-planes; these are designed to build up thought-forms upon the astral which shall serve as channels for the descending spiritual force. The group-mind of the congregation is placed in touch with these thought-forms, and into that group-mind the descending force enters. Each individual member of the group thus formed is then filled with the descending force in such measure as he is capable of receiving.

In the process of our ritual the group-mind of the congregation is then focussed, purified, and exalted. In the atmosphere thus prepared the priest or celebrant is then able in his turn to rise into yet higher consciousness and touch lofty spiritual sources of realisation. The power thus contacted is brought through into the thought-form that the congregation has assisted in building and creates a powerful psychic atmosphere in the sanctuary, which is highly charged with spiritual forces. These forces thus brought within reach of normal consciousness are apprehended by the psychism that is latent in each one of us.

Ritual is meditation expressed in action. Unless we understand the esoteric psychology of meditation, we shall not understand ritual. To those unaccustomed to meditation, it may seem a simple thing to think about something for a given time; and so it may be if the thing thought about is well within the range of our experience and interests us. But if the object of our meditation is below the horizon of our experience, dimly sensed as the glow of a hidden sun, if it is just beyond the range of our consciousness, and we see the light it reflects, but not itself, then meditation is a different matter, and the subject of our concentration is a will-o'-the-wisp, ever eluding us. This, and this alone, is true mystic meditation, the out-reaching of the mind, at fullest stretch, from the known to the unknown.

The occultist, unblessed with the winged mind of the mystic, has his own devices for securing these elusive things of vision. He takes for his meditation not the elusive light reflected like the aurora borealis, but a landmark which has a definite bearing in relation to the place whence light arises. He cannot see the light from where he stands, but he knows that if he directs his steps towards the chosen landmark, from that spot, when he arrives there, he will see the light, its very self.

The symbols upon which he meditates are for him the cairns of the Hill of Vision, and he finds that when he has identified himself with the chosen symbol, when, in other words, he stands beside the landmark that he has used to guide his steps, he will then see the light of the uncreated reality which was all the time the real object of his worship.

For the occultist, meditation is performed by means of symbols, each of which is ultimately resolved into its essence. For the ceremonialist, ritual is a series of acted symbols by means of which he causes the congregation who witness the rite to accompany him in his meditation until they, too, shall, all and severally, stand beside the landmark and see the Very Light, and for them also the symbol shall be resolved into its essence. In this manner those who could not of themselves perform any deep and coherent mystical meditation are led in thought through the astral corridors to the Mounts of Illumination. The celebrant exalts the consciousness of the congregation by enabling them to travel upon the wings of imagination where they cannot walk upon the feet of reason, setting one foot before another in the logical processes.

In order to secure a focussed exaltation of consciousness, the occultist uses certain conventional symbols; when he performs a ritual he uses these selected symbols to correspond with the ritual symbols. This is the ancient language of mime, which came before speech, and which is used by the animals. Ritual is a cosmic mime in which ideas are expressed by gestures. And just as in the classical school of the ballet there are a series of stereotyped gestures expressive of such things as the counting of money, or the stroking of a beard that indicate an old man, so in ritual there is a series of conventional gestures that indicate the calling down of power, the sending forth of power, and all the needs and activities of the human soul.

These are not arbitrary, but are the natural attitudes that the human form assumes, and anyone who uses the pictorial methods of the Composition of Place in meditation finds that he spontaneously pictures himself as assuming these attitudes so universal that they are enshrined in sacred sculpture in all parts of the world.

But not only are there symbolic gestures, but also symbolic objects, and these objects are the natural counterpart of the gestures and arose as spontaneously, for they are the instruments of the gestures, the tools that extend their action. The rod, the sword, the cup, all these things are the product of the gesturing hand. Were there a magician who could petrify, like the Gorgon's head, the prayers, the aspirations, and the strivings of the soul, we should see rendered visible before us the furniture of the lodge or the decorations of the sanctuary. Cathedrals have been called prayers in stone, and the writer spoke more truly than he knew; but they might be more truly called souls in stone, for the ancient cruciform shape is the type of the crucified.

The place of working, whether the lodge or the sanctuary, is the type of the soul of man. It represents the form side of his being. But into the form plays a force if it is a living soul, and that force is typified by the gestures of the celebrant. It is by means of action, not word, that power is called down from on high. The celebrant could perform his rite voicelessly, but he could not perform it motionlessly. The words of a ritual are designed for the ears of the participants, not for the ears of God. By the images called forth by the words, the thoughts of the congregation are directed and exalted.

Phase by phase, the ritual unrolls itself; passing from the preliminary invocation, which is the preparation of the place, through purification to the prayer for grace and help in human things; thence to the summoning of power into the world of form, the priest functioning as magician in materialising in his own soul and in the group-mind of the congregation the living sense of a contact with invisible and awful potencies. Out of the majesty of this invocation arises the mighty ritual of the Mass and the power to perform it.

The Mass itself is the Ritual of the Cup; it is the calling down of power into a receptacle, that receptacle being the soul of man. It is not the raying forth of power, as in the rituals in which the Rod takes part; nor is it the cut and thrust of the Sword rituals, nor the bludgeoning of the Hammer of Thor; these are positive rituals; but the Cup is a negative, receptive ritual.

The empty Cup is lifted on high, and the downpouring power fills it. Macrocosmically the priest uplifts the Cup, and microcosmically the hearts of the participants are lifted up with it; for in the microcosm the heart-centre is the Cup.

But the Cup is no ordinary cup that is thus uplifted. It is sacred, and sacred in a special way. It is not the cup of Dionysius consecrated to a divine inebriation; it is not the cup of hemlock that ends all things for an aeon; it is the Cup which Our Lord first prayed might pass from Him, and of which ultimately He drank. It is the Cup of the Last Supper.

The ritual, as it advances in its traditional majesty, builds up before the inner eye an image of the table spread in the upper chamber. The scene, familiar from our earliest memories of things sacred, appears before us. The disciples rejoicing that the bridegroom is still with them; the Master overshadowed and yet illuminated by His knowledge of the impending crisis. He holds out to them the Cup and says, "Drink ye all of this". They think He means the wine, but we know He meant the experience. And again, He gives them the broken bread and says, "This is my body". It is the immemorial symbol of the sacrificed god, slain that the people may live. In the atmosphere of earth is built up a mighty image of the sacrificed god. Osiris, Balder, Qetzlcoatl, Prometheus, all held out that Cup in turn. Into that vast image entered Our Lord, the Christ, the Messiah, the Anointed, and identified Himself with it. Thus did He become the Christ whose sacrifice had power to save His people from their sins.

And as this image forms before the eyes of the imagination, we too enter into that vast and mighty presence, the presence of the Christ eternal, co-existent with the Father from the beginning of life. The Cup is formulated in our midst. The Power descends. The atmosphere of the sanctuary is charged to the highest tension. Then, at the summons of the celebrant, the congregation comes up to the altar rails and partakes; the priest reaches out to them across the invisible barrier between the Inner and the Outer, which is marked by the threshold of the sanctuary, and they receive, each one, his modicum of the power, conveyed magically and imaginatively in the bread and wine; the bread, which is the negative aspect of that power, and the wine, which is its positive and dynamic aspect. The bread which sustains, and the wine which is the pure juice that consecrates the vision of the initiate. The Roman Church gives the bread to the people and reserves the wine for the priest in order that he, and he alone, may function with power; but at the Reformation Martin Luther said "Every man shall be his own priest" and gave the wine to the people.

We, in the Church of the Initiates, give the wine to the people also. And not only do we give the wine, but we call upon them to participate in the invisible aspect of the ceremony. With this end in view, the ritual of our service is worked by two persons instead of one, and the two are not chief and subordinate, but the positive and negative poles of the dynamism of the Mass. The Lector works with the group-mind of the congregation and leads them out through the astral corridors up into the heights of the Mount of Vision.

Throughout the ceremony he makes no movement, save to rise when they rise at the points where they enter into the action of the ritual. He leads them, too, in their responses, where the group-mind of the congregation links up with the force that is being formulated on the other side of the altar rails. He is, in fact, the bellwether of the flock; he is the archetypal penitent, the archetypal communicant.

In him are exemplified the aspirations of the whole congregation when he reads the words of Holy Scripture which form the body of his ritual.

In these words are expressed the immemorial cravings of the soul and the promises that have given relief. They are hallowed for all those marked with the Cross of Christ by their association with childhood's memories, the most potent of all associations. They found their way to our hearts when those hearts were still open to spiritual influences, before they had been hardened and closed in defence against the blows of life. Long before we could understand the significance of the words, our childish ears were accustomed to the great cadences of the Authorised Version; to us they were a chant before they were a teaching. The very beak and roll of the sonorous Elizabethan English, the matrix of our tongue, is mantric. And these earliest rhythms, made holy by association, find their way by their accustomed tracks into the depths of our hearts, which today we call our unconsciousness, and evoke therein the deva forms of vision and prophecy that live ever in the group-souls of peoples. These are the images of the gods riding out from Asgaard; these are the Beautiful Ones in the hollow hills. We do not worship graven images with superstitious observances, but we evoke the forms not made with hands, eternal in the heavens of the imagination, which are the channels of manifestation to us of the powers of the Great Unmanifest. These are the rainbow rays of the invisible light that blinds us in its whiteness. These are the powers of the ineffable brightness which are revealed and displayed by the image-making faculty of the mind, working beyond the threshold of consciousness according to its immemorial fashion, and building those palaces of heaven and peopling them with the celestial forms which are the spiritual heritage of every race. By these means do we evoke the astral images which represent to our minds the eternal uncreated realities which we can only hope to see as in a glass darkly, while we yet dwell in the tabernacle of the flesh. There are times and seasons when the soul unlatches the door of its dwelling and slips forth into the starry deeps of consciousness and sees God face to face. It steps forth in sleep, and in trance and in death; but for the most part it takes no pitcher to the waters of life, and returns empty-handed. The symbolic expression of scripture and ritual is the pitcher in which the waters of life are brought back to the world of men and shown to their mortal eyes that they may see and, seeing, believe and, believing, drink and thirst no more.

ORDER OF THE SERVICE

Our ritual requires two persons for its celebration, whom we call the Ministrant and the Lector. The Ministrant performs the actual rite, and the Lector reads the passages of Scripture and leads the responses of the congregation. The teaching may be given by either of these, or by a third person, who need not necessarily be a member of the Guild.

The service itself falls into four main divisions. Firstly, the opening service, in which the Lector takes the lead, and which is designed to prepare the congregation and place for the performance of the great rite of the Eucharist, and which has several subdivisions within itself. Secondly, the teaching and instruction is given to the congregation. Thirdly, the Eucharist itself, in which the Ministrant is the dominant figure; and fourthly, the concluding service, in which the major part of the working again falls to the Lector.

The opening part of the service is designed, as has already been said, to purify the consciousness of the congregation for the mystical rite, and prepare what is called in esoteric terminology, the place of working.

Opening Prayer

The Ministrant, standing before the altar, raises his hands in the Sign of the Chalice, which consists in lifting the arms above the head with the hands cupped, as if about to catch something falling from above. In this position the head is involuntarily thrown back and the face turned upwards, and the whole attitude is that of one who awaits the descent of power. These symbolic attitudes, called in esoteric terminology, *signs,* are very important, for they render in the universal language of mime or gesture the idea which should have been inwardly formulated. And even in the case of an ignorant operator, who does not understand the significance of the inner processes of ceremonial, the very assumption to an attitude tends to induce the corresponding state of consciousness, and automatically renders him an adequate celebrant apart from his personal co-operation. Let the reader experiment with the attitude of the Sign of the Chalice and note its effect upon consciousness. He will then be in a much better position to understand what is going on in the consciousness of the Ministrant, standing at the focus of power.

In this attitude the Ministrant makes the opening prayer:

"Oh Holy Jesus, Master of Love and Compassion, we Thy children, dedicated to Thy service, approach Thee in faith in the Living Christ, the unseen companion of the Heart.

Prepare us, O Lord, to drink of the living waters of life, soon to be made manifest unto us; open our eyes that we may see, and our hearts that we may understand. Make the way plain, O Lord, that we fail not in Thy service.

May we be a channel whereby Thy Holy Ones may approach the world. May we be a centre of radiation of Thy power. Teach us to travel light, as do all who travel upon the Path; to give ourselves to Thy service; to attune ourselves to Thy will; to suffer gladly for Thy sake; to lay down the small personal life in the great cosmic life, and to love with the Love of God."

It will be observed that each prayer in our ritual opens with a different phrase of invocation; no two are alike. This is not a mere literary device to avoid unpleasant repetition but has a definite esoteric significance. Each prayer is designed to call down a different aspect of Divine force; and the ceremony builds up out of them as a symphony builds up out of the unfolding motifs.

In this, the Opening Prayer, we have the invocation of Our Lord as Master of Love and Compassion, and we who pray approach in humility as little children. We recognise our own helplessness and need of compassionate help. We approach God from the side of mercy. We recognise our own limitations and the difficulties of the Path. This honesty and humility is not only the beginning of wisdom, it is also the beginning of strength, for it causes us to cast aside all that is coarse and unsound in our character or position and plant our feet firmly on the rock of reality. This prayer of humility brings down those of high estate and fills them with honesty and self-knowing; it raises up the lowly and meek of heart and gives them strength and confidence because they have cast themselves upon the mercy of the Master of Love and Compassion, who knoweth the needs they cannot utter and answereth to them with His unfailing love. It is this attitude of confiding love, which is the surest invocation of the Christ, and it is the bedrock of mystical attainment. Intellect will not take us very far on this Path of the Bhakta Yoga. God is found through the heart.

But even for those of intellectual capacity and vigour of character this prayer is needful, for the night cometh when no man can work, and there comes a time for all when life has beaten them to their knees and they have found the limits of their own strength. This is one of the tests of the Path, and none who set out on that road can hope to escape it. Those who are meek and lowly in heart meet this test at the outset; they are easily brought low and shaken in their self-confidence; for them to come to the Master of Love and Compassion is to find rest for their souls; they escape onto the Path.

But strong and positive natures do not find it so easy. Going in their own strength, they evade this test until the evening is far advanced and the dark night of the soul closes about them in good earnest. It is now that they need to know how to change their polarity and come to the Master of Compassion as little children, for no one else can help them. Until we have been through that experience, and found that Master, we cannot reckon that we are more than neophytes upon the Mystic Path.

So then, in this the Opening Prayer of our ritual, we bring the soul to its knees, for that is the starting place of the Path.

But the soul does not remain upon its knees, but at the bidding of the angel, which God sendeth to those who cry for light, it stands upright upon its feet and grows strong. Just as it is necessary that the soul should come to its knees at the threshold of the Path, so is it needful that it should rise to its feet in firmness and resolution if it is to tread that Path. For it is not our concept that the soul should grovel before its God, but that it should arrive at the right starting point before it tries to set out on its journey. And so the prayer goes on to invoke the Master under another name; and again this change of phrase is not fanciful, but has its exact esoteric significance. "We approach Thee in faith in the Living Christ, the Unseen Companion of the Heart." This is the invocation of the initiate who seeks his Master in the Hidden Church of the Holy Grail. The exoteric churches stress the Slain Christ, Christ crucified; it is in His Name that they call to the lost sheep and seek to raise the submerged tenth. But in the Church of the Initiates we seek to find the Risen Christ, the ever-living Master, who comes to meet us on the inner-planes and shall be for us the Great Initiator. This is the unseen companion of the heart with whom the initiate seeks to make contact.

The prayer continues with its plea for Divine aid in the heavy task of self-preparation for the Great Work, and concludes its first clause with the words, "Make plain the way, O Lord, that we fail not in Thy service."

How needful is this guidance, for with the strongest *will* our unresolved karma causes us to wander from the Path. Everybody has a blind spot in his soul; there are things that each one of us will never face voluntarily; there are preconceived ideas that fit in with the bias of our temperament and which we defend at all costs, even the cost of relationship with reality. It is these dissociated complexes, nothing more, that give us our first test upon the Path.

Well-meaning people reiterate the assurance that if our intentions are right, no harm shall befall us. But is this promise confirmed by experience? We know only too well that it is not. So long as our intentions are right, it is true that God will never lose touch with us, but if we make a misstep and slide into extreme depression, no miracle is going to be performed for our benefit. Too many souls make that commonplace mistake. The Eastern Tradition speaks truly when it makes discrimination one of the qualifications for the Path. The Christian faith lacks its Jnana Yoga; it has an inadequate appreciation of the place of the mind in the scheme of salvation. We do well to pray that the way may be made plain to our understanding that we fail not therein, for if it is not plain, and we make mistakes, even with good intention, we must bear the consequences of those mistakes and retrace our steps.

See - Feel - Act

The second phase of our service opens as the Ministrant, kneeling before the altar, humbly requests the mystical presence of the Christ.

"Oh Lord Jesus, most holy and beloved Master, be with us in Thy wisdom and compassion that that which we are about to do may be potent in spiritual power. Amen."

As in all true ceremonial, each word is chosen designedly in order that it may evoke the precise aspect of the force it is intended to use. An occult invocation is like a medical prescription — it is an exact formula. As our ritual proceeds, it will be observed that different aspects of the Divine power are invoked, gradually working up to the climax of invocation in the supreme moment of the Mass. In the Opening Prayer we each make ready our own soul; we draw near to God as individuals; in this prayer the Ministrant invokes the descent of the Christ-force into the group-mind made ready to receive it.

We now come to an important point in our consideration of the principles of ritual. A point known to every trained occultist, but of which the uninitiated are unaware. We propose, however, to make it known, in order that all who care to utilise it may do so, because we are anxious that all who come to our service may share in the mystical experiences the communion service is designed to bestow.

It is generally realised that in the performance of any ritual or act of devotion it is not enough to repeat the words parrot-fashion, it is necessary to realise them and pour into them strong devotional feeling if the act is to be effective. It is not so generally realised, however, that the act of devotion is much more powerful if it is accompanied by the formulation of a clear-cut visual image and the whole process pictured symbolically in the imagination. The occultist who works through ceremonial is taught to do this with the utmost precision, and the working of an occult ritual is accompanied by the formulation of a carefully arranged series of astral images built up by the participants. It is this that marks the difference between a ritual done by a trained occultist and the same ritual performed by an untrained person who by some means has succeeded in obtaining the printed words.

In the present case the Ministrant is invoking the descent of the Christ-force and for this the appropriate symbol is the Chalice. All present should therefore visualise a mighty Chalice of gold, greater than the stature of a man, suspended in the air immediately over the Zodiac which lies upon the floor in the centre of the sanctuary, and at such height to enable those moving about the sanctuary in the performance of the ritual, to pass beneath it, and not through it. This thought-form should be held steadily in the imagination throughout the whole service when it has once been formulated at the appropriate point in the service, and those who have psychic powers will be interested to observe the astral phenomenon connected with it. It is not desirable to formulate the Cup sooner, because the psychic atmosphere must be purified before any formulation takes place lest we should find ourselves working on a mixed contact.

Prayer Of Invocations

It will be observed that the invocation is to the Lord Jesus. The word Lord is the English rendering of the Hebrew Adonai, which is one of the forms of the Holy Names of God. In the Qabalah, the mysticism of Israel, these Holy Names are used as indicating the modes of the manifestation of the Divine power, and that which is assigned to the Sphere of Earth (Heb: Malkuth) is Adonai ha Aretz, Lord of the Earth-plane. In bringing in the magical formula of our ceremony we therefore invoke Him as Lord. When we desire the Christ-force to manifest in our own higher selves, we invoke Him as Master, for He is to us the Great Initiator, and when thus invoked we are not summoning Him to manifest in the Sphere of Earth but ourselves are risen up to meet Him upon the highest plane to which the incarnated soul can aspire while in full consciousness (Heb: Tiphareth). There are, of course, higher planes of trance consciousness, but we need not concern ourselves with them here.

But with the invocation to the Lord Jesus is coupled another "Most holy and beloved Master". It may appear at first sight that, in view of what has just been said, we have here a linking of incompatibles, but this is not the case. It must be borne in mind that the services in our sanctuary, though they are thrown open to all who care to attend, are in reality the celebration of the rites of the

Church of the Initiates, and are so used by the members of our inner group who are instructed in these matters. The employment of the word Master in this respect indicates the relationship of initiator and initiate, and this invocation is equivalent to saying, "O great Initiator, we, Thy initiates, are about to celebrate Thy rites. Be Thou with us in that form under which Thou hast taught us to know Thee." This cannot be revealed to the uninitiated.

Let it be observed, finally, that this prayer emphasises the triune mode of the manifestation of the divine presence as wisdom, compassion or love, and power. Western religions tend to subdivide themselves into cults and offer devotion to a single aspect of the Godhead to the exclusion of all others, forgetting that the Godhead must of necessity be as many-sided as creation. God is a Trinity of Father, Son, and Holy Spirit, represented in the moral qualities as power, love and wisdom. Each of these aspects must equally be represented as triune, for we cannot divide the substance. In the Father aspect of God, the creator and sustainer of our universe, we have the power aspect predominating, yet not without wisdom and love, which may be imaged as the basal angles of the triangles whose apex is power. In the Son love predominates because He is the Saviour, the equilibrator, the reconciler between the pairs of opposites whose action and reaction determine manifestation. In Him too, however, the other qualities are present, for the Son is neither mindless nor powerless, though His mode of function is through love. Herein the apex of the triangle is love, and its basal angles wisdom and power. And in the Holy Spirit we have for the apex wisdom, for it is the illuminator. It is under this aspect of the Godhead that initiation is conducted and the adept works. It will thus be seen that the key to the Mystery of the Trinity lies in the eye of the beholder. God is One, manifesting as Three. From whatever angle we view that celestial triangle will it appear to our finite vision as a person of the Trinity. Whatever aspect we invoke, that form of power will predominate.

In this prayer, then, we invoke the love aspect of our Saviour, yet not unmindful that He is a Trinity within Himself, and we remind ourselves of His other aspects in order that we may have a balanced conception, leaning neither to an undue severity nor an undue leniency, but equilibrated in wisdom.

One of the problems of Christianity as a world-religion is due to the limitation of its appeal owing to its onesideness. It can only initiate a certain type of temperament. It has a Bhakta-yoga, and none other. Moreover, its limitations cause it to take no account of much that God implanted in man, who is thus left to solve his problems as best he may, unhelped by any sacramental aid. This leads to two kinds of disaster — repression and laissez-faire — with their consequent mental and social pathology.

When we criticise Christianity, however, it must not be thought that we are condemning the Christ. He was to us the manifestation of the very God, beyond our criticism because He is beyond our comprehension. We are criticising what has come down to us as His system, and we criticise it on the grounds that are within our knowledge in that its results in practice are both inadequate and disastrous. We consider that we give a truer loyalty to Our Lord in thus criticising the system than in justifying its limitations and imperfections that are attributed to Him.

We believe that what we possess now as Christianity is but the distorted and battered remains of what He gave us. Nor are we unique in feeling this. Every reformer from Luther onwards has said the same thing, and has sought to discover what Our Lord really taught and to re-establish the faith on its original basis. We, however, approach the problem in a different way. We are not concerned so much with the determination of true doctrine as with the practical task of exalting consciousness to realisation of the Christ-nature. Doctrine is secondary and can follow after.

In concluding our study of this prayer, let us note one final lesson that may be deduced from it. It says, "Be with us. . . that that which we are about to do may be potent in spiritual power".

It will be observed that the whole of the work is not left to the other side. We on earth are going to do something and having made our invocation we proceed to do it, relying upon our Master's promise that He will come at the appointed time to turn the water into wine.

Priests Of The Sacrament

We are functioning as adepts in a magical ceremony. We are making a channel of invocation. We are not helplessly leaning upon the Good Shepherd but are as skilled craftsmen preparing the structure for the Master to use. Thus are we able to cause spiritual power to manifest itself upon a level of consciousness normally inaccessible to it, and thus give mystical experiences to those who would be exceedingly unlikely to obtain them unaided. The magical joins the spiritual with the material. That is its function and its justification.

The sacramental side of religion is magical, as is stated by such authorities as Evelyn Underhill and Sir James Frazer. The Roman Church knows this and uses the knowledge but does not impart it to the laity. Protestant Christianity is entirely ignorant of this inner side of its own faith. We, for our part, hold with Martin Luther that every man and every woman should be a priest and work directly with God. To this end we not only employ the magical sacramental method but also teach its significance.

Meditation Follows Invocation

"Let us meditate upon the Master Jesus as the Risen Christ."

These words follow immediately upon the first prayer of invocation. The Ministrant, kneeling to invoke, and remaining kneeling, invites the congregation to join with him in the meditation which shall place all present in touch with the power called down. For it is not enough that the priest should invoke on behalf of the people; each individual member of the congregation must play his part if he is to receive any spiritual benefit; he himself must set open the door of his consciousness that the Christ may enter in. Therefore, meditation must always follow invocation.

It will be observed that in this invocation a particular form of meditation is indicated. It is not enough that we should sit silent with our hearts raised in aspiration. Our aspirations must be given a definite form if they are to be effectual as means of contacting spiritual forces, for forces at the levels at which we can contact them are specialised and differentiated. We shall find that we receive quite a different type of spiritual impulse if we invoke God the Father to that which we receive if we invoke God the Son. And even in our invocations of God the Son there are different aspects under which we can invoke Him, and in this knowledge lies one of the most important keys to spiritual experience.

The invocation here is of the Master Jesus as the Risen Christ. In order to understand the significance of this invocation, we must explain our concept of the different levels of the Christ-contact.

SPIRITUAL NATURE OF CHRIST

Because human beings are at different levels of development, there must be different grades of spiritual teaching and discipline to meet their needs. We classify these as the exoteric Church, the mystical Church, and the esoteric Church.

It is the task of the exoteric Church to seek the lost sheep and help assist them in their spiritual needs. The Church must see that every soul is given the opportunity to reach the normal standard of human development of its race and age. It should save the sinner and heal those whose sickness has its roots in spiritual conditions. It should comfort the afflicted, help the weak, instruct the young, and give to the simple in heart a message that they can understand.

The central symbol of the exoteric Church is the Christ as the Good Shepherd, compassionate and beloved. Under this aspect, the Christ force comforts and protects. It is this element that says "Suffer the little children to come unto Me, and forbid them not, for of such is the kingdom of heaven". This part of the Christ rules over the young souls, whether young in years or in understanding and character-development. He never puts out the smoking flax, but tenderly nurses the tiny spark through many incarnations until the time comes when it can be fanned to flame.

But this is not the only aspect of the Christ-force. If it were, there would be many souls not of the child-like type who would remain uncalled and unfed. For it is needless to say to the strong man in his pride, "Come unto Me, all ye that labour and are heavy laden, and I will give you rest". It is not rest he wants, but an ideal to inspire him as he goes into battle to fight the good fight; a beacon to guide him as he runs the straight race. He does not need rest and comfort, but direction of energy and a strong hand on the reins to guide the forces that are in him into the right path. It is one of the cardinal defects of the Christian sects that they are too highly specialised. They do not recognise the needs of temperaments other than those whose needs they are designed to meet. They must not forget that the Good Shepherd has sheep dogs as well as sheep, and that the sheep dog is a stronger and more intelligent beast than the sheep. If Christianity is to be a universal religion it must find a place and a message for the noble pagan who can become the Warrior of Christ, but never His lamb. It is the strength of Roman Catholicism that it has different spiritual disciplines in the different great monastic Orders, and that men of one temperament find their spiritual home in the Franciscan Order, and of another temperament with the Dominicans or Jesuits. It is the weakness of Protestant Christianity that instead of maintaining the different aspects as sections, it has allowed them to break up into sects.

Mystical Church Of Christ

And this brings us to the question of the Mystical Church of Christ to which the monastic Orders may be said to belong. It will be observed that we do not distinguish between the different Christian Communions upon the ground of their theological beliefs; our classification is horizontal, not vertical; for the initiate cares little for theology, which appears to him a very idle science as handled by the uninitiated, who do not possess the key to the symbolism of the Sacred Books; he judges entirely by results, and assesses the grade of a Church by the level of development of the souls it is dealing with, and despises no teaching that is helping any soul to tread its path.

The inner aspect of the Christian Churches is mystical, as distinguished from the outer, which is ethical. The part of the Christ contacted in the mystical Church is Christ Crucified, and the symbol of its meditation is the black Calvary Cross, the Cross of suffering and renunciation, the Cross in which the shaft is three times the length of the limbs. It is a curious fact that if anyone meditates upon the black Calvary Cross, he will receive illumination through sorrow, pain and loss; and if he meditates upon the bent-limbed, or whirling cross, called the swastika and the Hammer of Thor, he will feel the contact of the fiery nature forces, for meditation symbols are the means of contacting the various invisible potencies, and there are many more forms of the cross than most people are aware of.

It is an undeniable fact that the average man is only awakened to a desire for spiritual things by the lessons of suffering and helplessness; he will seldom turn to Christ for help as long as he is in any way able to help himself. "O Lord we come to Thee because we have nowhere else to go" is his prayer. The outer forms of the Christian faith therefore do rightly when they make the black Calvary Cross of suffering and renunciation the central symbol of their method, for it is only suffering that can awaken the average soul.

It is one of the great lessons of the spiritual life that power and freedom can only be won through meekness and renunciation; yet this is not to be thought of as the whole aim of the Christian discipline, but rather as a stage upon the path, yet an essential and unavoidable stage. Until we have mastered the discipline of this stage, we are unfit to be entrusted with the dynamic powers wielded by the adept, for we dare not unleash forces unless we can be sure of controlling them; and how can we hope to control the forces of the macrocosm if we cannot control the forces of the microcosm?

The cult of the Crucified Christ, therefore, is a grade of initiation, and no more the be-all and end-all of the Christian faith than is the cult of the Good Shepherd as exemplified in evangelical Christianity.

What, then, is the Third Degree of Christian initiation, the three stages of which are symbolised by the three-fold proportion of shaft to limb of the Latin Cross? We call it the Church of the Risen Christ, as distinguished from the Church of the Good Shepherd and the Church of the Crucified Christ. Let us now consider the significance of this concept and the kind of force that is contacted under the symbol of the Risen Christ.

CONFESSION AND ABSOLUTION

We now come to the third section of our service wherein we make confession, learn the conditions of forgiveness, and receive absolution. Sin is as old as mankind, and its forgiveness as old as the Church; it has been dealt with in many ways, and our way of dealing with it is but one among many, and each way must be judged by its effectiveness. Does it quench smoking flax? Does it let evil multiply and grow strong? If it does either of these things, it is inefficient. Let me point out yet again that the thing that matters in the formal side of religion is its effect on the souls of those who believe in it.

Our method of dealing with sin is simple and non-specific. It is simple because the end we wish to attain is very simple, being unity itself, the union of the soul with God in oneness of nature. It is non-specific because human problems are so infinitely complex that only a formula as comprehensive as the horizon can be made to cover them.

This section of our service opens with the words of the Ministrant reading from I John 1:5:

> *"God is Light, and in Him is no darkness at all. If we say we have fellowship with Him, and walk in darkness, we lie, and do not tell truth. But if we walk in the Light, we have fellowship one with another, and the blood of Jesus Christ cleanseth us from all sin. If we say we have no sin, we deceive ourselves, and the truth is not in us."*

Here we have a clear and explicit pronouncement. None but the pure in heart can have communion with God, and if we say we have no sin, we deceive ourselves.

Different things are taken for granted in different circles. Those who come to the services of the Guild of the Master Jesus are mostly drawn from among groups already interested in advanced thought, who have already broken away from conventional thinking and are seeking more satisfying solutions to life's questions than orthodoxy affords them. Such a breakaway very often results in a reaction on more levels than one, and the old barriers being down, they are sometimes not replaced with anything else until it is learned by experience that they guarded unwary footsteps from a slough of despondency.

It will be observed that at no point in our service do we define sin. We do not say, this and that are sinful and you must not do them. We simply say, only the good can come to God. We do not feel we know enough about God to be dogmatic in the matter. Each soul knows well enough what deteriorates it, and different things damage different souls. The coward who practices persistent meekness is weakening himself. Chastity is no virtue in the frigid. It is all a matter between the soul and God. We are like children playing "I spy", and our conscience tells us "Hot" or "Cold" as we draw nearer to goodness or depart from it.

But equally plainly do we say, He who thinks he has no sin deceives himself. We are none of us perfect. If we were, we should not be here. We should have gone on to higher planes. The very fact of our presence on this earth is a certificate of imperfection. It means that we have something still to learn, and it is for each one of us to face that something. We know what it is well enough if we compare ourselves with the pattern shown us on the Mount.

But having said these necessary things to awaken the soul from its self-satisfaction, there follow words from the most beautiful of all the parables; Luke *15:18:*

> "*I will arise and go to my father, and will say unto Him: 'Father, I have sinned against heaven and before thee, and am no more worthy to be called thy son. Make me as one of thy hired servants.' And he arose and came to his father. But when he was yet a great way off, his father saw him, and had compassion, and ran, and fell on his neck, and kissed him.*"

In our main service we make no conditions and ask no questions. We put before the soul the issues of sin and repentance and tell the story of the Prodigal Son, Sunday by Sunday reminding those who come to our services that when he was yet a great way off, his father saw him, and ran, and fell on his neck, and kissed him. While we are yet a very long way from reformation, God welcomes us home.

Then follows the prayer of the Ministrant:

> *"O Master of Love and Compassion, show us wherein we have erred, and give us strength and understanding to make amends."*

It will be seen here clearly implied that we do not look upon sin as an offence against God, but rather as an erring, or wandering from the right path, a losing of the way of life, an injury inflicted primarily upon ourselves. We do not apologise to God, but ask for His help to put us back again on the right path in order that we may tread it, and we believe this attitude to be more truly God-fearing than any amount of beating of breasts and tearing of hair. Repentance is indeed the first of the acts of devotion, but remorse is a psychopathology.

GOD IS A TRIUNE GOD

Once again we stress that fundamental point in our teaching, that God is a Triune God of wisdom, strength and love, and that love alone will not put us on the right path, but that strength and understanding also are necessary.

Following these readings there is a silence, in which each one looks into his own soul and prays in his heart the prayer of the Ministrant. And then there follows an invocation and response, the congregation again being drawn into the movement of the ritual.

Ministrant: *"O Lord, show Thy mercy upon us."*
People: *"And grant us Thy salvation."*

Then the Lector reads again, and the words, taken from the 15th Psalm, tell clearly upon what conditions God will receive us into His holy place.

"Lord, who shall abide in thy Tabernacle? Who shall dwell in Thy holy hill?

And the Lord answered saying:

He that walketh uprightly, and worketh righteousness and speaketh the truth in his heart.

He that backbiteth not with his tongue, nor doeth evil to his neighbour, not taketh up a reproach against his neighbour.

He that sweareth to his own hurt and changeth not.

He that putteth not out his money to usury, not taketh reward against the innocent.

He that doeth these things shall never be moved."

Psalms 15 and Leviticus 19

And what does God require of us in our daily lives? Freed of their archaic verbiage, these words tell us that we must be honest and kindly, that is all. Simple enough, but God will not overlook a failure to fulfil these requirements.

Then the Ministrant turning to the people, recites to them the brief instruction the members of the Society of the Inner Light received from the inner-planes at the time of its foundation.

"Let the brethren dwell together in love and harmony; in loyalty and trust; thinking no evil of one another. Let compassion temper justice, and justice balance compassion. Let us be serene and diligent, courageous and strong, wise and temperate. There is a blessing on all who serve."

In this passage it will be observed that every quality is balanced by it's opposite: compassion by justice, serenity by diligence, and that of the Sign of the Cross is made by the Ministrant with two fingers. Thus do we represent symbolically one of the teachings of esoteric science, that all things manifest as pairs of opposites and that it is only between them, in equilibrium, that is found the Path of Life. There is no blessing on diligence unless it is serene, as Our Lord pointed out to Martha, whose temper had worn thin with much serving. There is no blessing on justice unless it is merciful and aims not at the death of the sinner, but rather that he should turn from his wickedness and live. There is no blessing on mercy unless it is also just, and does not deteriorate into an unwise sentimentality that gratifies our emotions, saves us trouble, and leaves the evil-doer free to go and do it again. We hold that justice should always rob sin of its profits and make the sinner thoroughly uncomfortable as long as he elects to remain a sinner.

And now the Lector reads again, using the words of Our Lord.

"Judge not that ye be not judged: and with what measure ye give, it shall be measured to you again. And why beholdest thou the irritation that is in thy brother's eye, and considereth not the annoyance that is in thine own eye? Thou hypocrite, first cast out the sting that is in thine own eye, and then thou shalt see clearly to cast out the speck that is in thy brother's eye. Love your enemies; bless them that curse you; do good to them that hate you and use you and persecute you, that ye may be the children of your Father which is in Heaven, for He maketh His Sun to rise on the evil and on the good, and sendeth rain on the just and the unjust. For if you love only them that love you, what reward have ye? And if ye salute your brethren only, what do ye more than others? Be ye therefore perfect, even as your Father in Heaven is perfect."

Here we learn the demands of the Christ-life, which separates it with a great gulf from the life of the world. Our Lord says, "Do not react to evil on its own plane, for you do more harm than good by so doing, deal with it from a higher plane, by spiritual realisation, not human resentment."

Now all stand for the Lord's Prayer, which is repeated in unison. And then the Ministrant gives that conditional absolution which leaves the final issue between the soul and God, which is the only place where it can rest.

"For if ye forgive men their mistakes, your Heavenly Father will also forgive you. But if ye forgive not men their faults, neither will your Heavenly Father forgive you your errors."

Can we expect the Father of us all to treat us better than we treat our brethren, His other children? The measure of His love for us is also the measure of His love for them. "As you have done it unto the least of these, so have you done unto Me."

If we do not show mercy, how can we hope for mercy? And however secure we may feel our position to be, can we be absolutely sure that the time will never come when we would be very thankful for a little mercy ourselves, and see no hope left for us unless we get it? Shall we not in that day remember in bitterness the time when we ourselves refused to temper justice with mercy, and therefore have no claim on the divine compassion?

It is a true saying that it is unwise to demand perfection unless you are prepared to give it; so let us realise that we are all human with human failings, and when taken by surprise, we are liable to do things we shall afterwards regret, and so need to make allowances for each other and lend a helping hand to the undeserving as well as the worthy, for all who breathe the breath of life have the capacity to feel pain.

GUILD OF THE MASTER JESUS

CELEBRATION OF THE HOLY COMMUNION

Two celebrants participate in this Rite representing the positive and negative poles of the dynamism of the MASS.

The *MINISTRANT* works with the invisible forces and builds forms to channel their manifestation.

The *LECTOR* works with the group-mind of the congregation.

The Temple is formed symbolically with the Altar in the East and the congregation seated in the West. As the congregation views the Altar, the *MINISTRANT* is seated to the left on the North side of Altar and the *LECTOR* is seated on the right-South side of the Altar.

Order Of Service

MINISTRANT: *(Moves to stand between the Altar and the congregation, facing the Altar and the East . . . Raises his hands in the Sign of the Chalice - lifting his arms in front and above the head with the hands cupped, the head is thrown back and the face turned upward awaiting the descent of power.)*

"O Holy Jesus, Master of Love and Compassion, we Thy children, dedicated to Thy service, approach Thee in faith in the Living Christ, the unseen companion of the heart.

Prepare us, O Lord, to drink of the living waters of life, soon to be made manifest to us, open our eyes that we may see, and our hearts that we may understand. Make the way plain, O Lord, that we fail not in Thy service. May we be a channel whereby Thy Holy Ones may approach the World. May we be a centre of radiation of Thy power.

Teach us to travel light as do all who travel upon the path; to give ourselves entirely to Thy service; to attune ourselves to Thy will; to suffer gladly for Thy sake; to lay down the small personal life in the great cosmic life, and to love with the love of God.

Lift up your hearts."

ALL: We lift them up unto the Lord.

LECTOR: *(Stands on South side of Altar facing West towards the congregation.)*

"I will lift mine eyes unto the hills, whence cometh my help. My help cometh from the Lord, which made heaven and earth.

He will not suffer thy foot to be moved; He that keepeth thee will not slumber. Behold, He that keepeth Israel will neither slumber nor sleep. The Lord is Thy keeper; the Lord is thy shade upon thy right hand. The sun shall not smite thee by day nor the moon by night. The Lord shall preserve thee from all evil; He shall preserve thy soul. The Lord shall preserve thy going out and thy coming in, from this time forth and even for evermore."

MINISTRANT: *(Kneeling, facing Altar and the East.)*

"O Lord Jesus, Most Holy and Beloved Master, be with us in Thy wisdom and compassion, that what we are about to do may be potent in spiritual power. Amen."

"Let us meditate upon the Master Jesus as the Risen Christ."

Remains kneeling - Silence - Pause for meditation. Ministrant rises and stands facing Altar and the East

LECTOR: (*Standing on South side of Altar facing West toward the congregation.*)

"God is light and in Him is no darkness at all. If we say we have fellowship with Him and walk in darkness we do not speak the truth. But if we walk in the light, we have fellowship one with another, and the blood of Jesus Christ cleanseth us from all sin. If we say we have no sin, we deceive ourselves and the truth is not in us.

I will arise and go to my Father and will say unto Him: "Father, I have sinned against heaven and before Thee, and am no more worthy to be called Thy son. Make me as one of Thy hired servants."

And he arose and came to his Father. But when he was yet a great way off, his Father saw him and had compassion, and ran to meet him, and fell on his neck and kissed him."

MINISTRANT: (*Standing, facing Altar and the East.*)

"O Master of Love and Compassion, show us wherein we have erred and give us strength and understanding to make amends."

Short Silence

MINISTRANT: (*Standing, facing Altar and the East.*)

"O Lord show Thy mercy upon us."

ALL: "And grant us Thy salvation."

LECTOR: (*Standing on South side of Altar facing congregation in the West.*)

"Lord, who shall abide in Thy Tabernacle? Who shall dwell in Thy Holy Hill? He that walketh uprightly and worketh righteousness and speaketh the Truth in his heart. He that backbiteth not with his tongue, nor doeth evil to his neighbour, nor taketh up a reproach against his neighbour. He that sweareth to his own hurt and changeth not. He that putteth not out his money to usury, not taketh reward against the innocent. He that doeth these things shall never be moved."

MINISTRANT: *(Turns, facing congregation from West side of Altar.)*

"Let the brethren dwell together in love and harmony, in loyalty and truth, thinking no evil of one another. Let compassion temper justice and justice balance compassion. Let us be serene and diligent, courageous and strong, wise and temperate. There is a blessing on all who serve."

Makes the sign + over the brethren and turns to Altar.

LECTOR: *(Standing on South side of Altar facing congregation in West.)*

"Jesus saith: Judge not that ye be not judged: and with what measure ye give, it shall be measured to you again. And why beholdest thou the irritation that is in thy brother's eye, and considereth not the annoyance that is in thine own eye? Thou hypocrite, first cast out the sting that is in thine own eye, and then thou shalt see clearly to cast out the speck that is in thy brother's eye. Love your enemies; bless them that curse you; do good to them that hate you and use you and persecute you, that ye may be the children of your Father which is in Heaven; for He maketh His Sun to rise on the evil and on the good, and sendeth rain on the just and the unjust. For if you love them that love you, what reward have ye? And if ye salute your brethren only, what do ye more than others?

Be ye therefore perfect, even as your Father in Heaven is perfect."

MINISTRANT: (Facing congregation from West side of Altar.)

"Let us join together in the Lord's Prayer."

ALL: *(Stand)*

"Our Father, who art in heaven,
Hallowed be thy Name.
Thy Kingdom come,
Thy will be done,
On earth as it is in Heaven.
Give us this day our daily bread.
Forgive us our trespasses,
As we forgive those who trespass against us.
Lead us not into temptation,
But deliver us from evil.
For thine is the kingdom, and the power and
the glory, for ever and ever,
Amen."

MINISTRANT: (Facing congregation from West side of Altar.)

"For if ye forgive men their mistakes, your Heavenly Father
will also forgive you. But if ye forgive not men their faults,
neither will your Heavenly Father forgive you your errors."

ALL: *(Sit)*

MINISTRANT: (Turns, facing the Altar and the East.)

"O Master of Love and Compassion, our human needs are
ever with us. May Thy wisdom give us understanding, and
Thy love give us strength to bear our burdens to the honour
and glory of Thy Holy Name. Amen."

MINISTRANT: Returns to seat on North side of Altar

LECTOR: *(Standing on South side of Altar facing congregation in the West.)*

"Jesus saith: "Come unto Me all ye that labour and are heavy laden, and I will give you rest. Take my yoke upon you and learn of Me, for I am humble and lowly of heart, and ye shall find rest for your souls. For My yoke is easy and My burden is light.""

ALL: *(Stand)*

"The Lord is my shepherd, I shall not want.
He maketh me to lie down in green pastures,
He leadeth me beside the still waters, He restoreth my soul;
He leadeth me in the paths of righteousness for His Name's
    sake.
Yea, though I walk through the Valley of the Shadow of Death,
I will fear no evil, for Thou art with me, Thy rod and Thy
    staff they comfort me.
Thou preparest a table before me in the presence of mine
    enemies;
Thou annointest my head with oil, my cup runneth over.
Surely goodness and mercy shall follow me all the days of
    my life,
And I shall dwell in the House of the Lord forever.""

ALL: *(Sit)*

MINISTRANT: *(Rises. Takes position between congregation and Altar, facing East.)*

Prayer For The Nation

"May the blessing and the mercy and the goodness of God rest upon our people, and on all peoples. May there be peace and goodwill between us and them. May there be brotherly love, good faith, and kindness between man and man throughout our heritage. May the spirit of liberty, equality and justice be maintained among us.

Keep far from us both poverty and riches, that we be not led into temptation, but give us a sufficiency of all good things and Thy blessing thereon. May the Sword of Thy Might deal justice between man and man, nation and nation, may we be fearless and merciful ministers of Thy justice and truth. Bless all who serve their fellow men; may we be numbered among the servers."

Prayer For The Home

"Bless, O Lord, all homes and consecrate them. Bless the marriage bond between man and woman, that it may be natural and beautiful, a source of joy and peace and security. Sanctify it with Thy blessing that it may be sacred unto Thee; bless with a special blessing all who open the gates of life unto incoming souls.

Heal, we beseech Thee, O Lord, all strife and quarrel within the home and bless the peacemakers."

Prayer For Others

"O Master Jesus, we bring to Thy Compassion and Wisdom all those of our friends who are sick or in trouble; may Thy Infinite Love meet all their needs. May Thy Help comfort those for whom our prayers have been asked.

Especially...

Let us remember those dear to us who have entered into the Light. May that Light shine upon them perpetually.

O Thou Most Holy and Powerful Lord Jesus Christ, Son of God Most High, we invoke Thy Most Potent Name and Sign, in the Name of the Father and of the Son and of the Holy Ghost. Amen."

LECTOR: *(Standing on South side of Altar facing congregation in the West.)*

May the Lord hear thee in the day of trouble; may the God of Jacob defend thee, and send thee help from the sanctuary and strength out of Zion. We will rejoice in Thy salvation and in the name of our God we will set up our banners. May the Lord fulfil all thy petitions. Now know I that the Lord saveth His anointed. He will hear him from His Holy Heaven, with the saving strength of His right hand. Some trust in chariots and some in horses, but we will remember the Name of the Lord our God.

And the seventy returned with joy, saying: "Lord, even the devils are subject unto us through Thy Name." And He said unto them: "I beheld Satan as lightning falling from Heaven. Behold I give you power to tread on serpents and scorpions, and over all the power of the enemy, and nothing shall hurt you."

He that dwelleth in the secret place of the Most High, shall abide under the shadow of the Almighty. I will say of the Lord: He is my refuge and my fortress; my God, in Him will I trust.

I shalt not be afraid of the terror by night, nor for danger by day because the Lord is my protection and no evil befall me nor any plague come unto my home. For He shall give His angels charge over me, to keep and honour me.

He shall call upon Me and with long life will I satisfy Him and show Him my salvation.

MINISTRANT: *(Standing between congregation and the Altar, facing East.)*

"O Master Jesus, Lord of Love and Compassion, we worship Thee with love, obedience and pride in being your own.

O Holy Mary, Mother of Jesus, draw thy compassionate mantle of blue around us.

O Holy Michael, Saint and Angel, with thy rod of power

protecting us from the satanic forces, we salute you with love, honour and gratitude for thy protection.

O Holy Men of our race, great Saints of old with whom we join, we salute you with love and respect. Give us of your strength, your faith and fearlessness."

MINISTRANT: *(Remains at Altar)*

LECTOR: *(Standing on South side of Altar, facing congregation in the West.)*

"Jesus saith: The Comforter, which is the Holy Spirit, whom the Father will send in My Name, He shall teach you all things and bring all things to your remembrance."

LECTOR: *(Seats himself in South)*

MINISTRANT: *(Returns to seat to the North of Altar)*

Teaching And Instruction
by designated Speaker

TEACHER: *(Stands, between congregation and Altar, facing congregation in the West.)*

Holy Communion Service

Opening Invitation

MINISTRANT: *(Standing on East side of Altar facing Altar and congregation.)*

"Dearly beloved in Christ, I bid you to the Holy Communion of the Body and Blood of Christ our Saviour.

Consider how He bids us all to try and examine ourselves before we presume to eat of that Bread and drink of that Cup.

Let us examine ourselves in thought, word and deed."

ALL: *Silence for Self Examination*

"The Lord Almighty pardon + and deliver you from all your sins, confirm and strengthen you in all goodness, and bring you to the Life of the Ages. Amen."

"Lift up your hearts"

ALL: "We lift them up unto the Lord."

MINISTRANT: *(Standing on East side of Altar facing Altar and congregation.)*

"Let us give thanks to our Lord God."

ALL: "It is worthy and right to do so."

MINISTRANT:

"It is very true, proper and our bounden duty that we should at all times and in all places give thanks unto Thee.

Company of Heaven, we praise and magnify Thy glorious name, evermore singing and saying:

HOLY! (bell) HOLY! (bell) HOLY! (bell)
Lord God of Hosts,
Heaven and Earth are full of Thy glory;
Glory to Thee, O God Most High.
Blessed is He that cometh in the Name of the Lord.
Hosanna in the Highest.

Prayer of Consecration

"All glory to Thee, Almighty God, our Heavenly Father, Whose only-born Son, Jesus Christ didst suffer death upon the Cross, and by that death didst overcome death, and by that sacrifice didst cleanse the world of the domination of evil, opening the way into the heavenly places and commanding us to continue this blessed sacrament of His Love.

Hear us, O Almighty God, and with Thy Holy Spirit, bless + approve + and sanctify + these gifts of bread and wine, that they may become the channels and signs of His life and strength.

Who, on the day before He suffered, took bread and when He had given thanks, be blessed + brake, and gave it to His disciples, saying:

'Take, and eat ye all of this, for *THIS IS MY BODY.*'

Likewise, after supper, He took the cup, and when He had given thanks, He blessed it + and gave it to them, saying:

'Take, and drink ye all of this, for *THIS IS MY BLOOD.*'

Wherefore, O Lord and Heavenly Father, we Thy children, having in remembrance the precious death of Thy Son, His mighty resurrection, and glorious ascension, according to His holy institution, do celebrate and set forth before Thy divine majesty, with these Thy holy gifts, the memorial which He hath willed us to make.

And here we offer and present unto Thee, O Lord, ourselves, our souls and bodies, to be a reasonable, holy, and living sacrifice unto Thee, beseeching Thee that all we who are partakers of this Holy Communion may be filled with Thy grace and heavenly benediction, through Jesus Christ our Lord, by whom, and with whom, in the unity of the Holy Spirit, all honour and glory be unto Thee, O Father Almighty, world without end. Amen."

MINISTRANT: Communicates

LECTOR: *(Kneels)* Communicates

BRETHREN   Come to Altar, kneel and Communicate

MINISTRANT: (Upon completion of the serving, moves to the East side and stands in the centre of the symbol of the universe, facing East with Altar and congregation to his back, exalts the Cup with both hands.)

> "Glory be to God on High, and
>   On Earth peace to men of goodwill.
>   We praise Thee, we bless Thee,
>   we worship Thee,
>   We honour Thee, we give thanks to
>   Thee for Thy great Glory.
>   Amen."

ALL:

> "O Holy Spirit, my soul inspire, Thou Flame of Fire descend
>   on me."

ALL: *Sit*

MINISTRANT: (On East side of Altar, turns to West, kneels at Altar, after replacing cup. Rises, circles Altar, stops in West, faces West and congregation.)

LECTOR: *(Standing on South side of Altar facing congregation in West.)*

> "Now on the first day of the week, very early in the morning,
>   they came to the tomb, bringing spices which they had
>   prepared. And they found the stone rolled away.
>   And they entered in and found not the body of the Lord Jesus.

And it came to pass, as they were much confused, two men stood by them in shining garments. And as they were afraid and bowed down their faces to the Earth, those shining beings said unto them: 'Why seek ye the living among the dead? He is not here, but is risen.'

And when the day of Pentecost was fully come, the disciples were all with one accord in one place. And suddenly, there came a sound from Heaven as of a rushing mighty wind, and it filled all the house where they were sitting. And there appeared unto them cloven tongues like as of fire which touched them, and they were all filled with the Holy Spirit.

But we speak of the wisdom of God as a mystery, even the hidden wisdom which God ordained from the foundation of the world unto our glory. As it is written: 'Eye hath not seen, nor ear heard, neither have entered into the heart of man the things that God has prepared for them that love Him.' But God has revealed them unto us by His Spirit; for the Spirit searched all things, yea, the deep things of God.

Jesus saith: 'I will pray to the Father and He shall give you another Comforter, that He may abide with you for ever, even the Spirit of Truth, when the world cannot receive because it seeth Him not, neither knoweth Him. Ye know Him, for He dwelleth with you, and shall be in you; I will not leave you comfortless.

I will come to you. Peace I leave with you. My Peace I give unto you, not as the world giveth I unto you. Let not your heart be troubled, neither let it be afraid. Lo, I am with you always, even unto the end of the world."

MINISTRANT: (*West side of Altar facing congregation.*)

"The Peace of God, which passeth all understanding, keep your hearts and minds in the knowledge and love of God and of His Son, Christ our Lord; and the blessing of God Almighty, the Father + the Son, and the Holy Spirit, be amongst you and remain with you always. Amen."

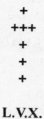

L.V.X.

If you are sincerely interested in the ideas expressed in this book and want to take further steps, then write to:

The Secretary,
B.M. Vixack
LONDON
WC1N 3XX.

Other titles from Thoth Publications

AN INTRODUCTION TO RITUAL MAGIC
By Dion Fortune & Gareth Knight

At the time this was something of a unique event in esoteric publishing - a new book by the legendary Dion Fortune. Especially with its teachings on the theory and practice of ritual or ceremonial magic, by one who, like the heroine of two of her other novels, was undoubtedly "a mistress of that art".

In this work Dion Fortune deals in successive chapters with Types of Mind Working; Mind Training; The Use of Ritual; Psychic Perception; Ritual Initiation; The Reality of the Subtle Planes; Focusing the Magic Mirror; Channelling the Forces; The Form of the Ceremony; and The Purpose of Magic - with appendices on Talisman Magic and Astral Forms.

Each chapter is supplemented and expanded by a companion chapter on the same subject by Gareth Knight. In Dion Fortune's day the conventions of occult secrecy prevented her from being too explicit on the practical details of magic, except in works of fiction. These veils of secrecy having now been drawn back, Gareth Knight has taken the opportunity to fill in much practical information that Dion Fortune might well have included had she been writing today.

In short, in this unique collaboration of two magical practitioners and teachers, we are presented with a valuable and up-to-date text on the practice of ritual or ceremonial magic "as it is". That is to say, as a practical, spiritual, and psychic discipline, far removed from the lurid superstition and speculation that are the hall mark of its treatment in sensational journalism and channels of popular entertainment.

ISBN 1-870450 31 0 Deluxe Hardback Limited edition
ISBN 1-870450 26 4 Soft cover edition

THE CIRCUIT OF FORCE

by Dion Fortune.

With commentaries by Gareth Knight.

In "The Circuit of Force", Dion Fortune describes techniques for raising the personal magnetic forces within the human aura and their control and direction in magic and in life, which she regards as 'the Lost Secrets of the Western Esoteric Tradition'.

To recover these secrets she turns to three sources.

a) the Eastern Tradition of Hatha Yoga and Tantra and their teaching on raising the "sleeping serpent power" or kundalini;

b) the circle working by means of which spiritualist seances concentrate power for the manifestation of some of their results;

c) the linking up of cosmic and earth energies by means of the structured symbol patterns of the Qabalistic Tree of Life.

Originally produced for the instruction of members of her group, this is the first time that this material has been published for the general public in volume form.

Gareth Knight provides subject commentaries on various aspects of the etheric vehicle, filling in some of the practical details and implications that she left unsaid in the more secretive esoteric climate of the times in which she wrote.

Some quotes from Dion Fortune's text:

"When, in order to concentrate exclusively on God, we cut ourselves off from nature, we destroy our own roots. There must be in us a circuit between heaven and earth, not a one-way flow, draining us of all vitality. It is not enough that we draw up the Kundalini from the base of the spine; we must also draw down the divine light through the Thousand-Petalled Lotus. Equally, it is not enough for out mental health and spiritual development that we draw down the Divine Light, we must also draw up the earth forces. Only too often mental health is sacrificed to spiritual development through ignorance of, or denial of, this fact."

"....the clue to all these Mysteries is to be sought in the Tree of Life. Understand the significance of the Tree; arrange the symbols you are working with in the correct manner upon it, and all is clear and you can work out your sum. Equate the Danda with the Central Pillar, and the Lotuses with the Sephiroth and the bi-sections of the Paths thereon, and you have the necessary bilingual dictionary at your disposal - if you known how to use it."

ISBN 1-870450 28 0

ENTRANCE TO THE MAGICAL QABALAH
By Melita Denning & Osborne Phillips.

In this significant new work, Denning and Phillips set forth the essential traditions and teachings of the treasury of mystical and arcane learning which is known as the Qabalah.

Everything that is, ourselves included, is seen by the Qabalah as existing in some or all of four "Worlds" or levels of being.

These Worlds supply the whole fabric of our existence, and we in turn are integral parts of them. It is from this primal unity of person and kosmos that our great aspirations spring: our longing to know and to experience the reality, not only of that mystery which encompasses us, but also of that mystery of selfhood which is within us. For each of these mysteries reflects the other.

This very fact of the reflected likeness gives us a key to both mysteries, a key to mystical and to psychological understanding. It is this fact which makes magic possible. It is this same fact which makes the Qabalah a coherent system in which the aspirant does not follow blindly but with a comprehension ever increasing, and without ever losing that uplifting sense of wonder and of adventure which are rightfully a part of life itself.

With clarity and insight, the authors explore the origins and spirit of this system, its relationship to the Hermetic writings and the Zohar, its great patterns of thought and method, its spiritual sources of power and its tremendous creative potential. The question of evil is addressed in a study of the Qlipphoth and unbalanced force. Here also, among many other vital topics, are considered the role of the Supernal Mother in the cosmic scheme, the structure and functions of the psyche, spiritual realms, the destiny of the soul after death, the nature of the Gods, the way of magical attainment and the crossing of the Abyss.

ISBN1-870450-35-3